on top of spaghetti...

Other books by Johanne Killeen and George Germon

Cucina Simpatica

on
top
of
spaghetti...

...macaroni, linguine,
penne, and pasta
of every kind

Johanne Killeen
and George Germon

WILLIAM MORROW
An Imprint of HarperCollinsPublishers

To more than a quarter century
of
loyal staff
and
dedicated, caring clients
at
Al Forno Restaurant

HarperCollins books may be purchased for educational, business, or sales promotional use. For information please write: Special Markets Department, HarperCollins Publishers, 10 East 53rd Street, New York, NY 10022.

FIRST EDITION

Printed on acid-free paper

Library of Congress Cataloging-in-Publication Data

Killeen, Johanne, 1949–
    On top of spaghetti . . . : . . . macaroni, linguine, penne, and pasta of every kind / Johanne Killeen and George Germon.
        p. cm.
    ISBN-13: 978-0-06-059873-0
    ISBN-10: 0-06-059873-5
    1. Cookery (Pasta) I. Germon, George, 1945– II. Title.

TX809.M17K47 2006
641.8'22—dc22
                                                                                2006043360

06 07 08 09 10   WBC/CW   10 9 8 7 6 5 4 3 2 1

Contents

Acknowledgments

We were sitting at a cramped table at Gino's, a raucous family-owned trattoria in Rome with our editor Susan Friedland, when she said, "Why don't you two do a pasta book?" We couldn't say "Yes!" fast enough. Thank you Susan for your invaluable help, for whipping the recipes into an organized shape, and for getting your hands in the dough with us. Mat Schaffer was there, too, and he came up with the perfect title. Thanks, Mat.

The only thing better than one brilliant editor is two: Thank you Harriet Bell for bringing this book to completion with great style, a critical eye, graciousness, and enthusiasm.

We thank our team at HarperCollins, especially Lucy Baker for keeping everything together with great cheer; Roberto de Vicq de Cumptich for the delightful jacket; and Leah Carlson-Stanisic for the lighthearted and jolly interior.

Thank you Beatriz da Costa for the delicious photographs.

Thanks to our friends, the tasters, testers, and contributors who always inspire us: Patricia and Walter Wells, Maryanne Ziegler, Eli Zabar and Devon Fredericks, Christina and Santiago Quijano-Caballero, Donna Paul, Shiela and Julian More, Vivi and Colette Viviani, Ruth Phillips and Julian Merrow-Smith, Uda Strydom and Linda Vicquery, Ric Marx and Deborah Benson, Wendy Suntay, Ryan Duffy, Traci and Bernie Maceroni, Jeannie Rogers, Mike Leppizzera, René Becker, Rolando Beramendi, Tamario, Norma Jean and Ken Castellucci, Anthony Michelletti, the supper club gang: Jannie and Jean-Pierre Ottaviani, Florence and Georges Quintaine, Françoise and Jean-Claude Cavalière.

Thanks to our food and wine friends in Italy at whose tables and in whose kitchens we continue to learn: Faith Heller Willinger, the Contini Bonacosis—our Tuscan family at Tenuta di Capezzana, and their chef, Patrizio Cirri; Anna Tasca Lanza, Venceslao Lanza di Mazzarino, Costanza and Paolo di Camporeale, and the amazing kitchen staff at Regaleali—our Sicilian family; Natale and Connie Rusconi and Chef Renato Piccolotto at The Cipriani; Alessandro Laurenzi and Flaminia Mazziotti, Fausto Maculan, Giovanni Puiatti, Silvia and Giovanna Franza, Costanzo and Titina Vuotto, Cesare Giaccone, Cesare Cassella, Sandro Fabris.

Thank you Buddy Cianci for believing in us way back in 1980.

Thank you to our dear ones eating pasta in heaven:

Luis "Funcho" Mejia, Bree, Tullio De Robbio, Richard Sax, Hardu Keck.

Special thanks to Brian Kingsford for wearing *every* hat at Al Forno for more than half his life and for being like a son to us.

How Much Pasta to Cook?

In Italy, pasta is served as a first course followed by a main course. We enjoy pasta as an appetizer sometimes or as a main course at other times. If we are serving pasta as a first course we count on a pound for eight people followed by a substantial second course; or, a pound for six people if the main course is light.

When pasta is the main course accompanied by a salad and nothing else, we cook a pound for four servings. If we precede the pasta with an appetizer or antipasto, we find a pound sufficient for six portions, especially if it is followed by a salad and dessert.

For a midnight dinner we boil eight ounces of spaghetti or macaroni for the two of us and there is always some left over unless we're both famished—or cannot stop ourselves from finishing the last strands of spaghetti.

The rule of thumb is four ounces of pasta per person as the main meal and about half that for a first course. The amount you cook, however, should depend on your appetite and that of your guests. It is better to err on the generous side rather than the opposite. These recipes are simple and easily doubled or halved. Trust your judgment.

Don't trust people who don't like pasta.

Pasta: A Love Story

Neither one of us can remember the exact moment we fell in love with pasta. It's an emotion that existed earlier than our memories began—like the love of a parent. Certainly it was before we knew it as "pasta"—we called it "spaghetti" or "macaroni." In our childhood homes, cupboards were never without boxes of spaghetti, rigatoni, and pastina. We grew up with fresh pasta, too. George's Italian-American mom made homemade ravioli and lasagne. His Greek dad rolled out ribbon noodles to accompany rustic stews. Johanne's Polish-American family made pierogi (hearty potato and cheese or cabbage-filled half-moons of pasta) and kluski (irregular, hand-cut short lengths of pasta somewhat like späetzle, made from the left-over bits of pierogi dough). No matter whether it was dried or fresh, Italian, Greek, or Polish, pasta was a treat—food that brought a smile to every face at the table.

When we fell in love with each other, pasta was one of many shared passions. We were both artists who graduated from Rhode Island School of Design. We were both crazy about Italy. George lived in Rome, teaching the European Honors Program for RISD. Johanne, concurrently but separately, lived in Florence, pursuing postgrad photography studies. Though we were unaware of each other at the time, we were both experiencing the same thing in our adopted cities—enjoying the incredible riches of the museums and galleries, while unconsciously absorbing Italy's culture through its food. The freshness of the ingredients and the immediacy of the cooking made an indelible impression on each of us. Back in the States, our paths converged in the art world, but our rapture blossomed in the kitchen. Days in the photo lab or at the drafting table were followed by evenings cooking together. We wooed each other by re-creating dishes we were mad about in Italy. We enjoyed the Italian way of eating, too—pasta as a first course followed by a simple grilled meat or chicken with a crunchy salad to finish. Inevitably, we planned the pasta course first and let everything else revolve around it. We dazzled each other with food from our taste memories—George made linguine with a fiery clam sauce in the spirit of the Roman *arrabbiata*, or angry, tomato sauce. Johanne tossed penne with tomato, cream, and five cheeses, styled after her favorite "of the moment" Tuscan pasta. We were so focused on pasta that we decided to plan our first trip together to Italy, determined to find out why well-prepared pasta is something Italians excel at—almost a birthright.

We have been traveling to Italy ever since—for thirty years—and much of the time has been spent tasting, watching, cooking, and learning about pasta. The pursuit of perfect pasta started with stolen glances into restaurant kitchens in Rome. We were too shy to ask questions, but we were certain there were secrets to uncover. As we developed friendships with other food-crazed cooks, chefs, and winemakers in Italy, we were invited into their home kitchens to cook. We jumped at any opportunity to cook with Italian friends, always trying to figure out how and why in their hands pasta tasted so good. No matter where we went, we found professional chefs and home cooks alike using exactly the same simple techniques with utmost respect for fresh, seasonal ingredients. We found that there are no tricks—just good, straightforward cooking that results in honest food. The lessons we learned gave us confidence as we grew to understand the Italian kitchen. That understanding allows us to translate the pastas we love in Italy into recipes that reflect our style, personality, and taste. Some are bold and robust. Others are delicate and subtle. Some can be called fast food—prepared in minutes—while others are slow food suited to a lazy day. All mirror the sensibility and the accessibility of the Italian way with pasta.

We have cooked tens of thousands of pounds of pasta at Al Forno, our restaurant in Providence, Rhode Island, as well as plenty at home, too. It is the food we are most particular about representing in a pure Italian way, whether it is served to our customers at the restaurant or to our friends and family at home. Pasta is the food we love best. We want you to fall in love with pasta, too, and to experience anew the genius of this hearty food.

Whether you're in the mood to prepare packaged dry pasta or homemade, there are clear easy-to-follow recipes with accompanying sauces. Using techniques learned in Italy and basic kitchen skills, anyone can create his or her own superb spaghetti or rigatoni, or mix, roll out, and cook ethereal fresh noodles, lasagne, or ravioli. Classic favorites—Al Forno's baked pastas and sturdy macaroni—as well as innovative dishes such as Spaghettini with Tomatoes, Cinnamon, and Mint (page 79) or New World Pappardelle (page 84) are sure to give you joy and satisfaction. Many recipes are inspired by our late-night "midnight spaghetti" routine—pasta that we cook for each other at home after the last customer has left and the restaurant is locked up for the night. These dishes are perfectly suited to workdays—or nights—when time is tight and appetites are aroused. When you have time for a few fun-filled hours, reward yourself with one of our homemade vegetable lasagnes filled with fresh artichokes, mushrooms, or zucchini flowers. Their lightness and spunk will make you look at lasagne in a whole new way.

We continue to show our caring and love for each other by cooking. Johanne knows she can have her way with George by putting Spaghetti Aglio-Olio (page 51) on the table. George knows Johanne will melt if he makes Ricotta Ravioli (page 228). No matter what occasion or time of day or night, for us the unique, tangible, sensual enjoyment offered by pasta is among life's greatest pleasures.

Midnight Spaghetti

Work nights end late for us. At home, when the adrenaline of heading a supercharged restaurant kitchen wears off, we're hungry. That's when we depend on the immediacy of dried pasta and a quick sauce. We call these late-night pastas "midnight spaghetti." It began as a lighthearted competition between us that is fun and relaxing. The rules are simple: Prepare a delicious sauce in the time it takes for a pot of water to boil and the pasta to cook. Even when we're exhausted from the long day at Al Forno, we find great pleasure in cooking for each other and sharing this very private time. There's nothing to revive a lagging spirit like something good to eat.

Here are some of our favorites:

Spaghetti with Fresh Spinach and Gorgonzola
Pantry Spaghetti
Vintner's Spaghetti
Pappardelle with Olives, Thyme, and Lemon
George's Spaghetti with Raw Cucumber and Basil
Spaghetti with Sizzled Capers and Herbs
Spaghetti Aglio-Olio
4AM Spaghetti for One
Mostaccioli with Tomato "Pesto"
Spaghettini with Tomatoes, Cinnamon, and Mint
Salina-Style Spaghettini with Cherry Tomatoes
Spaghettini with Tomatoes, Garlic, and Hot Pepper
Midnight Meat Sauce for Spaghetti
Fettuccine with Mascarpone and Parmigiano-Reggiano
Penne with Anna's Idea

Pasta Pantry

Anchovies

Anchovies are good ensemble players; they can be subtle or aggressive. In small quantities—to add depth to a sauce or round out the salt—they will remain in the wings like stage prompters whispering in the dark. Give them a starring role, and they will shine in the spotlight and command the stage. Either way, it takes excellent quality and a judicious director to finesse a stunning performance. Handled properly, anchovies are delicious.

Start with the best anchovies you can find. A brand that stands out is the small, artisanal-quality producer Rustichella d'Abruzzo. Plump, pink fillets from Adriatic Sea swimmers are cured in salt, skinned, deboned, and packed in small jars with extra virgin olive oil. Use them right out of the container.

Most commercially canned anchovy fillets do not come with the same credentials. They are packed in inferior oil and must be rinsed in running water and dried on paper towels to remove the oil and excess salt. A better choice is whole anchovies cured and packed in salt. They are shipped in large tins and sold in small (or large) quantities in the deli section of well-stocked supermarkets or Italian specialty stores.

To separate whole, salted anchovies into fillets, rinse them under cold, running water to remove excess salt. If they are stiff, soak them for a few minutes in cool water until they are pliable. Rinse again under cold, running water while gently rubbing off their skin. Scrape away any remaining pesky bits of skin with a knife. Pull off the fins. Poke your finger into the tummy cavity and gently separate one fillet from the central bone. Now you can remove and discard the central bone and tail clinging to the second fillet. Rinse again and pat dry with paper towels. One salted anchovy will yield two fillets.

Bread and Bread Crumbs

A piece of bread is perfect for soaking up a puddle of sauce left in the pasta bowl after the spaghetti or macaroni has been eaten. We mean a simple, straightforward Italian loaf or country-style bread. Sourdough, although delicious on its own slathered with butter, is too aggressive and overwhelms subtle flavors rather than complementing them.

We make our bread crumbs from the same plain Italian or country bread. Cut up or tear apart any of your leftovers (smaller chunks are easier to grind up). Leave them on the counter in an open basket for a day or two to completely dry out. Whirl the pieces in a food processor until the crumbs are fine. There are always larger bits that don't break down completely. Use a mesh colander to sift the bread crumbs. Store the fine ones that slip through the screen in a clean, dry jar. We save the coarse crumbs in another jar to use on salads instead of croutons.

Capers

Since discovering sun-dried capers cured in salt in Sicily, we no longer buy those that are brined and put up in jars. Salted capers have the pure, direct taste of the flower bud without interference from vinegar or brine. Sun-dried capers seem to last forever, but their salt becomes more pronounced as the buds dehydrate from age. Best to buy small quantities.

Put the salted capers in a sieve and rinse under cool, running water (soak them for 15 to 20 minutes if you are particularly sensitive to salt). Drain and dry on paper towels. Occasionally, we use capers without rinsing but add no additional salt to the recipe.

Chicken Stock

Many cooks think making stock is the perfect way to use up vegetable peels, bits, pieces, and scraps of everything, but George has an entirely different philosophy. At home, we make stock from the bones from a carved bird whether it be roast chicken, turkey, or duck (or from freshly roasted poultry necks and backs). We break it up, carcass, skin, and all, and put it in a stockpot with any leftover drippings and juices with a good sprinkle of salt. Having set aside the innards—liver, gizzards, and heart—before cooking the bird, we put them into the pot. We add 1 or 2 peeled and chopped carrots, a cut-up stalk of celery with tender celery leaves, 2 large peeled and chopped onions, and cover with cold water. For aromatics, we put in a few sprigs of parsley, 2 cloves, 1 or 2 fresh bay leaves, a few fennel seeds, a dozen black peppercorns and, in summer, a cut-up garden tomato. We bring everything to a boil, then reduce the heat to maintain a gentle simmer for an hour or so. It's a very casual process that rewards with a delicious broth—all done after dinner in the time it takes to clear plates, wash the dishes, pots, and pans, and get the kitchen back in order. Before we go to bed we strain the stock into a bowl nesting in a larger bowl filled with ice. The cold stock is transferred to quart containers, covered, and refrigerated for up to 3 days—or frozen to have on hand for future use.

We used to be finicky about removing and discarding the roasted skin and every bit of fat before beginning a stock. But all that is wasted effort. After the stock has been strained and chilled, all the fat rises to the surface, solidifies, and is easily removed. What remains is flavor as the taste of fat is water-soluble. And that flavor is a welcome component in many of our recipes. It adds a richness and depth to even the most simple sauce—you'll see what we mean when you prepare Fettuccine with a Delicate Tomato Sauce (page 71) or Farfalle with Zucchini, Zucchini Flowers, and Broth (page 33).

Flour

All-purpose flour differs *in* composition regionally in the United States depending on where the wheat is grown and how it is milled. The South and Pacific Northwest national brands have a lower protein content than the national brands in other areas of the country, which is why biscuits in the South are fluffier and more tender than those produced in New England. When making pasta at home, a lower protein flour will produce a softer dough, while a higher protein flour will produce a sturdier one. Will it make a difference in your kitchen? Yes. Will it be critical? No. We tested George's Fresh Pasta (page 212) with Italian 00 flour, French #45 and #55 flour, and King Arthur unbleached all-purpose flour, available all over the Northeast (and through their mail-order catalog). With minor adjustments in the amount of water and flour (a dry mixture will require a bit more water while a sticky dough may need an extra tablespoon or two of flour), all produced very good pasta.

Garlic

While garlic is an important ingredient in Italian cooking, contrary to popular belief, it is used with moderation—especially in the north. In our kitchen, we use only fresh garlic, peeled from the cloves of tightly clustered heads. The fresher the garlic, the better; so choose heads of garlic that seem heavy for their size, the way one would choose citrus fruit. It is an indication of its moisture content and youth.

Do not be tempted by the convenience of peeled garlic cloves packed in jars. They are treated with a preservative to keep the cloves white, which is so effective that the garlic will not turn color when cooked in hot oil or butter. Pass right by the prepared chopped garlic in oil or water and—above all—garlic powder. Both are inferior to fresh garlic and will lend a pungent, harsh taste to your food.

Grana Padano

The only thing wrong with Grana Padano is that it isn't Parmigiano-Reggiano. For that reason, it gets a bum rap. But why get touchy about it? They are two distinctly different cheeses and should not be compared. True, they both fall under the category "grana," meaning they are hard, grainy-textured cheeses often used interchangeably; both are made from cow's milk. They each have the D.O.P. status (*Denominazione di Origine Protetta*, or Protected Designation of Origin).

Parmigiano-Reggiano is, without question, the more famous, complex, and regal cheese, produced in a small, concentrated area consisting of five neighboring provinces. It is made under stricter regulations, is aged longer, and is more costly to produce, which is why we pay more for it. Grana Padano casts a wider net. It is made in a larger territory—twenty-seven provinces—with a bigger, more industrial production. Each cheese should be appreciated as unique—related like stepsisters, not twins.

That said, you can find fine examples of Grana Padano, and a nice fresh hunk, eaten on its own or grated over pasta, can be very good indeed.

Mozzarella

Genuine mozzarella is made from buffalo's milk in Campania in the south of Italy. It must be eaten absolutely fresh. The cheese is a flat-out dream with a texture that is creamy, supple, soft, and velvety. When cut, it oozes its milky whey and makes a sensational partner with tomato and its juices (try the Spaghetti with Fresh Tomatoes and Mozzarella on page 87).

Much more widely available in Italy and in the United States is cow's milk mozzarella, called *fior di latte*. Though less lush than buffalo mozzarella, it is delicious and easily found in well-stocked supermarkets and specialty stores. When buying mozzarella, don't settle for inferior cheese! The individual roundish balls should be stored in a liquid bath (packed individually in sealed plastic bags or bobbing about en masse in a container). Fresh mozzarella is a gastronomic pleasure and a far cry from the dry, rubbery, yellow-hued, supermarket variety sold dry in shrink-wrap plastic.

Olive Oil—The Extra Virgin

Olive oil is an obvious choice when dressing salads, but it is also a wonderful cooking ingredient. As excellent olive oils have become available in the United States, our cooking has come to rely much less on butter and much more on extra virgin olive oil.

Though the olive oil industry in Italy has strict rules, you need a few facts to navigate the labels. First, look for the term "extra virgin" to identify the highest grade of cold-pressed olive oil containing no more than 1 percent acidity in the form of oleic acid. In the fine print, you should see the words "produced and bottled," *produtto e imbottigliato*, to be sure you are getting olive oil from a guaranteed source, the producer's own land. If the label simply says "produced" or "bottled," you may be paying for oil from olives grown in an entirely different country. A good tip is to look for olive oil produced by a wine estate you respect (we love the olive oils from Tenuta di Capezzana, Regaleali, Castello di Ama, and Frescobaldi Laudemio). Chances are if they are producing high-quality wines, they will not tarnish their reputation by putting their name on inferior oil. Just like wine, olive oil is different from harvest to harvest with some years better than others. A notable producer will make the best of the conditions in an off year, though their yields may be greatly reduced.

Olive oil does not have an infinite shelf life; it is best consumed within a year of its production. Many of the better olive oils are vintage dated so you know exactly how old it is and how long it has been on the grocery shelf. Once you have made your purchase, preserve the flavor of the olive oil by storing it in a cool, dark place. Heat and light will hasten its deterioration. Though you may be tempted to refrigerate your oil, resist. Any droplets of water from the condensation occurring from change in temperature from the cold fridge to your kitchen counter will eventually ruin the olive oil.

In terms of taste, extra virgin olive oils vary greatly from different regions and different producers. We like the assertive flavor of Tuscan olive oil, especially when it is first pressed and at its friskiest. It may be too strong, however, for delicate foods like fish and shellfish. In such cases, look for olive oils from coastal regions, such as Liguria.

This may sound like a lot to remember just to buy a bottle of olive oil. The best oil is costly. A little research will reward you with enjoyment enough to justify its price.

Pancetta

Pancetta is unsmoked pork belly cured in salt and spices. In Italy, it is eaten just like prosciutto as an antipasto or as a filling for a *panino*, or sandwich. Pancetta is also used as an ingredient in cooking, lending its distinctive taste to sauces, stews, braises, and vegetable dishes. American smoked bacon (also made from pork belly) looks like pancetta and for that reason is sometimes suggested as a substitute. We find it a mismatched pinch-hitter. The smoky taste is invasive rather than complementary. If you cannot find a satisfactory pancetta at a shop specializing in Italian products, use streaky salt pork instead—blanch it in boiling water before using to eliminate some of its salt.

Parmigiano-Reggiano

There is nothing comparable to authentic Parmigiano-Reggiano. The genuine article comes in large wheels weighing 60 to 70 pounds. The outside rind is stenciled with the words "PARMIGIANO-REGGIANO"—a guarantee you are buying the true cow's milk cheese produced and aged in the zones around Parma. Buy Parmigiano-Reggiano in a chunk—cut from the wheel to order—from a reputable market. Request a piece with the rind attached to the chunk as it will help retain its moisture content. Fresh is best, so buy according to the amount you will use within a few weeks. Store it in the fridge wrapped in deli paper or wax paper with an added outside layer of foil. Grate only as much as you will use right away. After the shredded bits are exposed to air, the cheese quickly loses its savor.

Parmigiano-Reggiano is pale gold in color with tiny white dots. It has a nutty, rich, complex, and slightly salty taste. It melts readily on top of hot pasta or pizza. Don't discard the rind; it's completely edible. Save the rinds (well wrapped and stored in the refrigerator) to add to soups, or to tomato or meat sauces for macaroni. The rind softens in cooking, lending its splendid flavor and adding extra richness to a dish.

A generous sprinkle of Parmigiano-Reggiano is used on many pasta dishes, especially those made with butter. It is not, however, appropriate or necessary for all pasta. For instance, Parmigiano-Reggiano is never combined with fish-based pastas—that's a no-no in Italy as home cooks and professionals alike agree it takes away from the fresh, briny flavor of seafood.

Pasta (Dried)

Our pantry is never without several packages of dried pasta made from hard wheat flour and water. George adores "string" pasta—spaghetti, cappellini, and linguine are his favorites. Johanne shares his lust for strands, but also craves the chewy texture of thicker-walled macaroni like rigatoni, orecchiette, or penne. We buy dried ribbon noodles, too, like tagliatelle, fettuccine, and pappardelle. These are available made from wheat flour and water or with wheat flour and eggs. Buy ribbon noodles packaged in nests rather than in long strands; the nests cook more evenly and are less prone to sticking together.

Certain pasta shapes complement different sauces. There are rules—but common sense and your judgment should be your guide (good news for anarchists). Whatever shape you choose, look for fine-quality dried pasta. The best comes from artisans who make pasta from excellent select wheat varieties and exceptional water. In the artisanal preparation, the ingredients are pampered—it's like a pasta spa. Everything is done slowly and carefully. The dough is mixed in small machines at a drowsy clip and kneaded at a snail's pace. Then, the shapes are created by extruding the pasta through various hand-carved bronze dies that are rough textured and cause enough of a drag to delay its arrival at the other end. Drying the pasta is another leisurely process—it can take as long as forty-eight to fifty-six hours. The resulting pasta has a characteristically chapped surface and matte finish as though it had been dusted with the finest powder. All the gentle coddling pays off in satisfyingly dense, rustic, flavorful pasta with a chewy mouth-feel. When you drop it into boiling water, you can smell its wheaty aroma rising up in the steam. It tastes great unadorned, but sings with sauces. The uneven exterior of the noodles hugs and draws flavors to it. Two exceptional brands to look for are Rustichella d'Abruzzo and Latini. More widely available brands of quality are De Cecco and Del Verde.

Industrial pasta is easy to find stacked chockablock on the shelves of our supermarkets. Their production is fast paced and heat enhanced (warm water to mix with the wheat; smooth-surfaced Teflon-coated dies to push the dough speedily into shapes; and high temperatures to dry the pasta pronto). The warmth robs the wheat of flavor and the extrusion creates a smooth, slick surface that sauces slide away from rather than attract. Quality does come at a price—you can expect to pay more for artisanal pasta. Still, pound for pound, it's a comparative bargain.

Pecorino Romano

Pecorino Romano, sometimes simply called Romano, is a sharp, aged cheese made from ewe's milk. Freshly grated, it enhances macaroni sauces that benefit from a forceful flavor like Spaghettini with Paprika, Garlic, and Pecorino (page 53), or Linguine with Frenched Green Beans and Parsley "Pesto" (page 58). It should be purchased in a chunk like Parmigiano-Reggiano. The cheeses are not interchangeable. Where Parmigiano is lush, mild, and mellow, Romano is heady and keen. The two cheeses are sometimes used in combination, though one must be careful not to overpower the more delicate Parmigiano.

Pine Nuts, or *Pignoli*

Buy pine nuts, called pignoli in Italian, with your nose and palate. They should have a delicate smell and taste sweet and creamy. Ask a reputable merchant for pignoli (or pinoli) imported from Europe as they have a higher protein and lower oil content than either the Asian or American varieties. European pine nuts are long and thin; Asian ones are shorter, plumper, and rounded at one end. Like all nuts, pine nuts do not age well. Keep them well wrapped so as not to absorb other flavors, and store them away from heat in the fridge or freezer. Buy only the amount you know you will use quickly.

Portion Scale

Bakers are familiar with portion scales that measure grams and ounces (grams are slightly more accurate). They know the portion scale is the only tool that provides absolute precision in their formulas. It is indispensable in our restaurant kitchen, too, not only for an accurate baking blueprint, but also for assembling ingredients for any recipe to ensure consistency.

At home, we use an inexpensive electronic scale that measures from 5 grams to 5 kilos; or roughly from ¼ ounce to 10 pounds. It is especially useful in weighing the ingredients for homemade fresh pasta (and for measuring out portions of dried pasta, too). To give you an example, flour measured in a cup can vary in weight depending on whether it was fluffed, sifted, scooped, spooned, or leveled. One person's cup can be another person's ¾ cup. Grams and ounces do not change; 250 grams or 8 ounces today will be the same tomorrow.

Prosciutto di Parma and Prosciutto Cotto

Prosciutto di Parma, or Parma ham, is cured pork that is aged on average for 14 months. It is deep, rosy pink with a sweet taste and supple texture. It is more expensive than domestically produced prosciutto and it is worth every dime. The hams from U.S. manufacturers tend to be rather salty and dry. Prosciutto di Parma is available in well-stocked grocery and specialty shops featuring Italian products. If you buy it sliced, keep it well wrapped and refrigerated as it can dry out quickly.

Produced in Italy and imported into the United States, *prosciutto cotto* is boned pork thigh pickled in salt and spices, then steamed and pressed into a rounded oblong mold. Light pink in color, it resembles cooked ham, widely available in supermarkets everywhere. The two are interchangeable.

Ricotta

Ricotta was originally made from sheep's milk. Today, in Italy and in the United States, it is more common to find ricotta made with cow's milk. It is a soft, pure white whey cheese with a creamy texture. It has many uses in the kitchen from appetizers and pasta right through desserts. When purchasing ricotta, look for purity. Buy cheese made without additives like guar gum. It is worth the effort to find a store specializing in good Italian products where you might find an artisanally produced fresh ricotta.

Faith Willinger, born-again Tuscan, author of *Eating In Italy* and *Red, White & Greens*, is our official muse in all things gastronomic in Italy. She has lived in Florence for more than two decades and spends every waking hour discovering and promoting the food and wine of her adopted country. It was Faith who gave us the idea to make our own ricotta. Made from readily available ingredients, it is superior to the packaged brands in the supermarket. And vegetarians, take note: It is made with lemon juice rather than rennet. This is our adaptation of Faith's recipe.

4 cups whole milk
1 cup heavy cream
½ teaspoon fine sea salt (optional)
Juice of 1 lemon

1. Combine the milk, heavy cream, and salt (if using) in a nonreactive saucepan with a heavy bottom. Bring to a boil over moderately high heat.

2. Add the lemon juice and continue to boil, stirring constantly and adjusting the heat so the cream does not overflow, until the curds separate, about 1 minute.

3. Pour into a very fine-mesh stainless steel strainer, or an open-mesh strainer lined with several layers of cheesecloth. Place the strainer over a deep enough bowl or saucepan so that the bottom does not sit in liquid. Allow the cheese to drain for 1 hour in the refrigerator. Discard the liquid and transfer the ricotta to a covered container. Refrigerate until ready to use. The cheese will keep for 2 or 3 days.

Makes 1 cup

Ricotta Infornata

Ricotta infornata, or baked ricotta, is sold in toasty, brunette-hued wheels and has a nutty, faintly smoky flavor. Unable to find ricotta infornata in the United States, we experimented with making it ourselves. Here is our recipe. Cut it into wedges and serve it accompanied by a young, fresh Sicilian white wine—or try it on Salina-Style Spaghettini with Cherry Tomatoes (page 81).

The longer you bake the ricotta, the deeper the color and the richer and more flavorful the cheese will be.

1 pound fresh ricotta
Pinch to ¾ teaspoon sea salt, plus more for baking
Unsalted butter

1. Taste the ricotta. If it needs salt, mix it with a pinch or up to ¾ teaspoon. Transfer to a perforated cheese mold or fine-mesh strainer or colander to allow excess liquid to drain. Place the mold or strainer over a bowl to catch the liquid. Loosely cover and refrigerate for at least 24 to 36 hours.

2. Preheat the oven to 350 degrees.

3. Butter the bottom and sides of a small ceramic baking dish. Cover with a thin layer of salt. Gently turn the cheese out onto the baking dish without disturbing its form. Sprinkle salt lightly over the surface of the cheese to create a protective layer.

4. Bake for at least 60 minutes or up to 90 minutes until the ricotta becomes a rich, nutty brown.

5. Cool to room temperature, then cover and store in the refrigerator for up to 1 week.

Makes 1 ricotta infornata

Salt: Kosher and Sea

At our restaurant, Al Forno, we like light and flaky kosher salt that falls from your fingers without leaving grains sticking to them. Be sure to check the ingredients on the label. Some brands of kosher salt (the blue box) contain an anticaking agent. Look for one (white, red, and yellow box) without the added chemical.

We also use sea salt at Al Forno and at home. It has a pure taste—sweeter and rounder than kosher. At home we keep three saltcellars next to the stove: one for kosher, one for fine-grained sea salt, and the other for coarse-grained sea salt. The fine goes into any preparation that requires the salt to "melt" into the food quickly. The coarse sea salt goes into the pasta pot, where the boiling water quickly dissolves it.

Sea salt has become rather fashionable recently, with store shelves groaning under the weight of myriad choices. Prices can be staggering, too, and ingredients confusing. Take nothing for granted. Read the label. It should say "sea salt." Pass on those that are iodized or those with any additives.

Table salt never touches our food because it contains a metallic-tasting chemical—best left in the laboratory—to keep the salt from reacting to humidity and clogging the shaker.

Our recipes call for sea salt, but you can substitute kosher salt if you like. If you are not used to using sea salt, you may find it "saltier." Adjust the amount to your taste and health requirements.

Tomatoes: Fresh, Canned, and Juice

Tomatoes are indispensable in the Italian kitchen. It's hard to imagine the *cucina* before their introduction from the New World in the sixteenth century. What did they eat on their maca-roni? Catherine de' Medici, the Tuscan dauphine, brought her cooks from Italy to France in 1533 before her marriage to the future King Henri II. There were two pasta dishes prepared for her wedding: one moistened with pan juices from roast meats tossed with cheese; the other one sweet with butter, honey, cinnamon, and saffron.

The Neapolitans were the first Italians to embrace tomatoes and add them to their culinary repertoire. It took the rest of the people on the peninsula many more years to be wooed by and wed to them. In Italy today, tomatoes are used in all sorts of preparations: in sauces for pasta or rice, eaten raw in salads, stewed, stuffed, sautéed—just to name a few.

In our kitchen (restaurant or home), fresh tomatoes are used with abandon—but only in the summer when they are picked from the vine ripe and juicy. We use both plum tomatoes and the rounder "salad" tomatoes for pasta sauces. The plum type is fleshier with fewer seeds. The round ones are generally juicier. Either way, use fresh tomatoes that have a rich, deep taste with a good acid balance. Avoid overly sweet varieties as they can dull the palate rather than excite it.

Out of season, canned tomatoes are the preference. Imported tins of San Marzano plum tomatoes are excellent (brands will naturally vary in taste and quality). Look for those that boast the D.O.P. (*Denominazione di Origine Protetta*—Protected Designation of Origin) pedigree. There are plenty of good choices for California canned tomatoes, too. Opt for ones that have no additives, such as the organic tomatoes from Muir Glen. They produce a quality tomato paste, too.

When we want a smooth, light tomato sauce, we use bottled organic tomato juice for all or part of the recipe—the Fettuccine with a Delicate Tomato Sauce (page 71) and the Macaroni with Hidden Asset Meat Sauce (page 128) are good examples. Tomato juice is also good to have on hand when you want to thin a thick sauce in a jiffy without losing the tomato taste.

Pasta Tips

Here are our pasta tips:

First and foremost, pasta is the star of the show. Complement it with a sauce or a condiment, but don't overwhelm it. When cooked properly and sauced judiciously, pasta is the most dazzling of dishes.

Get ready before you begin so you can proceed through all the steps quickly and efficiently. The pasta should not wait between draining and saucing.

Choose your pot, fill it with an adequate amount of water (we use a large pot filled with 6 quarts of water for up to one pound of pasta and set it to boil on the stove. It is important that the pasta cook in rapidly boiling water, so put the pot on the burner with the most Btus to maintain a strong boil over high heat. Reduce the heat if the water threatens to boil over. If you are cooking a large quantity, it is best to use more than one pot to avoid overcrowding. (Pasta needs enough water around it to dilute its starch. Too much pasta in too little water will give you a gummy result.)

We use a large stockpot for packaged "string" cuts like spaghetti and linguine (and we place a colander in the sink for draining—you don't want to be rummaging around for it when the pasta is ready. A few extra minutes sitting in water will overcook the noodles). For sturdy macaroni like rigatoni, and for homemade and filled pastas, we use a pasta cooker with a built-in strainer. The Alessi pasta pot is exquisite aesthetically; it also works better than any other built-in-strainer type of pot we have used. If you are draining pasta from a stockpot into a colander in the sink, use this tip we learned from Martha Stewart while filming a pasta segment for her TV show: Run the cold water on the side of the sink (not in the pot, of course). It will prevent the "all steam facial" and, ladies, your mascara won't run.

A handy tool:

Spring-loaded tongs are great for stirring pasta in boiling water and tossing it in sauces. They also make perfect serving utensils along with a serving spoon for more sauce.

Get your bowls or plates ready:

To keep your pasta steaming as you enjoy it, heat the serving and/or individual serving bowls or plates. Thick china will hold the heat best. Be careful not to heat them to the point that the pasta and sauce sizzle when added. They should not be so hot that you need mitts to pick them up. For delicate sauces like the creamy egg-based ones, or pesto, which should never be heated, use warm, not hot bowls. For uncooked sauces, especially those meant to be served less than piping hot, you can use a room-temperature bowl.

If you don't have a plate warmer in your kitchen, soak the bowls in a tub of hot water for 5 minutes before serving. A large serving bowl can be filled with hot water, set next to the sink, and drained just before adding the pasta.

We use individual, shallow—never deep—soup bowls with a wide rim for most of our pastas. Some varieties, especially homemade ribbon noodles or lasagnette, are better served on a flat plate (also with a wide rim) so they can spread out. As fluffy as the noodles seem, they weigh each other down if stacked too high and stick together.

Time to cook:

Put the salt (we use additive-free sea salt) in the boiling water just before adding the pasta; and remember to salt generously to pump up the neutral taste of the pasta. Salt in the water also helps prevent noodles from sticking together. We use 3½ tablespoons salt to 6 quarts of water.

Never add oil to the water (some cooks believe it prevents the pasta from sticking together). It's a waste of money and could prove hazardous if the pot boils over. Plus, any oil clinging to the pasta will make it slippery and prevent the sauce from absorbing into it. The best way to prevent pasta from sticking together is to stir it as soon as you drop it into the pot. Then stir frequently in abundant, rapidly boiling water.

Don't trust the suggested cooking time on the package. The pasta generally takes less time to cook. Testing is the only reliable way to determine whether the pasta has cooked enough or not. Remember, too, each brand of pasta cooks differently. There are some, like Latini, that go from firm to overcooked in the time it takes to drain and sauce it (cook it less than you think is necessary; it will soften further in its sauce). Experience must be your guide—start testing by tasting at least 2 minutes before the recommended cooking time, then every 30 seconds until it is al dente. Stick to a particular brand until you know its specific qualities and quirks.

When is the pasta cooked?

Pasta continues to soften in water (or in sauce) even if the heat is turned off. Drain it just before you think it is perfectly done—the center should be quite firm—so that you have enough time to put it together with the sauce and serve it al dente.

The string cuts, from the thinnest cappellini to the thicker spaghetti and linguine, are most vulnerable and can overcook easily. If preparing a large quantity of pasta, choose a sturdy macaroni like rigatoni, penne, ziti, or bowties.

Homemade pasta will be softer and its texture silkier than any dried boxed pasta, but it should still offer some resistance under your teeth.

Before and after you drain the pasta:

Always reserve some of the pasta cooking water. You don't always need it, but if a sauce is too thick you can use some of the hot liquid to thin it out. If the sauce is too thin, add some pasta water and boil vigorously for a few minutes. The starch in the pasta cooking water will help to thicken your sauce.

Never rinse the pasta after it is drained. The starch clinging to it is important to its taste and texture and allows the sauce to "stick" to the pasta.

Combining the pasta with its sauce:

Pasta is porous and sometimes benefits from a few last minutes' cooking in its sauce to absorb flavor (follow the advice of individual recipes). For this technique, boil the pasta until it is firm and slightly underdone. Drain, and toss in sauce prepared in a skillet or sauté pan. Finish cooking the pasta over high heat to reduce the sauce, or over a gentle flame if the sauce is the perfect consistency.

With rare exceptions, pasta benefits from a good toss in its sauce. If it is an oil-based one, you could toss the drained pasta with a little extra oil to keep it moist and moving freely. If the sauce is butter based, toss the pasta with a few extra tablespoons of butter before adding the sauce. The butter trick is especially beneficial to homemade pasta, which can clump if not sufficiently lubricated. It, too, should move freely, sliding upon itself rather than sticking together.

A note on cheese:

Not all pasta is meant to be served with grated cheese (follow the suggestions of individual recipes). Sauces containing seafood, for example, are prepared and served without cheese. There are exceptions to the rule (in Italy, there are always exceptions to the rule) where sharp, salty Pecorino Romano is a welcome addition to some seafood dishes, but not Parmigiano-Reggiano (the accepted belief is that cheese can dull the fresh taste of seafood and make it seem less pristine).

For pasta that goes well with cheese, keep a grater and chunks of cheese at the table to add if appropriate. We use the plastic hand-cranked Zyliss grater with a stainless steel drum. It's sturdy, handy, and efficient.

Finally:

Pasta waits for no one. Savvy cooks have their guests seated at the table before dropping pasta into boiling water. As soon as it is served, compliment the cook by picking up your fork and eating.

  on top of spaghetti...

Pasta with Vegetables, Legumes, and Herbs

◆ Spaghetti La Bomba or Spaghetti Boom Boom ◆

Serves 6 to 8 as a first course or 4 to 6 as a main course

We found a gas station in Italy worth mentioning in a cookbook. The nondescript service area Irpinia Sud, on the autostrada in Campania south of Naples, turned out to have a cornucopia of delicious edibles. The shelves were lined with quality wines, too, from the area, other regions of Italy, and even France. They had a small, but remarkable, selection of food, including locally prepared products and fresh mozzarella. We couldn't resist buying a jarred pasta sauce of chopped vegetables with an ample amount of hot peppers aptly named "La Bomba"—"the bomb" in English—or Boom Boom as George calls it. This is our homemade version. You can make it as explosive as you like with the quantity and intensity of hot peppers you add. It is delicious on pasta and makes a superb spread for crostini, too.

Even though the sauce is puréed at the end, it helps to cut the vegetables into a very small dice—less than ½-inch cubes—for even cooking and absorption of the olive oil.

½ cup extra virgin olive oil
1 tablespoon minced fresh garlic
1 to 2 fresh hot peppers
½ cup diced green bell pepper
½ teaspoon or more fine sea salt
1 heaping cup diced fresh artichoke bottoms, all traces of choke removed (about 6 medium artichokes)
1 heaping cup peeled and diced eggplant
1 heaping cup diced zucchini
5 to 6 fresh basil leaves
1 pound dried spaghetti or spaghettini

1. Combine the olive oil, garlic, and hot peppers in a large straight-sided sauté pan. Sauté over moderate heat for about 5 minutes until soft. Add the green pepper and salt, and sauté an additional 5 minutes. Add the artichoke bottoms, eggplant, and zucchini. Sauté the vegetables over moderately high heat, stirring constantly, until every morsel is well coated. Most of the olive oil will disappear into the eggplant, which is like a sponge. Lower the heat to moderate and sauté, stirring often, until the vegetables are very soft without browning, about 25 minutes. During this time the eggplant will give up much of the oil and its natural juices to keep everything moist. Roughly tear the basil into the mixture and cook for 3 minutes more.

2. Allow the vegetables to cool for 10 minutes. Transfer them to the bowl of a food processor. Coarsely chop the vegetables with on and off pulses until you have a chunky purée. Taste for salt and add more if necessary. You may use the sauce right away or allow it to cool to room temperature, cover, and store in the refrigerator for up to 3 days.

3. To serve, bring plenty of water to a boil in a large pot. Generously salt the water and drop in the pasta. Cook, stirring often, until al dente. Drain, and transfer the pasta to a heated serving dish. Toss with enough sauce to coat the strands of spaghetti, reserving ½ cup or so to pass at the table. Serve immediately.

◆ Penne with Easy Norma ◆

Serves 6 to 8 as a first course or 4 to 6 as a main course

Pasta alla Norma is a Sicilian dish made with eggplant deep-fried in an abundant quantity of hot oil. This is an excellent technique but tricky, expensive, and time-consuming. We omit the frying step and cook the eggplant in the sauce until it is meltingly tender.

1¼ cups finely chopped onions
3 cups tomato juice, preferably organic
4 to 4½ cups cubed unpeeled eggplant
1 teaspoon or more sea salt
½ cup extra virgin olive oil
¼ teaspoon cayenne (optional)
1 pound dried penne or spaghetti
Freshly grated ricotta salata

1. Combine the onions, tomato juice, and 1 cup water in a large saucepan. Bring to a boil, cover, reduce the heat, and simmer for 8 to 10 minutes. Add the eggplant and salt. Pour over the olive oil, sprinkle in the cayenne if you like, and stir to combine. Cover, bring to a boil, reduce the heat, and simmer gently for 40 minutes, stirring occasionally, until the eggplant is meltingly tender and the sauce has thickened. If the sauce seems too thin, uncover and boil over moderately high heat, stirring constantly, for 5 minutes to thicken. Set aside over very low heat.

2. Bring a large pot of water to a boil for the pasta. Generously salt the water and drop in the penne. Cook, stirring often, until al dente. Drain the penne in a colander. Return the pasta to the pot and ladle over enough of the eggplant sauce to coat the penne generously. Sprinkle with some of the ricotta salata and toss. Serve right away in heated bowls, passing extra sauce and cheese at the table.

◆ Spaghetti "Spaghettata" ◆

Makes about ¾ cup chunky spaghettata or ½ cup finely ground

All over Italy, little sacks of dried herb and spice mixtures are sold in farmers' markets, butcher shops, and coffee bars along the autostrada, or in any big supermercato. There's an endless variety of these mixtures—some labeled to use with fish, others with meat, etc. George snatches up the ones designed for pasta, the "spaghettata" blend. These aromatic grab bags vary from package to package. Some are blow-your-head-off spicy with a predominance of hot pepper; others are tamer with oregano or chives standing out. The best are noncommercially made, prepared by artisans who forage for wild herbs or grow their own.

George loves the stuff and keeps a little jar on the table when he makes a simple pasta. He's also been known to sneak a pinch or two from his pocket to jazz up his pie at the local pizzeria. When his stash from Italy runs out, he concocts his own spaghettata. Unlike the merchants at daily markets in the Campo dei Fiori in Rome, or the Mercato di Sant'Ambrogio in Florence, who would never divulge the exact proportions of their secret blends, George is happy to share his recipe. Tucked away in the pantry, it's a secret weapon ready to liven up a quick bowl of spaghetti.

George's mix is heady with garlic and quite spicy. You can tone down the heat by using less pepper flakes. The oregano taste should be pronounced, so add more if yours doesn't have a strong aroma.

George dries his spaghettata on the kitchen counter during cool months, or outside in the sun with a mesh fly cover over it in the summer. If your climate is very humid or moist, use a fruit and vegetable dehydrator or an oven set on very low heat instead of air-drying the mix.

George's Spaghettata Blend

1 cup tightly packed fresh flat-leaf parsley leaves
2 tablespoons fine sea salt
¼ cup crushed red pepper flakes
1 teaspoon dried oregano
2 tablespoons finely chopped fresh garlic

1. Combine all the ingredients in a food processor. Pulse on and off until finely chopped.

2. Transfer to a plate and spread out the mixture. Keep in the open air, tossing every now and then (perhaps two or three times a day) until completely dried—3 to 5 days. If you live in a moist climate, this could take more time. Be sure there is no moisture in the mixture before you transfer to a clean, dry jar. If you would like a less chunky texture, pulse it in the food processor to a fine powder before storing.

The Spaghetti

Cook 2 ounces spaghetti per person for a first course or 4 ounces spaghetti per person as a main course.

The No-Fuss Choices for George's Favorite Sauces

Olive oil: Drizzle the cooked and drained pasta with extra virgin olive oil, a few tablespoons of pasta water, and a sprinkle of spaghettata. Pass more at the table for extra seasoning. Or warm the olive oil and spaghettata together in a sauté pan until the mixture softens and becomes very aromatic before adding cooked and drained spaghetti with a little pasta water. It is a small change that results in a different taste.

Butter: Toss the cooked and drained spaghetti with softened butter and a little pasta water. Sprinkle with spaghettata.

Ricotta: Toss the cooked and drained spaghetti with fork-fluffed ricotta—a few tablespoons for each 4-ounce portion. Soften the cheese with a few tablespoons of pasta water and sprinkle with spaghettata.

4AM Spaghetti for One (page 54): Prepare the recipe, adding as much spaghettata as you like to bolster the spices.

Tomato: Spaghettata enhances many tomato sauces for pasta. Try it when you dress spaghetti with Pomodoro—Al Forno's Tomato Sauce (page 70), or sprinkle it on Bucatini with Fresh Tomatoes, Pancetta, and Onion (page 80).

on top of spaghetti...

◆ Spaghetti with Mushroom Ragù ◆

Serves 6 to 8 as a first course or 4 to 6 as a main course

This is what meat-loving Tuscans call *sugo finto*, or fake sauce, because it contains no meat even though it tastes like it does. Mushrooms create the pretense here, imparting their "meaty" taste and texture to the sauce. Use the best mushrooms available—cultivated white, cremini, or portobello—in the produce section of your supermarket or at the farmers' market.

This recipe makes 3½ to 4 cups of sugo—more than ample for a pound of spaghetti. Sauce the pasta judiciously and save any leftover ragù for another meal or as a topping for crostini.

1 ounce dried porcini mushrooms
¾ cup finely diced onions
½ cup peeled and finely diced carrots
½ cup trimmed and finely diced celery
1 teaspoon finely chopped fresh garlic
2 to 3 sprigs fresh flat-leaf parsley, finely chopped
¼ cup extra virgin olive oil
1 teaspoon or more sea salt
¼ teaspoon crushed red pepper flakes
2¼ to 2½ cups finely chopped mushrooms (white, cremini, or portobello)
2 to 3 fresh sage leaves
1 sprig fresh rosemary, stemmed
1 bay leaf
½ cup dry white wine
3 cups canned puréed tomatoes
1 pound dried spaghetti or spaghettini
2 tablespoons unsalted butter
Freshly grated Parmigiano-Reggiano

1. Soak the porcini mushrooms in 2½ cups warm water for 1 hour. We like to use a 4-cup Pyrex measuring cup. With a slotted spoon or tongs, transfer the mushrooms to drain on paper towels. Gently pour most of the soaking liquid through a fine-mesh strainer suspended over a small bowl (or another Pyrex measuring cup), being careful not to disturb the particles of sand that have sunk to the bottom. Save about 2 cups of the liq-

uid and discard the remainder. Finely chop the porcini and set aside.

2. Put the onions, carrots, celery, garlic, parsley, olive oil, salt, and red pepper flakes in a large straight-sided sauté pan. Sauté over moderately high heat until the vegetables are soft, about 10 minutes. Add the mushrooms, sage, rosemary, and bay leaf, and sauté over high heat for 5 minutes, stirring often. Add the porcini and wine. Cook, stirring frequently, until most of the wine has evaporated. Add 1 cup of the reserved mushroom water and the tomatoes. Bring to a boil, reduce the heat, and simmer for 20 minutes. If the sauce seems too dry, add a bit more of the mushroom soaking liquid. Taste the sauce and add more salt if necessary.

3. To serve, bring plenty of water to a boil in a large pot. Generously salt the water and drop in the spaghetti. Cook, stirring often, until al dente, then drain and transfer to a large serving bowl. Spoon some of the sauce over the spaghetti, dot with butter, and toss; sprinkle with Parmigiano-Reggiano and toss again. Serve right away, passing more sauce and cheese at the table.

on top of spaghetti...

◆ Penne with Fresh Artichokes ◆

Serves 6 to 8 as a first course or 4 to 6 as a main course

When we were testing this recipe recently, our friends Deborah Benson and Ric Marx were visiting us from Boston. Looking at the prepped vegetables laid out on the table, we remarked that it seemed like too many artichokes for the quantity of pasta. Deborah encouraged us to use all of them, as Ric adores artichokes. It turned out to be just the right amount for an artichoke lover.

6 tablespoons extra virgin olive oil
2 cups chopped onions
3 plump garlic cloves, peeled, trimmed, and finely chopped
8 to 10 fresh artichokes, trimmed down to the hearts, chokes removed, and thinly sliced
1 teaspoon fine sea salt
1 pound dried penne
1½ to 2 tablespoons freshly squeezed lemon juice
5 to 6 tablespoons unsalted butter, at room temperature
Freshly grated Parmigiano-Reggiano

1. Bring a large pot of water to a boil for the pasta.

2. Combine 3 tablespoons of the olive oil, onions, garlic, artichokes, and half of the salt in a large straight-sided skillet. Cover and sauté over moderate heat, stirring often, until the artichokes are tender, about 15 minutes. Taste and add more salt if necessary. If the mixture seems dry, add up to 3 more tablespoons olive oil.

3. Generously salt the pasta water and drop in the penne. Cook, stirring often, until the penne are tender. Drain, saving about 1 cup of the cooking water, and transfer the penne to the sauté pan with the vegetables.

4. Add the lemon juice and butter, and toss to combine. If the mixture seems dry, add the cooking water, a few tablespoons at a time, until you have a nice, moist consistency. Serve right away, sprinkled with Parmigiano-Reggiano.

◆ Spaghetti with Fresh Spinach and Gorgonzola ◆

Serves 6 to 8 as a first course or 4 to 6 as a main course

In early spring, look for tender spinach with small leaves at the local farmers' market. It is so flavorful that it needs nothing more than a bit of Gorgonzola and butter to make a memorable dish.

4 ounces Gorgonzola, at room temperature

4 tablespoons unsalted butter, at room temperature

8 cups firmly packed trimmed young, fresh spinach

2 tablespoons extra virgin olive oil

2 teaspoons sea salt

1 pound dried spaghetti or spaghettini

10 to 12 large fresh basil leaves (optional)

1. Bring a large pot of water to a boil for the pasta.

2. In a small bowl, mush together the Gorgonzola and butter until you have a smooth paste. Set aside but do not refrigerate.

3. Wash the spinach in plenty of cold water. Drain in a colander, leaving the water clinging to the leaves.

4. Heat the olive oil in a large straight-sided skillet over moderately high heat. Add the spinach and 1 teaspoon of the salt. Toss the spinach with tongs until it has wilted. Taste it and add more salt if necessary. Turn off the heat, but keep the spinach warm on the side of the stove.

5. Generously salt the pasta water and drop in the spaghetti. Cook at a rolling boil, stirring often, until al dente. Drain the pasta, reserving about 1 cup of the cooking water. Transfer the spaghetti to the skillet and toss with the spinach. Add the Gorgonzola-butter mixture and toss to coat each strand of spaghetti. If the pasta seems dry, add a bit of cooking water and toss again. Add as much of the cooking water as you need to make a creamy consistency. If you have fresh basil, tear the leaves and toss into the spaghetti. Serve right away.

 on top of spaghetti...

Spaghettini with Creamy Spinach and Parmigiano-Reggiano

Makes 6 small first-course portions or 3 main-course portions

A pound of raw spinach equals about 8 cups, which may seem like a mountain of greens, but it will shrink considerably when cooked. This is quite a rich sauce, so 12 ounces of spaghettini are more than ample for 6 people as a first course.

12 ounces dried spaghettini
8 cups firmly packed washed and trimmed young, fresh spinach
1 cup heavy cream
10 swipes of nutmeg across a grater or more if you like
20 to 25 turns of a pepper mill filled with white peppercorns
¼ to ½ teaspoon sea salt
1 cup freshly grated Parmigiano-Reggiano

1. Bring a large pot of water to a boil for the pasta. Stir in a generous amount of salt and drop in the spaghettini. After a minute or two, add the spinach handful by handful so the water doesn't lose its boil at any time (that would cause the pasta to cook unevenly). Cook, stirring often, until al dente.

2. Meanwhile, warm the cream over moderate heat with the nutmeg, pepper, and salt. Bring it to a boil, but don't let it reduce at all. Taste the cream. It should be well flavored with nutmeg and pepper. Add more if you like.

3. Drain the spaghettini and spinach in a colander, reserving about 1 cup of the pasta cooking water. Over low heat, stir the spaghettini into the cream mixture along with most of the Parmigiano-Reggiano (the rest can be passed at the table or used to garnish the top just before serving). If the noodles absorb too much cream, add pasta water, a tablespoon at a time, until you have the consistency of heavy cream, with each serving having a little puddle on the bottom of the bowl. Serve right away.

◆ Rigatoni with Zucchini Sauce ◆

Serves 6 to 8 as a first course or 4 to 6 as a main course

Make this when zucchini is young, sweet, and tender during the early summer. Allow the vegetables to cool a bit once they are sautéed before puréeing them to retain the brilliant green of the parsley leaves.

8 tablespoons (1 stick) unsalted butter
2 pounds firm, young zucchini (5 or 6), trimmed and chopped
3 cups chopped onions
1 teaspoon or more fine sea salt
1 cup loosely packed fresh flat-leaf parsley leaves
1 pound dried rigatoni or farfalle
½ cup finely shredded zucchinio (optional)
Freshly grated Parmigiano-Reggiano
Extra virgin olive oil (optional)

1. Melt the butter in a large straight-sided sauté pan. Add the chopped zucchini, onions, and salt, and sauté over moderate heat until the vegetables are very soft without browning, 10 to 15 minutes. Set aside to cool for 20 minutes.

2. In batches, purée the zucchini-onion mixture with the parsley leaves. Return the sauce to a clean sauté pan and place over very low heat.

3. Bring a large pot of water to a boil. Generously salt the water and drop in the rigatoni. Boil the pasta, stirring often, until it is al dente. Drain, reserving ½ cup of the pasta water. Toss the pasta in the sauce, adding some of the pasta water if the sauce is too thick. Serve right away, sprinkled with shredded zucchini, if you like, Parmigiano-Reggiano, and drizzle with olive oil, if you wish.

◆ Farfalle with Zucchini, Zucchini Flowers, and Broth ◆

Serves 6 to 8 as a first course or 4 as a main course

Lucky you if you have your own vegetable garden to raid each day for fragile zucchini blossoms. The rest of us must make do with their hoped-for availability at farmers' markets. In this recipe, the flowers add their delicate taste and texture to the zucchini and broth. The combination of bright yellow petals and summer green zucchini makes a dish as pretty as it is delicious.

Look for a dried farfalle made with eggs. Be sure to test the cooking time of the pasta you choose so you can judge when to begin cooking the zucchini. The little dice will be tender after simmering 5 to 6 minutes in the broth. The zucchini should be cooked through but still firm enough to retain its shape and color without being at all mushy.

4 cups homemade chicken stock (see Pasta Pantry)
12 ounces dried egg farfalle or bowties
1 heaping cup diced tender young zucchini
48 zucchini flowers, cleaned and cut vertically into a fine julienne
8 tablespoons (1 stick) unsalted butter
Freshly grated Parmigiano-Reggiano

1. Bring a large pot of water to a boil. Use a pasta cooker with a built-in strainer if you have one.

2. Bring the chicken stock to a boil in a large straight-sided sauté pan.

3. Generously salt the boiling water and drop in the farfalle. Be sure to stir the water frequently so the pasta does not stick together.

4. After the pasta has been boiling for 4 to 5 minutes, drop the diced zucchini into the broth. Lower the heat to a lively simmer.

5. Drain the pasta while it is still very firm—about 2 minutes before al dente. Transfer the pasta to the broth. Add the flowers and butter, raise the heat, and toss together. Cook, stirring often, for 2 minutes. The sauce should be slightly thickened and glossy from the butter. Serve immediately with Parmigiano-Reggiano to pass at the table.

◆ Orecchiette with Cool Chickpeas ◆

Serves 4 as a first course or 2 to 3 as a main course

This room-temperature dish is a snap to make. All the ingredients but the pasta are assembled in advance and the orecchiette are cooked just before serving. If you want to get fancy, peel the chickpeas beforehand. Does it make a difference? Yes, the pasta dish will be more refined. Elegant or rustic? It is your choice. Either way you will have a delicious pasta.

Orecchiette, or little pasta ears, are ideal for this combination as they cuddle with the chickpeas and collect them in their little concave interiors. Slices of bread from a crusty loaf are a good accompaniment to soak up every drop of sauce in the bottom of the bowl.

1 heaping tablespoon finely chopped red onion
4 tablespoons extra virgin olive oil
1 teaspoon or more finely chopped fresh hot pepper
1 cup cooked chickpeas
1 tablespoon finely chopped fresh flat-leaf parsley
1½ tablespoons freshly squeezed lemon juice
5 large fresh mint leaves
8 ounces dried orecchiette or pasta shells
Lemon wedges (optional)

1. In a large bowl, combine the onion, olive oil, hot pepper, chickpeas, parsley, and lemon juice. Slice the mint into a fine chiffonade and stir into the chickpeas. Allow to marinate at room temperature for at least 20 minutes or up to an hour.

2. Bring a large pot of water to a boil. Add a generous amount of salt and drop in the pasta. Cook, stirring often, until al dente.

3. Drain the pasta and toss in the bowl with the chickpeas. Set aside for 5 minutes to allow the pasta to absorb the flavors. Serve with a crusty loaf of bread to dip into the sauce and lemon wedges to spritz each serving, if you like.

◆ Linguine with Spicy Lentil Sauce ◆

Serves 10 to 12 as a first course or 6 to 8 as a main course.
This recipe may be divided for fewer servings or multiplied to accommodate more guests.

We love the combination of pasta and beans or lentils and find it a great way to get a good balanced meal in one bowl.

Browning the vegetables in olive oil is a technique we learned from our friend Patrizio, a gifted chef in Tuscany. This method caramelizes the natural sugars in vegetables and boosts their flavors. It gives the sauce a richer, deeper taste—a useful tip, especially for vegetarian cooking.

George insists on cooking a string pasta—one he can twirl on his fork—for this recipe, but a sturdier macaroni, like penne or short fusilli, works equally well.

6 tablespoons extra virgin olive oil, plus additional to drizzle on the pasta
1 cup (2 stalks) finely chopped celery
1 cup finely chopped carrots
2 cups chopped onions
2 plump garlic cloves, peeled and coarsely chopped
1 to 2 fresh hot peppers, seeded and chopped
1 teaspoon fine sea salt
½ teaspoon crushed red pepper flakes
8 ounces (1½ cups) lentils
1½ pounds dried linguine or penne
1 scant tablespoon minced lemon zest
½ cup coarsely chopped fresh flat-leaf parsley

1. Heat the olive oil in a heavy saucepan. Add the celery, carrots, onions, and garlic. Sauté over moderately high heat, stirring from time to time, until the vegetables are soft and beginning to brown, about 15 minutes. Add the fresh hot peppers, salt, and red pepper flakes. Continue to sauté, allowing the vegetables to brown. This should take an additional 5 to 10 minutes. At this point it's a good idea to keep a close watch on the vegetables, stirring often, so they don't burn.

2. Add the lentils and 5 cups water. Cover, bring to a boil, lower the heat, and simmer until the lentils are soft but not falling apart, 18 to 22 minutes. (If your lentils have been gathering dust in your pantry, they can take as much as 40 minutes to cook. For a longer cooking time, you may have to add an additional cup or two of water.)

3. When the lentils are tender, bring at least 5 quarts of water to a boil in a large pot. Generously salt the water and drop in the pasta. Cook, stirring often, until al dente.

4. Drain the pasta and toss it into the lentil sauce. Drizzle with an additional tablespoon or two of olive oil. Fold in the lemon zest and parsley, and serve right away.

on top of spaghetti...

◆ Pantry Spaghetti ◆

Serves 6 to 8 as a first course or 4 to 6 as a main course

We always have garlic in the house as well as tomato paste and a selection of olive oils. And what house can call itself a home without a cupboard full of pasta? With these simple ingredients, a last-minute meal is always possible. Consider yourself even luckier if you happen to have some fresh parsley and basil on hand.

½ cup extra virgin olive oil
4 plump garlic cloves, peeled and finely minced
4 tablespoons tomato paste
1 teaspoon fine sea salt
1 pound dried spaghettini
4 tablespoons chopped fresh flat-leaf parsley (optional)
8 fresh basil leaves, cut into a chiffonade (optional)

1. Bring a large pot of water to a boil.

2. Heat the olive oil in a 10- to 12-inch skillet over moderately high heat. Add the garlic and sauté until it becomes golden. Reduce the heat and immediately add the tomato paste to cool the pan and prevent the garlic from burning. Stir in the salt. Cook the mixture over low heat, breaking the tomato paste into small bits with a fork without trying to create a smooth puree. When the tomato paste has become aromatic and darkened a shade, remove the pan from the heat.

3. Meanwhile, add a generous amount of salt to the boiling water and drop in the spaghettini. Cook at a rolling boil, stirring often, until the pasta is al dente. Drain the spaghettini, add to the sauté pan, and toss to coat the pasta. Garnish with the parsley and basil, if you wish, and serve immediately.

Spaghetti alla Chitarra with Potatoes, Sage, and Gorgonzola

Serves 6 to 8 as a first course or 4 to 6 as a main course

Pasta and potatoes may seem like an odd combination, but the two are joined together in several Italian dishes. To round out the bland nature of the pasta and potatoes, we add two ingredients with bold flavors—fresh sage and Gorgonzola. In judicious amounts, they work remarkably well together, creating a surprising balance. If fresh sage is unavailable, substitute ½ to 1 teaspoon of aromatic dried oregano. Crush it between your fingers before adding it to the Gorgonzola butter to release its scent.

4 small Red Bliss potatoes (8 ounces total), peeled and cut into ½-inch cubes

6 tablespoons unsalted butter, cut into small dice

4 tablespoons (2½ ounces) crumbled Gorgonzola

1½ to 2 tablespoons finely minced fresh sage (do not substitute dried sage)

1 pound dried spaghetti alla chitarra or spaghettini

10 to 12 turns of a pepper mill

1. Combine the cubed potatoes and at least 6 quarts of water in a large pot. Bring to a rapid boil and cook the potatoes for 5 minutes.

2. Meanwhile, with a fork, mash the butter, Gorgonzola, and sage together in a serving bowl large enough to accommodate the cooked pasta. Set aside in a warm place.

3. After the potatoes have boiled 5 minutes, add a generous amount of salt to the boiling water and drop in the spaghetti. Cook at a full rolling boil until the pasta is al dente. Drain the pasta and potatoes in a colander, reserving about ½ cup of the cooking water.

4. Transfer the potato cubes and pasta to the serving bowl. Gently toss with the Gorgonzola and butter. Grind the pepper over, add ¼ cup of the pasta water, and toss again. Add more water if necessary. The sauce should be glossy, with the consistency of heavy cream. Serve immediately.

◆ Vintner's Spaghetti ◆

Serves 6 to 8 as a first course or 4 to 6 as a main course

This recipe qualifies as "midnight spaghetti": There are very few components, the ingredients are staples in our kitchen, and the dish is assembled in just minutes. Perfect for satisfying late-night hunger or to enjoy any other time.

We like the interplay of sweet onions used here to offset the acid in the wine. The garlic adds pungency and the hot pepper adds a little zip.

2 plump garlic cloves, peeled and finely minced
1½ cups finely diced onions
6 tablespoons extra virgin olive oil
1 teaspoon crushed red pepper flakes
½ cup dry red wine
1 pound dried spaghettini
Parmigiano-Reggiano for serving (optional)

1. Bring a large pot of water to a boil.

2. Combine the garlic, onions, olive oil, and red pepper flakes in a large straight-sided sauté pan. Cook over high heat, stirring frequently, until the garlic becomes golden and the onions have started to brown, about 5 minutes. Add the wine and continue to cook over brisk heat, allowing the wine to boil until it is almost completely reduced and you are left with a glossy purple glaze on the onions. Remove from the heat.

3. Stir a generous amount of salt into the boiling water and drop in the spaghettini. Cook at a full rolling boil, stirring frequently, until the pasta is al dente, 4 to 6 minutes. Transfer ½ cup of the pasta cooking water to the sauté pan set over a medium flame. Drain the spaghettini, transfer to the sauté pan, increase the heat, and cook, stirring and tossing the pasta until most of the water is absorbed. Serve immediately. Pass the Parmigiano-Reggiano, if desired.

◆ Pappardelle with Olives, Thyme, and Lemon ◆

Serves 6 to 8 as a first course or 4 to 6 as a main course

Inspired by a classic Tuscan appetizer—really just a little nibble—of deep-fried sage and anchovy sandwiches, we have since played with pairing aggressive flavors in our cooking. Here, the saltiness of the olives plays remarkably well to the pungency of fresh thyme. Citrus peel is added for a bright note, and the pepper flakes contribute a little pep.

30 to 35 kalamata olives, pitted
1 tablespoon coarsely chopped lemon peel without white pith, preferably organic
1 to 2 teaspoons coarsely chopped orange peel
½ teaspoon crushed red pepper flakes
2 tablespoons fresh thyme leaves
1 cup fresh flat-leaf parsley leaves
1 teaspoon fine sea salt
4 tablespoons extra virgin olive oil
1 pound dried pappardelle

1. Bring a large pot of water to a boil.

2. Combine all the ingredients except the pappardelle in the bowl of a food processor. Pulse on and off until you have a chunky purée. Transfer to a warmed serving bowl large enough to accommodate the cooked pappardelle and set aside in a warm place—either in an oven with a pilot light or beside the stove.

3. Stir a generous amount of salt into the boiling water and drop in the pappardelle. Cook at a full rolling boil, stirring frequently, until the pasta is al dente. Drain the pappardelle, reserving 1 cup of the cooking water. Toss the pasta into the serving bowl with the olive mixture. Add ¼ cup of the cooking water and toss well. Add more liquid if necessary. Pappardelle has a tendency to absorb liquid quickly so you may need to add more water. The sauce should cling to the ribbons of pasta but should not be dry. Serve immediately.

on top of spaghetti...

◆ Linguine with Bitter Greens and Pancetta ◆

Serves 6 to 8 as a first course or 4 to 6 as a main course

Our idea of comfort food is a steaming bowl of cappellini, or angel hair pasta, in chicken broth with a shower of Parmigiano-Reggiano. We call it Italian penicillin—but we don't wait for the first sign of a cold to enjoy it. This is a variation of that dish—a grown-up version—adding a little hot pepper and garlic to wake up the taste buds, pancetta for its distinct salty flavor, and the sophistication and balance of bitter greens. Linguine replaces the very fine strands of cappellini, since the sturdier sauce demands a thicker string pasta. We always keep a small supply of homemade chicken stock in our refrigerator or freezer so our hunger for this dish can be satisfied at any time.

4 tablespoons extra virgin olive oil
2 plump garlic cloves, peeled and finely minced
Packed ¼ cup (2 ounces) diced pancetta
¼ teaspoon crushed red pepper flakes
3 cups homemade chicken stock (see Pasta Pantry)
1 pound dried linguine or spaghettini
8 cups gently packed tender arugula or watercress leaves, tough stems removed
3 tablespoons freshly grated Parmigiano-Reggiano (optional)

1. Bring a large pot of water to a boil.

2. In a large straight-sided sauté pan, heat the olive oil, garlic, pancetta, and red pepper flakes over high heat, stirring frequently. When the garlic becomes golden, add the chicken stock, being careful not to burn yourself as the oil may sputter. Bring to a boil over moderately high heat, and then adjust the heat to maintain a boil to reduce and concentrate the stock. When the stock has reduced by half, set it aside over a very low flame.

3. Stir a generous amount of salt into the boiling water and drop in the pasta. Cook at a full rolling boil, stirring frequently, until the pasta is

still very firm. Drain the pasta, reserving about ⅓ cup of the cooking water, and toss the pasta in the sauce. Continue to toss over medium heat until al dente, about 2 minutes. During this time the pasta will absorb some of the sauce and reduce a bit further. You should have some broth left in the pan. If not, add the reserved pasta water, a tablespoon at a time, until the pasta is nice and moist. Finely chop the arugula or watercress and fold into the pasta. Serve immediately with or without the cheese.

◆ George's Spaghetti with Raw Cucumber and Basil ◆

Serves 6 to 8 as a first course or 4 to 6 as a main course

~~~~~~

When we want something fresh and light for pasta, George often makes this spaghetti with raw cucumber and olive oil. To make the cucumber pieces extra crisp and infused with the taste of basil, George chops them up together with salt and allows them to stand for 10 minutes before adding the olive oil. Sweet varieties of cucumbers with no trace of bitterness—like little Kirby pickling cucumbers and the long, thin cucumbers marketed as "English"—work well in this recipe.

~~~~~~

2 cups peeled and seeded coarsely chopped cucumber

⅔ cup gently packed fresh basil leaves

2 teaspoons sea salt

½ cup extra virgin olive oil

1 pound dried spaghetti

1. Bring a large pot of water to a boil for the pasta.

2. Layer the cucumber, basil, and salt on a cutting board and chop them together into a coarse purée (the cucumber should be chopped into ¼-inch pieces). Transfer to a large serving bowl. Set aside for 10 minutes.

3. Add the olive oil to the cucumber and set aside while you cook the pasta.

4. Generously salt the boiling water and drop in the spaghetti. Cook, stirring often, until al dente. Drain the pasta and toss in the bowl with the cucumbers. Serve right away.

◆ Jo's Spaghettini with Cooked Cucumbers and Mint ◆

Serves 6 to 8 as a first course or 4 to 6 as a main course

Johanne loves George's Spaghetti with Raw Cucumbers and Basil (page 43), but prefers the taste of cooked cucumbers. When she's in charge of dinner this is the version she prepares.

4 to 6 Kirby cucumbers or 1 large cucumber
6 tablespoons unsalted butter, at room temperature
1 teaspoon fine sea salt
1 pound dried spaghettini or linguine
1 cup gently packed fresh mint leaves

1. Bring a large pot of water to a boil.

2. Peel the cucumbers, cut them in half lengthwise, and with a spoon, scoop out and discard the seeds. Slice the cucumbers into ⅛-inch-thick half-moons.

3. Combine the cucumbers, butter, and salt in a large straight-sided sauté pan. Toss the cucumbers over high heat to melt the butter. Once they have begun to sizzle, lower the heat and cook gently for 5 to 7 minutes, or until they have become translucent. They should still be a little crunchy.

4. Meanwhile, stir a generous amount of salt into the boiling water and drop in the pasta. Cook at a full rolling boil, stirring often, until al dente. Drain the pasta, reserving ½ cup of the cooking water. Toss the pasta into the sauté pan with the cucumbers. Continue to toss until all the strands of pasta are coated with butter. Add some of the pasta water, a tablespoon at a time, until the pasta is nice and moist and the sauce is the consistency of heavy cream. Chop the mint and stir into the spaghettini. Serve immediately.

◆ Spaghetti with Sizzled Capers and Herbs ◆

Serves 6 to 8 as a first course or 4 to 6 as a main course

Our friend Costanza lives on the island of Pantelleria off the coast of Sicily where capers flourish. Capers love the sun, the volcanic soil, and the hot, dry climate—ideal growing conditions for the little buds. Costanza keeps us well supplied with capers packed in sea salt—the best and tastiest way to preserve their unique flavor.

We add no additional salt in this recipe (and we reduce the normal amount of salt in the pasta water), as the capers provide plenty. If your capers are supersalty, or if you have low tolerance for salt, soak them for at least 20 minutes in cool water, then drain well on paper towels before preparing the recipe.

As delicious as capers are uncooked, their flavor when sizzled and browned a little in olive oil is even better.

1 pound dried spaghetti
1 tablespoon salt
½ cup extra virgin olive oil
2 garlic cloves, trimmed and smashed with the flat surface of a chef's knife and peeled
2 tablespoons capers in salt
2 teaspoons dried oregano
½ cup loosely packed fresh oregano or marjoram leaves
2 teaspoons chopped fresh flat-leaf parsley

1. Bring a large pot of water to boil for the pasta. Add the salt and drop in the spaghetti. Cook, stirring frequently, to keep the strands from sticking together.

2. At the same time, put the olive oil, garlic, and capers in a large straight-sided sauté pan. Set the pan over moderately high heat and cook, swirling the pan from time to time, until the garlic is golden and the capers are sizzling and popping. Remove and discard the garlic. Take the pan off the heat and sprinkle in the dried oregano. Stir to combine.

3. When the pasta is al dente, drain it, reserving ½ cup of the water. Transfer the pasta to the sauté pan with the capers. Add the fresh herbs and toss. If the pasta seems dry, add a little pasta water, a tablespoon at a time. Serve right away.

pasta with vegetables, legumes, and herbs

◆ Rigatoni with Peperonata ◆

Serves 6 to 8 as a first course or 4 to 6 as a main course

In Italy, there are as many recipes for peperonata as there are cooks. Just about the only thing they would all agree on is the main ingredient—peppers. Originally from the south, peperonata can now be found as far north as Piemonte as a sauce for *capunet*, or stuffed cabbage. It is a versatile accompaniment to meats, chicken, or even grilled steak. Leftover peperonata is often used to sauce spaghetti. We make this condiment specifically for pasta and save the leftovers for boiled or grilled meats.

1½ cups chopped onions

4 plump garlic cloves, trimmed, smashed with the flat blade of a chef's knife, and peeled

1 cup chopped green bell pepper

2 cups chopped red bell pepper

2 long spicy finger peppers or 3 to 4 jalapeño peppers

1 cup finely chopped celery

1 teaspoon sea salt

1 cup extra virgin olive oil

2 cups tomato juice, preferably organic

1 pound dried rigatoni or spaghetti

1. Combine the onions, garlic, peppers, celery, salt, and ½ cup of the olive oil in a large straight-sided sauté pan. Cook over high heat, stirring often. There will be lots of moisture coming out of the vegetables. As they cook, much of the liquid will evaporate or reduce. Add more oil as needed to keep the vegetables moist. After 5 minutes, cover, lower the heat, and continue to cook gently for 10 minutes. Add the tomato juice, bring to a boil, reduce the heat, and cook, covered, for another 5 to 10 minutes, until the vegetables are very soft.

2. Bring a large pot of water to a boil. Add a generous amount of salt and drop in the rigatoni. Cook, stirring often, until tender (the pasta cylinders should collapse a bit). Drain, reserving 1 cup of the pasta water. Transfer the rigatoni to a heated serving bowl. Add enough sauce to generously coat the pasta. If the sauce seems too thick, add some of the cooking water, a tablespoon at a time. Reserve the rest of the peperonata to pass at the table or save it for the next day to accompany a main course or as a topping for bruschetta. Serve right away.

◆ Fedelini with Hot, Hot Pepper Oil ◆

Serves 8 as a first course or 4 as a main course

Try this when you're in the mood for a devilishly hot dish. The racy oil packs a wallop as the hot peppers breathe fire into it. The faint of heart can create a delectable sissy version of their own by substituting sweet yellow banana peppers, light green finger peppers, or Hungarian peppers for the spicy ones. Whichever peppers you choose, they will provide a unique flavor to the limpid oil, making a perfect condiment for pasta. The strained peppers make a great contribution to an antipasto course, or they can be used as an accompaniment to grilled leg of lamb or roasted chicken for a *secondo*, or main course.

Fedelini is a skinny spaghetti that goes well with oil-based sauces. Somewhere between spaghettini and cappellini in thickness, the lanky pasta strands have a great mouth-feel and collapse under the gentlest pressure of chewing. It is one of the more satisfying pastas and a small amount can assuage a big hunger. To prevent overcooking it, remove the fedelini from the boiling water about a minute before it is al dente as it will continue to soften after being drained and tossed with its sauce.

8 ounces (4 to 6) long hot or sweet finger peppers
1 cup extra virgin olive oil
1 plump garlic clove, peeled and cut into 3 or 4 slices
Sea salt
12 ounces dried fedelini or spaghettini
1 tablespoon finely chopped chives

1. Cut the peppers in half lengthwise and remove the stem, core, and seeds. Toss them into a large straight-sided sauté pan with the olive oil, garlic, and salt. Cook over moderately low heat, turning occasionally, until the peppers are very tender, about 15 minutes. Keep a close watch on them as they should just begin to brown but have no evidence of burned edges. Remove from the heat, set aside, and allow the peppers to cool in the oil.

2. Bring a large pot of water to a boil for the pasta.

3. With tongs, transfer the cooled peppers and a scant ½ cup of the flavored oil to a dish. Reserve for another use. Leave the rest of the oil (you should have about ½ cup) in the sauté pan. You can remove the garlic or not, as you wish. Reheat the oil on a low flame.

4. Generously salt the boiling pasta water and drop in the fedelini. Cook, stirring often, until it is about 1 minute before al dente. Drain the pasta, reserving 1 cup of the cooking water. Transfer the fedelini to the sauté pan and add the chives. Toss over moderate heat for about 1 minute to coat the pasta with the oil and distribute the tiny green flecks of chives. The pasta may soak up some of the oil and look dry. Add just enough of the reserved water, a tablespoon at a time, to prevent the strands from clumping and sticking together—you may need only a fraction of the reserved water. It should look oily rather than soupy. Taste, and add more salt if necessary. Serve right away in warmed bowls.

◆ Bucatini with Five-Pepper Sauce ◆

Serves 6 to 8 as a first course or 4 to 6 as a main course

This beautiful red-orange sauce can be aggressive or subdued depending on the kick of the hot peppers. There are literally hundreds of types of peppers, both hot and sweet—all members of the Capsicum family. And even within a particular variety—let's say jalapeño—the taste can differ from one pod to the next. If you are particularly sensitive to hot, spicy food, it is best to determine the pepper's potency before using it. Do this by cutting off a tiny bit from the stem end of the pepper where it is hottest and taste it with the tip of your tongue. Then decide how much to use.

Play with the proportion of jalapeños and hot paprika in this recipe to arrive at the taste that is most pleasing to you. More spice can be added individually at the table by passing around extra hot paprika, cayenne, or crushed red pepper.

This pasta benefits from a liberal amount of Pecorino Romano tossed in just before serving.

3 large red bell peppers
3 long sweet light green Italian frying peppers or yellow banana peppers
3 to 4 coarsely chopped red jalapeño peppers (or substitute any red or yellow hot pepper)
1 to 2 teaspoons hot Hungarian paprika or cayenne
4 teaspoons sweet Hungarian paprika
½ cup extra virgin olive oil
2 plump garlic cloves, peeled and roughly chopped
4 anchovy fillets (see Pasta Pantry)
1 cup homemade chicken stock (see Pasta Pantry)
1 cup puréed canned tomatoes
1 pound dried bucatini or spaghetti
Freshly grated Pecorino Romano

1. Roast and peel the red bell and Italian sweet peppers. This is most easily done by charring them on all sides directly over a charcoal fire, the gas burner on the stove, or under the broiler. When the skin has blackened all over, transfer the peppers to a plastic container with a tight-fitting lid. The steam will loosen the skins from the flesh. When cool enough to handle, rub the skins off the peppers, scraping away any stubborn black bits with a knife. Seed the peppers and remove the ribs, reserving any juices. Trans-

fer the peppers and juice to the bowl of a food processor. Add the jalapeño peppers, the hot and sweet paprikas, olive oil, garlic, and anchovy fillets. Pulse on and off until you have a rough purée; it should not be perfectly smooth. Pour into a large straight-sided sauté pan and add the chicken stock and tomatoes.

2. Bring the sauce to a boil over moderate heat, stirring often. Lower the heat and maintain a gentle simmer while you cook the pasta.

3. Bring a large pot of water to a boil, add a generous amount of salt, and drop in the bucatini. Cook, stirring often, until al dente. Drain and transfer the pasta to a heated serving bowl. Ladle over enough of the sauce to coat each strand generously. Sprinkle on some Pecorino Romano and toss together. Serve right away with the remaining sauce and more cheese.

on top of spaghetti...

◆ Spaghetti Aglio-Olio ◆

Serves 6 to 8 as a first course or 4 to 6 as a main course

There is no more elemental or delicious sauce for spaghetti than *aglio-olio*—garlic and olive oil heated together and tossed with pasta. With an additional ingredient or two, a basic aglio-olio can spawn an infinite variety of pasta sauces.

George learned to make aglio-olio in his mom's kitchen. The most important lesson in making aglio-olio, however, came from a very talented chef, Frank Gaudiano, who worked with George at the University Club in Providence. The trick is to add some water, broth, or wine just as the garlic takes on a light golden color as it sizzles in the olive oil. The liquid prevents the garlic from browning and softens and mellows the taste of the garlic, resulting in a sauce that clings nicely to the spaghetti with bits of almost delicate, nutty-tasting garlic.

The simplicity of this sauce puts the spotlight on its ingredients. This is the moment to trot out an excellent olive oil and impeccably fresh, plump cloves of garlic.

½ cup extra virgin olive oil
2 tablespoons minced fresh garlic
½ teaspoon or more fine sea salt
1 pound imported spaghetti or spaghettini

1. Bring a large pot of water to a boil for the pasta.

2. Heat the olive oil, garlic, and salt in a large straight-sided skillet over moderate heat, stirring often. Keep a close watch here and adjust the heat as necessary because you want the garlic to slowly turn from opaque white to a slightly translucent golden without a hint of browning. As soon as the garlic is golden, immediately add 2 cups water. Be careful not to burn yourself as the oil has a tendency to spatter. Raise the heat and boil vigorously until the garlic is soft and the liquid has reduced by half. Taste and add additional salt if necessary.

3. Add a generous amount of salt to the boiling pasta water. As soon as the water comes back to a rolling boil, drop in the spaghetti. Stir often until the spaghetti is al dente. Drain and transfer the pasta to the skillet. Over moderately high heat toss the spaghetti in the aglio-olio until it is nicely coated. Serve right away in heated bowls.

Variations

Spice up aglio-olio with crushed red pepper flakes. Add ½ to 1 teaspoon to the garlic and oil in step 2.

Substitute a light chicken stock (see page 7) for the water in the sauce for a richer, more mellow taste.

Substitute half the water with 1 cup dry white wine. The wine will lend a fresh and vibrant acidity to the aglio-olio.

Herbs are a nice addition to aglio-olio: Add 1 to 2 tablespoons chopped fresh flat-leaf parsley or fresh basil just before serving. Or sizzle 1 to 2 tablespoons chopped fresh parsley with the garlic and oil in step 2 before adding the liquid. The sautéed parsley has a completely different taste than raw parsley. It becomes fragrant with a hint of cinnamon in the aroma. (Curly-leafed parsley has an even more pronounced cinnamon scent.)

Add 2 tablespoons pitted, finely chopped cured olives to the aglio-olio about 3 minutes after adding the liquid in step 2. Or add an equal amount of prepared tapenade instead.

◆ Spaghettini with Paprika, Garlic, and Pecorino ◆

Serves 6 to 8 as a first course or 4 to 6 as a main course

Italo Scanga, an internationally acclaimed artist, was a passionate cook. For Italo, art and food were inextricably connected. In the kitchen, he was a fearless creator, always experimenting with ingredients. He loved paprika and used excessive amounts. Rather than sprinkling it on food as a spice, he focused on it as a main ingredient. We loved his exuberantly gutsy pasta made with a blizzard of paprika and hot pepper. It was a reflection of his zest for life.

We share Italo's enthusiasm for spicy food and use hot paprika in this recipe as well as cayenne. You can tone down the heat by using sweet paprika and omitting the cayenne.

½ cup extra virgin olive oil
2 tablespoons minced fresh garlic
½ teaspoon or more fine sea salt
2 tablespoons hot paprika
⅛ to ½ teaspoon cayenne (optional)
1 pound dried spaghettini
1 to 1½ cups freshly grated Pecorino
    Romano

1. Bring a large pot of water to a boil for the pasta.

2. Heat the olive oil, garlic, and salt in a large straight-sided skillet over moderate heat, stirring often. After 2 minutes add the paprika and the cayenne if you wish. Sauté until the garlic turns golden, keeping a close watch as the paprika will tint the garlic reddish, making it more difficult to see its transformation. Be careful not to let the garlic brown. As soon as the garlic is golden, immediately add 2 cups water. Be careful not to burn yourself as the oil tends to spatter. Raise the heat and boil vigorously until the garlic is soft and the liquid has reduced by half. Taste and add additional salt if necessary.

3. Add a generous amount of salt to the pasta water. As soon as the water comes back to a rolling boil, drop in the spaghettini. Stir often until the spaghettini is al dente. Drain and transfer the pasta to the skillet. Over moderate heat toss the spaghettini in the oil until it is nicely coated. Add 1 cup of the cheese and toss again. Serve right away in heated bowls. Pass extra Pecorino Romano at the table.

◆ 4AM Spaghetti for One ◆

Makes 1 generous serving

〜〜〜〜〜〜〜〜〜〜〜〜〜〜〜〜〜〜〜〜〜〜

One summer Johanne hiked up Mont Ventoux in southern France with four friends. They left at 10 P.M. to reach the summit just in time to see the sun rise gloriously over Provence. George thought it was an insane idea and stayed home in a comfortable bed while the hiking party rested midway up the mountain in sleeping bags. It was probably a mixture of anxiety and concern for the group that awoke George in the middle of the night with great hunger pangs. He made himself a satisfying pasta and slept like a baby for the rest of the night.

Was it the Espelette pepper powder in George's pasta that calmed him? With a rich, deep flavor and a spicy kick, Espelette peppers hail from southwestern France and command controlled-name status much like Parmigiano-Reggiano or San Marzano tomatoes of Italy. Christopher Columbus brought this uniquely New World crop to Europe from the Caribbean after his second voyage in 1493. Today the peppers are prized in Basque cooking—used fresh or sun-dried in their powdered form— and deserve wider recognition in America.

The piquant powder is great to have on hand in the spice cabinet. We use this French pepper to add an intriguing flavor to Italian pasta.

〜〜〜〜〜〜〜〜〜〜〜〜〜〜〜〜〜〜〜〜〜〜

4 ounces dried spaghettini
1 large garlic clove, peeled and trimmed
¼ cup extra virgin olive oil
½ to 1 teaspoon powdered Espelette pepper
   or hot or sweet paprika
Large pinch of dried oregano
Freshly ground black pepper
Pinch of sea salt

1. Bring a large pot of water to a boil for the pasta. Add a generous amount of salt and drop in the pasta. Cook, stirring often, until al dente.

2. While the pasta is cooking, rub the garlic clove all over the bottom of a heated pasta bowl. Pour in the olive oil and sprinkle over the Espelette pepper and oregano. Grind black pepper over the spices. Add a pinch of salt. The mixture should be quite aromatic with overtones of garlic.

3. Drain the pasta, leaving some moisture clinging to the spaghetti strands, and transfer to the pasta bowl. Sit down, toss the pasta in the flavored oil, and enjoy your peace and quiet.

  on **top** of spaghetti...

◆ Linguine with Classic Ligurian Pesto ◆

Serves 6 to 8 as a first course or 4 to 6 as a main course

Whether it is offered with trenette (the traditional regional homemade pasta similar to tagliatelle or the dried pasta called linguine); lasagne (silky square or rectangular flat sheets of fresh pasta so called in Liguria but broader and shorter than classic bolognese lasagne noodles, boiled till soft and slippery); spaghettini; or Ricotta Ravioli (page 228) pesto is irresistible. It's hard to believe that basil, olive oil, garlic, pine nuts, cheese, and salt pounded together can taste so good.

An exquisitely straightforward preparation, the ingredients and balance are key. Use only the freshest, most tender, aromatic basil leaves. Olive oil should be extra virgin and from Liguria. It is light, bright, perfectly suited to the food of the region, and exported to North America. Find the best-quality garlic—plump, moist cloves that are youthful and firm—and use it sparingly as too much will upstage and cloud the magic of the basil. The combination of Pecorino Romano and Parmigiano-Reggiano will successfully mimic the flavor of the traditional, more elusive fiore sardo. The pine nuts should be ultrafresh. Look for the long, thin, creamy Italian ones. Taste them, since pine nuts go stale and become rancid quickly due to their high oil content. Walnuts can be substituted for the more fragile pine nuts—but peel them; otherwise the bitter tannins in their skins can ruin the pesto. (To remove the skins: Drop a rounded $\frac{1}{4}$ cup walnut halves in boiling water for 2 minutes. Remove a few at a time from the water with a slotted spoon. Peel off the papery skin with the tip of a paring knife blade. Pull away the bits in the crannies, too. Set aside on paper towels to dry. Continue until all the walnut halves have been peeled. Coarsely chop the nuts and measure out the amount for the recipe.) Finally, only the fresh, clean taste of sea salt will do. It most closely echoes the proximity of the Mediterranean in the creation of this bright green sauce.

A good pesto will cast a spell on you. Resist the urge to put it on everything and anything. Its integrity and distinction are worth preserving by using it as an Italian would: tossed with pasta or spooned onto a minestrone, or vegetable soup, with Ligurian roots. Purists will use a mortar and pestle to make pesto.

The rest of us will haul out the blender or food processor (we prefer the blender) for the job. Get all the ingredients together and set up your machine before you begin. Pesto should never be warmed or cooked, so whirl it in the appliance of your choice as quickly as possible before the motor has a chance to heat up the container and taint the flavors.

3 cups gently packed young tender basil leaves
½ to ¾ cup light-flavored extra virgin olive oil
1 teaspoon minced fresh garlic
3 tablespoons pine nuts or peeled and chopped walnuts
½ cup freshly grated Parmigiano-Reggiano
¼ cup freshly grated Pecorino Romano
Sea salt
3 tablespoons unsalted butter, softened
1 to 2 tablespoons whole milk (optional—see Note)
1 pound dried linguine; 1 batch George's Fresh Pasta (page 212), cut into tagliatelle, lasagnette, or maltagliati; or 1 batch Ricotta Ravioli (page 228)

1. About an hour before you make the pesto, wash the basil in cold water, wrap in paper towels, and refrigerate. This will help to prevent the sauce from heating up in the machine.

2. Bring a large pot of water to a boil.

3. Set up the blender or food processor. Measure and assemble the olive oil, garlic, and nuts. Put the basil, ½ cup of the olive oil, garlic, and nuts in the blender or processor. Whirl to a thick paste. Add more oil if necessary.

4. Transfer to a mixing bowl and first stir in the cheeses, then taste to determine how much salt to add. The cheeses may provide enough.

5. In another mixing bowl, work the butter with a wooden spoon or rubber spatula as if creaming it for a cake. When it is very soft and smooth—but not at all melted—fold it into the pesto with the milk, if using. Set aside at room temperature while you cook the pasta.

6. Generously salt the boiling water and drop in the pasta. Cook, stirring often, until al dente. Drain the pasta without shaking it bone-dry and reserve about ½ cup of the pasta water. Transfer the pasta to a warmed serving bowl and nap it with the pesto. Toss gently, adding a little of the pasta water, a tablespoon at a time, to loosen the sauce. Pass any remaining pesto at the table along with some extra grated cheese. Serve at once.

Note: Pesto is a big topic of conversation. What makes it so much better in Liguria? Besides the obvious reasons—quality and freshness of ingredients—a new American friend who lives in Tuscany and loves Liguria as much as we do has it from a reputable authority that a little milk softens and mellows pesto, taking away any hard edges. Try it; it works.

on top of spaghetti...

◆ Rigatoni with Caper and Almond "Pesto" ◆

Serves 6 to 8 as a first course or 4 to 6 as a main course

We call the following seven recipes "pesto," although the name in Italy is most closely associated with the bright green Classic Ligurian Pesto (page 55). The word itself means pounded or ground and describes precisely how these sauces are made.

The ingredients for this pesto—capers, anchovies, almonds, and mint—remind us of sun-baked Sicilian days. Use this sauce with a sturdy macaroni like rigatoni, or string pasta like spaghetti or linguine, or as a condiment for grilled fish.

¾ cup salted capers, soaked for 15 to 20 minutes in cold water

6 anchovy fillets (see Pasta Pantry)

3½ ounces (1 cup) ground blanched almonds

2 tablespoons fine unflavored bread crumbs

1 plump garlic clove, peeled and trimmed

6 to 8 large fresh mint leaves

3 sprigs fresh flat-leaf parsley, leaves only

1 cup extra virgin olive oil

1 pound dried rigatoni

1. Bring a large pot of water to a boil.

2. Drain the capers and dry on paper towels.

3. Combine all the ingredients except the pasta in a blender jar. Blend until you obtain a chunky purée. Set aside. (You may cover and refrigerate the pesto for a day or two. Be sure to bring it to room temperature before you cook the rigatoni.)

4. Salt the boiling water and drop in the pasta. Cook, stirring often, until al dente. Drain the rigatoni, reserving about ½ cup of the pasta water. Transfer the pasta to a heated serving bowl. Toss with enough pesto to coat the rigatoni. Add a little pasta water, a tablespoon at a time, if the sauce seems too thick. Serve right away, passing any remaining sauce at the table.

◆ Linguine with Frenched Green Beans and Parsley "Pesto" ◆

Serves 6 as a first course

Frenching green beans fell out of fashion years ago, which is too bad because the technique is worth a comeback. Thinly sliced, slivered beans have a different, more appealing texture and taste. It is worthwhile finding the gadget (a closely spaced series of three or four blades through which the bean passes and results in julienne slices) that makes easy work of the cutting process. A good, sharp knife will also do the trick. If using a knife, cut the beans into as many vertical, thin slices as you can manage (the finer the slivers, the better they will twirl around your fork with the linguine). Take your time and tuck in your fingertips to avoid nicking them with the knife blade.

This spirited emerald green-on-green pasta sauce has a fresh flavor. The parsley and basil wake up the taste of the beans without overwhelming them. A hint of garlic and just a touch of hot pepper make all the components come alive.

In this recipe, there are equal amounts of green beans and pasta, so a mere 8 ounces of linguine will make 6 generous *primo*, or first-course, portions.

---

8 ounces fresh green beans, trimmed and sliced lengthwise into thin slivers
2 cups gently packed fresh flat-leaf parsley leaves
10 large fresh basil leaves
1 small garlic clove, trimmed and peeled
½ cup light-flavored extra virgin olive oil
½ teaspoon sea salt
Pinch or more of cayenne
½ cup freshly grated Pecorino Romano, plus more to pass at the table
8 ounces dried linguine

1. Cook the green beans in boiling salted water until tender. They should yield easily under the pressure of your teeth. Drain in a colander and set aside next to the sink to await the pasta.

2. Bring a large pot of water to a boil for the pasta.

3. Whirl the parsley, basil, garlic, olive oil, salt, and cayenne in a blender until you have a chunky

purée. Pour into a warmed, but not hot, serving bowl. Stir in ½ cup Pecorino Romano.

4. Generously salt the pasta water and drop in the linguine. Cook, stirring often, until al dente. Reserve about 1 cup of the cooking water, then pour the remaining water and pasta into the colander over the beans. This will warm the beans if they have cooled. Transfer the pasta and beans to the serving bowl and toss with the sauce and cheese. Add enough reserved cooking water, a tablespoon at a time, to loosen the pesto. There should be a small puddle of sauce on the bottom of the bowl. Serve right away with extra Pecorino Romano passed at the table.

◆ Spaghetti with Roasted Asparagus "Pesto" ◆

Serves 6 to 8 as a first course or 4 to 6 as a main course

As soon as we spotted the first lovely green stalks of fresh asparagus in the market this spring, we decided to make a pasta sauce with them. Our first thought was to do a pesto-type sauce, blending roasted asparagus with garlic, almonds or walnuts, and fruity olive oil. However, when we tasted the roasted asparagus puréed with only olive oil, all the other ingredients we intended to add seemed unnecessary. The sauce was pure and perfect. The only addition is freshly grated Pecorino Romano.

1 pound fresh asparagus
3 tablespoons plus ⅔ cup extra virgin
   olive oil
⅛ to ¼ teaspoon sea salt
1 pound dried spaghetti
Freshly grated Pecorino Romano

1. Heat the oven to 500 degrees.

2. Bring a large pot of water to a boil.

3. Trim off and discard any tough, woody ends of the asparagus spears. The trimmed weight should be about 12 ounces. Spread the asparagus out on a baking sheet in a single layer and brush with 3 tablespoons olive oil. Sprinkle with salt and roast the asparagus in the upper third of the oven until the spears are tender when pierced with the tip of a knife, 8 to 12 minutes, depending on their thickness. Set aside to cool for 5 minutes.

4. Transfer the asparagus to a cutting board and coarsely chop them. Put the asparagus and any oil left on the baking sheet in a blender. Add the remaining ⅔ cup olive oil and purée until smooth. Set aside. (You may cover and refrigerate the pesto at this point, but be sure to bring it to room temperature before you cook the spaghetti.)

5. Generously salt the boiling water and drop in the spaghetti. Cook, stirring often, until al dente. Drain the pasta, reserving about ½ cup of the cooking water. Transfer the spaghetti to a heated serving bowl. Toss with enough of the pesto to coat each strand. If the sauce seems too thick, add some of the pasta water, a tablespoon at a time. Serve right away with freshly grated Pecorino Romano passed at the table.

on top of spaghetti...

◆ Mostaccioli with Tomato "Pesto" ◆

Serves 6 to 8 as a first course or 4 to 6 as a main course

George developed this recipe for the Al Forno menu. The luxurious texture of pine nuts makes the pesto look creamier than it really is.

When we decided to include the pesto in this book, George handed me a slip of paper with the measurements of ingredients written in "tomato paste cans" instead of cups. While it works perfectly well his way, here is the translation in standard measures.

¾ cup (one 6-ounce can) tomato paste, preferably organic
¾ cup plus 2 tablespoons extra virgin olive oil
½ cup plus 1 tablespoon pine nuts (see Pasta Pantry)
¼ teaspoon sea salt
¼ to ½ teaspoon cayenne or crushed red pepper flakes
2 tablespoons tomato juice, preferably organic
2 plump garlic cloves, trimmed, peeled, and roughly chopped
1 pound dried mostaccioli, penne, or rigatoni
Freshly grated Pecorino Romano

1. Bring a large pot of water to a boil.

2. Combine the tomato paste, olive oil, pine nuts, salt, cayenne, tomato juice, and garlic in the bowl of a food processor. Run the motor until you have a smooth purée. Set aside at room temperature while you cook the pasta. (You can cover and refrigerate the pesto, but be sure to bring it to room temperature before boiling the pasta.)

3. Generously salt the boiling water and drop in the mostaccioli. Cook, stirring often, until al dente. Drain, reserving about ½ cup of the pasta water. Transfer the mostaccioli to a heated serving bowl. Add enough of the pesto to coat the noodles generously. Add a little pasta water, a tablespoon at a time, if it seems too thick. Sprinkle with cheese and pass more Pecorino Romano and any remaining pesto at the table.

◆ Spaghetti with Caper and Tomato "Pesto" ◆

Serves 6 to 8 as a first course or 4 to 6 as a main course

Our friend Gail escaped New York several years ago to live on the tiny island of Pantelleria between Sicily and North Africa. When she visits the United States, she brings capers she has preserved in salt gathered from the wild bushes growing between the black lava rocks surrounding her house. On one of her visits, Gail brought us a jar of caper paste, a traditional condiment of Pantelleria made with capers and sun-dried tomatoes. It was delicious spread on bruschetta.

The caper paste was the inspiration for this pasta sauce, which echoes the bold flavors of the sun-drenched island. For a lighter texture and taste, we use either fresh or good-quality canned tomatoes rather than sun-dried.

Salted capers may not be as widely available as the jarred ones in vinegar or brine, but they are worth seeking out as they have a pure, bright, fresh caper taste.

½ cup extra virgin olive oil
4 plump garlic cloves, peeled and coarsely chopped
½ cup chopped fresh or canned tomato pulp
3 tablespoons capers in salt, rinsed in warm water and patted dry
2 cups loosely packed fresh flat-leaf parsley leaves
½ cup loosely packed fresh oregano leaves or ¼ teaspoon excellent-quality dried oregano, preferably from Sicily or Greece
2 tablespoons best-quality red wine vinegar
Sea salt (optional)
1 pound dried spaghetti, linguine, or spaghettini
½ cup freshly grated Pecorino Romano (optional)

1. Bring a large pot of water to a boil.

2. Meanwhile, combine the olive oil and garlic in a very small saucepan. Bring to a boil and let boil briskly until the garlic is golden, turning two or three times. Remove from the heat and set aside, swirling the pan often, until it has cooled.

3. Pour the garlic and oil into a blender or food processor container. Add the tomato and the capers. Pulse on and off a few times to combine.

Add the parsley and oregano, and blend to a coarse purée. Stir in the vinegar. Taste and add salt if necessary. Set aside.

4. Stir some salt into the boiling water (keep in mind that the sauce may have a salty hit from the capers and you may not need as much to flavor the pasta). Drop in the spaghetti and cook, stirring often, until al dente. Drain, reserving about ½ cup of the pasta cooking water. Toss the spaghetti in a warmed bowl with the caper mixture. Add the pasta cooking water, a tablespoon at a time, to create a sauce that is a bit soupy. The sauce should not be so thick that there is no liquid on the bottom of the bowl. Serve right away with Pecorino Romano, if desired. George likes this pasta with cheese; Johanne prefers it without.

◆ Fusilli with Roasted Red Pepper "Pesto" ◆

Serves 6 to 8 as a first course or 4 to 6 as a main course

Roasted red peppers and sun-dried tomatoes share an essence equivalent to parallel tonality or timbre. On the palate they are equal but distinct. As in music, they have clear-cut pitch. As in color, they resemble one another in tint and value. Their flavors are concentrated—the peppers from roasting, the tomatoes from drying—giving each of them a more intense taste. Play them with anchovies and you have a magic brew.

Be sure the sun-dried tomatoes are nice and supple. If you buy the jarred ones steeped in olive oil, drain them well before using (often the olive oil is of inferior quality). This pesto needs no embellishment except a little crushed red pepper (Jo's choice) or a touch of grated Pecorino (George's preference) to gild the lily.

3 red bell peppers
½ cup extra virgin olive oil
Rounded ½ cup (about 12) sun-dried tomatoes
6 anchovy fillets (see Pasta Pantry)
Sea salt
1 pound dried fusilli
Crushed red pepper flakes (optional)
Freshly grated Pecorino Romano (optional)

1. Roast and peel the peppers. This is most easily done by charring them on all sides directly over a charcoal fire, the gas burner on the stove, or under the broiler. When the skin has blackened all over, transfer the peppers to a plastic container with a tight-fitting lid. The steam will loosen the skins from the flesh. When cool enough to handle, rub the skins off the peppers, scraping away any stubborn black bits with a knife. Seed the peppers and remove the ribs, reserving any juices. Transfer the peppers and juice to a blender. Add the olive oil, tomatoes, and anchovies. Whirl until you have a smooth purée. Taste the pesto and add salt if necessary (the anchovies may have added enough saltiness). Set aside while you cook the pasta.

2. Bring a large pot of water to a boil. Add a generous amount of salt and drop in the fusilli. Cook, stirring often, until al dente. Drain the

pasta, reserving about ½ cup of the cooking water. Transfer the fusilli to a warmed serving bowl and toss with enough pesto to coat the noodles generously. Add some of the pasta water, a tablespoon at a time, if the sauce seems too thick. It should be loose enough to puddle a bit on the bottom of the bowl. Serve right away with or without red pepper flakes or Pecorino Romano passed at the table.

✦ Spaghetti with Lemon Basil "Pesto" and Squash Blossoms ✦

Serves 6 to 8 as a first course or 4 to 6 as a main course

Our friend Patricia Wells has the best *potager,* or vegetable garden, in Provence. It is visually stunning, laid out in a classical pattern with pathways converging at the central core. There are red, yellow, and orange tomatoes—green-striped ones, too. Shiny black and snowy white eggplants hang from their thick stalks on perfectly straight stakes. Huge fans of chard—the all-green type and the flashy variety with red stalks and red-veined leaves—show off in one corner. And the squash patch, all perky green leaves and yellow blossoms reaching upward, hiding their treasures beneath: zucchini, sweet winter squash, and pumpkins. There are plenty of herbs. The choices for basil alone are staggering: large-leafed Italian, small aromatic lemon, spicy cinnamon, glossy aubergine-hued opal, and tiny green dwarfs.

Patricia harvests her treasures daily and creates superb dishes with them. This is one of our favorites—a bold triple lemony treat.

If lemon basil is not available, use regular fresh basil and add 1 teaspoon finely chopped lemon zest. If prepared lemon oil or lemon salt cannot be found, extra virgin olive oil and sea salt can stand in for them. Pump up the flavor with another ½ teaspoon lemon zest.

4 cups loosely packed fresh lemon basil leaves
3 tablespoons lemon olive oil
1 teaspoon lemon salt
1 pound dried spaghetti
20 to 24 squash blossoms, cut into a chiffonade (4 cups, loosely packed)
1 cup freshly grated Parmigiano-Reggiano

1. Bring a large pot of water to a boil for the pasta.

2. Make a chunky pesto by combining the basil, lemon oil, and lemon salt in the container of a blender or food processor. Whirl the mixture, stopping the motor before it is a completely smooth purée. Set aside.

3. Generously salt the boiling water and drop in the pasta. Cook, stirring often, until the pasta is still quite firm—about 2 minutes before it is

al dente. Drain the pasta, reserving 1½ cups of the water, and transfer the spaghetti to a large straight-sided sauté pan with a lid. Over low heat, toss the spaghetti with the squash blossoms and half the reserved pasta water. Cover and cook until the flowers wilt, about 2 minutes. Uncover, remove from the heat, and add the lemon basil purée and Parmigiano-Reggiano. If the mixture seems dry, add more water, a tablespoon at a time, until the spaghetti is well moistened without sticking together. Serve right away in warmed bowls.

Pasta with Tomato Sauces

◆ Pomodoro—Al Forno's Tomato Sauce ◆

Makes about 6 cups of sauce or enough for 1½ pounds of pasta, serving 10 to 12 as a main course.
The sauce freezes well.

This is the spur-of-the-moment sauce George put together on January 2, 1980—the day we opened Al Forno Restaurant. We needed a basic tomato sauce, something to have on hand to combine with pasta or chicken or the roasted potatoes we served that day. We wanted something with a fresh, sprightly flavor rather than a long-cooked sauce, but with some depth, a bit of character. The complexity in this sauce is a result of simmering sautéed garlic in wine and chicken stock until most of the liquid is absorbed by the garlic. In the cooking process, the garlic becomes mellow, the wine loses its harshness, and the chicken stock connects all the ingredients. Added to chopped canned tomatoes, it was just the right seasoning. We call this sauce *Pomodoro*, Italian for tomato.

In a sense the Pomodoro set the tone for the way we do things in the restaurant to this day—direct combining of ingredients. We use Pomodoro as a tool, a component, to add to a dish whenever tomato is needed. Making Pomodoro in our restaurant kitchen has become as much of a daily ritual as making chicken stock.

½ cup extra virgin olive oil
1 tablespoon minced fresh garlic
½ teaspoon fine sea salt
1 cup dry white wine
1 cup homemade chicken stock (see Pasta Pantry) or water
5 cups chopped canned tomatoes with their juices

1. Heat the olive oil, garlic, and salt in a medium saucepan over moderate heat, stirring often. Keep a close watch here and adjust the heat as necessary because you want the garlic to slowly turn from opaque white to a slightly translucent golden without a hint of browning. As soon as the garlic is golden, immediately add the wine and stock. Be careful not to burn yourself as the oil has a tendency to spatter. Bring to a boil, reduce the heat, and simmer until the garlic is soft and has taken on a nutty color, and the liquid has reduced to about 1 cup.

2. Add the tomatoes, bring to a boil, lower the heat, and simmer for 5 minutes.

 on top of spaghetti...

◆ Fettuccine with a Delicate Tomato Sauce ◆

Serves 6 to 8 as a first course or 4 to 6 as a main course

We all have busy days when we are hungry and tired and our brains are too fried to think about or cook anything the least bit complicated for dinner. That's when we pull out some chicken stock (always on hand in the fridge), organic tomato juice (always in the cupboard for an emergency Bloody Mary), and unsalted butter (another refrigerator staple). The combination of these three ingredients makes a light but elegant and satisfying sauce that can be put together in the time it takes to boil water for the fettuccine.

1½ cups homemade chicken stock
   (see Pasta Pantry)
¾ cup tomato juice, preferably organic
½ teaspoon sea salt
8 tablespoons (1 stick) unsalted butter, at
   room temperature
1 pound dried fettuccine
Freshly grated Parmigiano-Reggiano or
   Pecorino Romano (optional)

1. Bring a large pot of water to a boil for the pasta.

2. Combine the chicken stock, tomato juice, salt, and 4 tablespoons of the butter in a large straight-sided skillet. Bring to a boil, reduce the heat to moderate, and reduce by one-quarter.

3. Generously salt the pasta water and drop in the fettuccine. Cook until al dente.

4. Just before draining the pasta, add the remaining butter to the tomato mixture in the skillet. Swirl the butter in the pan until it is completely absorbed. Taste for seasoning and add more salt if necessary.

5. Drain the pasta and add to the skillet. Toss over moderate heat until every strand is coated. Serve right away in heated bowls. Pass the cheese at the table if you like.

◆ Spaghetti with a Simple Tomato Sauce ◆

Serves 6 to 8 as a first course or 4 to 6 as a main course

This sauce is cooked in one easy step. Every-thing stews together and simmers without fuss. Onions sweeten and balance the acidity of the tomatoes, while olive oil gives the sauce an unctuous quality. Blending the sauce gives it a great, orangey color and more finesse, but it is not a necessary step. If you prefer you can leave the sauce chunky.

1 cup finely chopped onions
3½ cups chopped canned tomato pulp and
  juice
½ cup extra virgin olive oil
½ to 1 teaspoon sea salt
1 pound dried spaghetti
Freshly grated Parmigiano-Reggiano
  (optional)

1. Combine the onions, 1 cup water, tomato, olive oil, and half the salt in a large saucepan. Bring to a boil, lower the heat, and simmer, covered, for about 45 minutes, or until the onions are melt-ingly soft. Taste and add more salt if necessary. Purée with an immersion blender and keep warm while you cook the pasta.

2. Bring a large pot of water to a boil. Add a gen-erous amount of salt and drop in the spaghetti. Cook, stirring often, until al dente. Drain the pasta and transfer to a heated serving bowl. Toss with enough of the tomato sauce to coat each strand generously. Sprinkle with Parmigiano-Reggiano, if you like, and serve at once in warmed bowls. Pass any remaining sauce at the table.

Spaghetti with "Authentic" Roman Tomato Sauce

Serves 6 to 8 as a first course or 4 to 6 as a main course

Pasta with tomato sauce could well be the national dish of Italy. This one comes from the Eternal City and an engaging young Roman named Piero. Piero was a bit of a show-off and loved to cook—especially when young women were around to impress. He often took over the student kitchen at the Palazzo Cenci, the European Honors Center for the Rhode Island School of Design, where he tried to woo the girls with his culinary skill. George, the resident professor at the time, chuckled at him but paid close attention, too.

Piero came armed with his mother's mezzaluna, a sharp knife with a curved blade and handles on each end, and the makings of his favorite recipe—a genuine Roman tomato sauce for spaghetti. Piero was precise, meticulous, and fussy. He commanded his post at the cutting board, philosophizing about this or that ingredient and the architecture of the sauce—the onions, carrots, celery, garlic, and herbs must be finely chopped and sautéed gently in olive oil until meltingly tender. The veggies had to be sufficiently soft and aromatic enough to give the sauce its foundation of taste. The wine—always dry and white—was added and reduced to eliminate any harshness and to release its tart/sweet properties. Only then was the tomato added. The sauce was cooked just enough to marry all the ingredients but keep its fresh taste. In the end, Piero certainly made a delicious sugo, one he must have watched his mother make hundreds of times. We don't know if Piero ever got a girl through his cooking, but his sauce is good enough to live on in our repertoire.

If you have a mezzaluna in your kitchen, use it to chop the vegetables; a sharp knife works just as well. Piero puréed his authentic sauce through a food mill; we use a modern immersion blender.

¼ cup extra virgin olive oil

¾ cup finely chopped onions

2 sprigs fresh flat-leaf parsley, leaves only,
   finely chopped

½ cup peeled and finely chopped carrots

½ cup finely chopped celery

1 large garlic clove, peeled and finely
   chopped

¼ teaspoon crushed red pepper flakes
   (optional)

1 teaspoon or more fine sea salt

½ cup dry white wine

3½ cups chopped canned tomato pulp and
   juice

1 pound dried spaghetti

Freshly grated Parmigiano-Reggiano or
   Pecorino Romano

1. Heat the olive oil in an earthenware pot or heavy-bottomed saucepan with the onions, parsley, carrots, celery, garlic, red pepper flakes, if you like, and ½ teaspoon salt. Sauté over moderate heat until the vegetables are very soft without allowing them to brown, 20 to 25 minutes. Add the wine, raise the heat, and allow the wine to all but evaporate, stirring often. Add the tomato and 1 cup water. Cover, bring to a boil, then lower the heat to maintain a gentle simmer. Cook for 30 minutes.

2. Purée the sauce with an immersion blender. You may use the sauce right away or cool to room temperature, cover, and refrigerate for up to 3 days, or freeze.

3. To serve, bring plenty of water to a boil in a large pot. Stir in a generous amount of salt. Drop in the spaghetti and cook, stirring often, until al dente. Drain and transfer the spaghetti to a heated serving bowl into which you have ladled some of the sauce topped with a sprinkle of grated cheese. Top the spaghetti with more sauce and another sprinkling of cheese. You may have more sauce than necessary. The pasta should be well napped but not swimming in sauce. Transfer the remaining sauce to a bowl and pass at the table if you like. Serve the spaghetti right away in warmed bowls.

◆ Tagliatelle with Little Girl's Tomato Sauce ◆

Serves 6 to 8 as a first course or 4 to 6 as a main course

Inspiration can come from anywhere. This sauce is an evolution of a tomato soup made for George by Mona, a precocious five-year-old. Too tiny to reach the counter or stovetop, she adeptly propped herself on a chair, chopped up tomatoes and butter, and put the whole lot—tomato skins and all—into a saucepan to cook. The soup was either truly delicious or it was the child's moxie that made it a most memorable lunch.

Here, the little girl's soup is transformed into a pasta sauce and dressed for dinner by peeling (and seeding if necessary) the tomatoes and adding a final flourish of Parmigiano-Reggiano. Sometimes the most basic things are the most satisfying.

¼ teaspoon sea salt
3½ cups (about 2 pounds) peeled and
  chopped fresh plum tomatoes
8 tablespoons unsalted butter
1 pound dried tagliatelle or spaghetti
Freshly grated Parmigiano-Reggiano

1. Bring a large pot of water to a boil.

2. Put the salt, tomatoes, and butter in a large straight-sided sauté pan. Bring to a boil over moderate heat, then lower the heat to maintain a simmer for 10 minutes. Taste the sauce and add more salt if necessary.

3. Generously salt the boiling water and drop in the pasta. Cook, stirring often, until al dente. Drain the pasta and transfer to the sauté pan. Toss until every strand is nicely coated with sauce. Transfer to heated bowls, sprinkle with Parmigiano-Reggiano, and serve right away.

◆ Spaghetti with Jo's Caper-and-Mint–Scented Green Tomato Sauce ◆

Serves 6 to 8 as a first course or 4 to 6 as a main course

Mint gives a great wake-up call to your palate. In this Sicilian-inspired sauce, it perks up and refreshes all the other ingredients.

3 tablespoons unsalted butter
3 tablespoons extra virgin olive oil
1½ cups chopped onions
2 Italian or Hungarian green finger peppers, seeded and chopped (see Note)
1 plump garlic clove, peeled and finely minced
6 to 7 medium (about 2½ pounds) green tomatoes, coarsely chopped
½ teaspoon sea salt
1 cup loosely packed fresh flat-leaf parsley leaves
¼ cup loosely packed fresh mint leaves
1 tablespoon capers in salt, rinsed and drained
1 pound dried spaghetti
Freshly grated Parmigiano-Reggiano

1. Heat the butter and olive oil in a large sauté pan. Add the onions, peppers, and garlic, and sauté over moderate heat until the vegetables are very soft but not browned, about 15 minutes. Add the tomatoes and salt, and cook an additional 10 minutes. Strain the mixture, reserving all the liquid, and transfer the solids to a food processor and purée. For a silky, smooth sauce, put the purée through a food mill. Transfer to a mixing bowl and set aside to cool.

2. When the reserved liquid has cooled to room temperature, put it in a blender with the parsley and mint. (Adding the fresh herbs to the cool liquid will keep the bright colors and fresh taste of the sauce. If you whirl the herbs in hot liquid, they will discolor and their flavors will dim.) Add the capers and purée. Transfer to the bowl with the tomato mixture. Stir to combine. Taste the sauce and add more salt if necessary.

3. Bring a large pot of water to a boil. Generously salt the water and drop in the spaghetti. Very gently reheat the sauce in a large sauté pan on another burner. When the spaghetti is al dente, drain, transfer to the sauté pan, and toss the pasta and sauce together. Transfer to warmed bowls and sprinkle with Parmigiano-Reggiano. Serve right away.

Note: Italian or Hungarian finger peppers have a distinctive, delicate flavor. Do not substitute green bell peppers. If finger peppers are unavailable, eliminate peppers from the recipe.

  on top of spaghetti...

◆ Rigatoni with George's Green Tomato Sauce ◆

Serves 6 to 8 as a first course or 4 to 6 as a main course

It's difficult to say goodbye to the all-too-short tomato season. To hang on, we gather all the tomatoes left on the vines just before the threat of the first frost. The red tomatoes go into salads or sauces, or are peeled, seeded, and chopped to fill a few precious containers to stash in the freezer for a treat during the long winter. We treasure the green tomatoes, too. Their bright taste and acidity complement many other ingredients. Here, they star in one of our favorite summer-into-fall recipes for pasta, which appears on the menu at Al Forno from September through Thanksgiving. We add a small amount of green bell pepper to the sauce—just enough for your taste buds to take notice without knowing exactly where the beguiling flavor is coming from.

We make this sauce with chicken stock to give it depth. You may use water instead with equally delicious results. The flavor will be more subtle, with a pure, vegetable taste. Most of the heat in the jalapeño is stored in the spongy inner tissue and seeds. Remove them if you want a less spicy result.

7 to 8 tablespoons unsalted butter, at room temperature
1 pound (about 2 large) green tomatoes, coarsely chopped
1½ cups coarsely chopped onions
½ green bell pepper, seeded and coarsely chopped
1 jalapeño pepper, seeded if you wish and coarsely chopped
1 garlic clove, peeled and sliced
1 to 2 teaspoons sea salt
2 cups homemade chicken stock (see Pasta Pantry) or water
1 pound dried rigatoni or penne
Freshly grated Parmigiano-Reggiano

1. Heat 4 tablespoons of the butter in a heavy straight-sided sauté pan with the tomatoes, onions, green pepper, jalapeño, garlic, and 1 teaspoon of the salt. Sweat the vegetables over low heat until they are very soft, about 30 minutes. Add the chicken stock, cover, and bring to a boil. Reduce the heat to moderately low and simmer for another 30 minutes.

2. Purée the sauce with an immersion blender. Taste, adding more of the salt if you wish. You may use the sauce right away or allow it to cool, then cover and refrigerate for up to 3 days.

3. To serve, heat up the sauce and keep it over the lowest possible heat.

4. Bring lots of water to a boil in a large pot. Add a generous amount of salt and drop in the pasta. Cook the pasta at a brisk boil until al dente—firm but not hard. Drain and transfer to a large, heated serving platter or pasta bowl. Toss in the remaining 3 to 4 tablespoons butter. Add enough of the green tomato sauce to generously coat the pasta. Serve at once in heated bowls and pass the Parmigiano-Reggiano.

on top of spaghetti...

◆ Spaghettini with Tomatoes, Cinnamon, and Mint ◆

Serves 6 to 8 as a first course or 4 to 6 as a main course

Crushed, rather than chopped, garlic is cooked in olive oil and removed from the sauce before adding the pasta—a technique that controls the garlic's influence. You can peel and smash the garlic in one motion. Cut off the stem end of the garlic cloves and place them on their sides on a cutting board. Crush them gently with a meat pounder or the wide blade of a chef's knife. The skins will slip off easily.

The cinnamon gives a mysterious flavor to the dish, while the mint provides a nice refreshing counterpoint to the taste of the garlic.

½ cup extra virgin olive oil

2 plump garlic cloves, trimmed, smashed, and peeled

2 cinnamon sticks (each 2½ to 3 inches long)

2 cups gently packed whole fresh mint leaves, finely chopped

4 fresh plum tomatoes, peeled, seeded, and chopped

1 pound dried spaghettini

1. Bring a large pot of water to a boil.

2. Heat the olive oil, garlic, and cinnamon sticks in a large straight-sided sauté pan over moderate heat. Cook, swirling the pan often, until the garlic becomes golden. Off the heat add half of the mint and stir it into the oil. Add the tomatoes, being careful not to burn yourself as they may sizzle and sputter in the hot oil.

3. Return the sauté pan to moderate heat and cook until the tomatoes are hot. Set aside on very low heat.

4. Generously salt the boiling water and drop in the pasta. Cook, stirring often, until al dente. Drain the spaghettini, reserving about 1 cup of the pasta water. Remove and discard the garlic and cinnamon stick from the sauté pan. Transfer the drained spaghettini to the sauté pan along with the remaining mint. Toss in the flavored oil until every strand of pasta is nicely coated with the sauce. Add a little of the pasta water if it seems too dry. Serve right away in warmed bowls.

Bucatini with Fresh Tomatoes, Pancetta, and Onion

Serves 6 to 8 as a first course or 4 to 6 as a main course

There are many arguments over the ingredients for classic Amatriciana sauce that we feel perfectly justified adding one more interpretation to the heap. The sauce contains tomatoes (usually canned), cured pork (classically *guanciale*, or salted and cured pork jowls, but often pancetta), onions (though some cooks think this is criminal), chile or crushed red pepper flakes (historians argue in favor of using black pepper instead), and white or red wine (we opt for no wine). There is even debate over what type of pasta one should use, bucatini or spaghetti. Both are delicious; you choose.

¼ cup plus 1 tablespoon (about 1¼ ounces) gently packed small cubes of pancetta
5 tablespoons extra virgin olive oil
3 cups (about 1½ pounds) peeled, seeded, and chopped fresh plum tomatoes
1 heaping cup diced onions
½ teaspoon sea salt
Pinch of crushed red pepper flakes or more to taste (optional)
1 pound dried bucatini or spaghetti
Freshly grated Pecorino Romano (optional)

1. Put the pancetta in a large straight-sided non-stick sauté pan over moderate heat. Toss often to prevent it from sticking. When the pancetta has rendered some of its fat and has browned on the edges, lower the heat and carefully add the olive oil along with the tomatoes, onions, and salt. Stir in some red pepper flakes if you like. Cover, bring to a boil, lower the heat to a simmer, and cook for 20 to 30 minutes until the onions are soft and completely cooked. Taste and add more salt if necessary.

2. To serve, bring plenty of water to a boil in a large pot. Stir in a generous amount of salt and drop in the bucatini. Cook, stirring often, until al dente. Drain the pasta, saving about 1 cup of the pasta water. Toss the bucatini into the sauce in the sauté pan. Stir over moderate heat until every strand is coated with sauce. Add some of the pasta water, a tablespoon at a time, if it seems too dry. Serve right away in heated bowls. Pass some Pecorino Romano and additional red pepper flakes at the table if you like.

on top of spaghetti...

◆ Salina-Style Spaghettini with Cherry Tomatoes ◆

Serves 6 to 8 as a first course or 4 to 6 as a main course

Salina is an unspoiled island of incredible beauty in the Tyrrhenian Sea, off the northeast coast of Sicily. The port of Santa Marina boasts a restaurant, Porto Bello, where the food competes with a dazzling view of the cobalt sea. At a memorable lunch, everything we tasted was bursting with flavor, but we were most impressed with a simple spaghetti tossed with warmed pomodorini—small, intense tomatoes—and fresh mint. The pasta was garnished with chopped garlic and a Sicilian cheese—*ricotta infornata*, or fresh ricotta cheese baked in the oven until it turns dark mahogany on the outside and caramel colored on the inside.

5 tablespoons extra virgin olive oil
6 dozen small (8 to 10 ounces) ripe cherry tomatoes, cut in half
Pinch or up to ¼ teaspoon cayenne
1 pound dried spaghettini
1 plump garlic clove, peeled and minced
½ cup heaping and loosely packed fresh mint leaves
1¼ cups (about 2¼ ounces) freshly grated ricotta infornata or ricotta salata

1. Bring a large pot of water to a boil.

2. Put the olive oil and cherry tomatoes in a large straight-sided sauté pan. Sprinkle with cayenne. Warm over medium heat until the tomatoes begin to give off some of their juice, shaking the pan every so often.

3. Meanwhile, generously salt the boiling water in the pot and add the spaghettini. Cook, stirring often, until al dente. Drain the pasta, reserving 1 cup of the pasta cooking water. Transfer the pasta to the sauté pan, add the garlic, and toss with the tomatoes. Add ⅓ cup of the reserved pasta water. Toss over medium heat until the water and oil emulsify. Add more water as necessary, a tablespoon at a time, until you have a nice creamy consistency and all the strands of spaghettini are well coated with sauce. Rip the mint leaves into small pieces and toss with the spaghettini. Transfer to heated bowls and top with the cheese. Serve right away.

◆ Spaghettini with Spicy Roasted Cherry Tomatoes ◆

Serves 6 to 8 as a first course or 4 to 6 as a main course

When roasted, the natural sugars in tomatoes become concentrated and distinctive. The hot peppers grab just enough of your attention and nicely offset the sweetness of the tomatoes.

Though buying tomatoes off-season rarely gives a reward (they are usually hard, unripe, and cottony in texture), you can occasionally find nice, juicy cherry tomatoes. If you do there is no need to relegate this recipe to "summer only."

1¼ pounds fresh, ripe cherry tomatoes, halved
½ to 1 teaspoon finely chopped fresh hot peppers
5 to 6 tablespoons extra virgin olive oil
1 pound dried spaghettini or linguine

1. Heat the oven to 400 degrees.

2. Toss the tomatoes, peppers, and olive oil together in a baking dish large enough to hold the tomatoes in a single layer. It is fine if they are a bit crowded. Roast for 20 to 30 minutes until the tomatoes are beginning to brown and have become very aromatic. Set aside.

3. Meanwhile, bring a large pot of water to a boil for the pasta. When the tomatoes are cooked, add a generous amount of salt to the pasta water and drop in the spaghettini. Cook, stirring often, until al dente. Drain the pasta, reserving about 1 cup of the pasta cooking water. Transfer the pasta to a heated serving bowl. Add the tomatoes with all their oil and hot peppers, scraping up every last bit with a rubber spatula. Toss together, adding enough of the reserved pasta water to keep the pasta very moist with a little puddle on the bottom. Serve immediately.

◆ Spaghettini with Tomatoes, Garlic, and Hot Pepper ◆

Serves 6 to 8 as a first course, 4 to 6 as a main course

Giovanni Puiatti makes some of the loveliest wines in Italy. When he was in Providence several years ago, we hosted a winemaker's dinner at Al Forno in his honor and created a sumptuous menu to complement his distinctive, varietal wines from Friuli in northern Italy. Late that night, when the last guest left, we sat down with Giovanni to unwind with a glass of his Pinot Bianco. Giovanni mentioned that in Italy he and his friends rejuvenate themselves at the end of the evening with a bowl of pasta. George put on his apron, returned to the kitchen, and prepared this spicy spaghetti. Indeed, we were all revitalized.

½ cup extra virgin olive oil
2 tablespoons minced fresh garlic
½ teaspoon crushed red pepper flakes
1 cup homemade chicken stock (see Pasta Pantry) or water
½ teaspoon fine sea salt
2 cups chopped canned tomatoes with their juice
1 pound dried spaghettini

1. Bring a large pot of water to a boil.

2. Heat the olive oil, garlic, and red pepper flakes in a 10- to 12-inch sauté pan over moderately high heat. As soon as the garlic becomes golden, slowly add the chicken stock or water and salt, being careful not to burn yourself as the oil may spatter. Let the liquid reduce for 2 to 3 minutes. Add the tomatoes, bring to a boil, lower the heat, and keep the sauce warm over very low heat while you cook the spaghettini.

3. Stir a generous amount of salt into the boiling water and add the spaghettini. Cook at a full rolling boil, stirring often, until the pasta is al dente. Drain the spaghettini, reserving about ½ cup of the pasta water. Transfer the spaghettini to the sauté pan with the sauce, stirring over very low heat until every strand is coated. If the sauce seems dry, add 1 to 2 tablespoons of the pasta water. Serve immediately.

◆ New World Pappardelle ◆

Serves 6 to 8 as a first course or 4 to 6 as a main course

〜〜〜〜〜〜〜〜〜〜〜〜〜〜〜〜〜〜〜〜〜〜〜〜〜〜〜〜〜〜〜〜

The food of Italy, even in this modern day, is distinctive by region. Each area of the country is known for its particular meats, vegetables, cheeses, or even salt. One eats what is freshest, best, and local. If it is mushroom season, every household and every restaurant menu will celebrate their short season by combining the *funghi* with crostini, pasta, and salads, or brushing them with olive oil to grill and serve as a main course. In New England, we follow the same drummer. When summer arrives with fresh-from-the-farm corn, we take full advantage of it. This "summer only" recipe combines the sweet corn with cool, ripe, juicy tomatoes, pungent cilantro, and habanero peppers for a kick of hot spice. A good, fruity Tuscan olive oil is perfect here. Old World and New share the stage.

〜〜〜〜〜〜〜〜〜〜〜〜〜〜〜〜

4 ears fresh corn, husked
8 small or 4 large (about 3 pounds) juicy, vine-ripened tomatoes, at room temperature
½ Scotch bonnet or habanero pepper, finely chopped
½ cup extra virgin olive oil
1 teaspoon fine sea salt
½ cup chopped fresh cilantro
1 pound dried pappardelle

1. Bring 6 quarts of water to a boil in a large pot for the pasta. Bring another pot of water to boil for the corn.

2. Salt the corn water to taste and add the corn. Boil for 2 minutes, drain, refresh under cold running water to stop the cooking, and drain again. With a sharp knife, remove the corn kernels from the husk and transfer to a large stainless steel mixing bowl. You should have 3 to 3½ cups of corn.

3. Core the tomatoes, cut them in half lengthwise, lay them on a cutting board, cut side down, cut them in half crosswise, then vertically into 1-inch chunks. Add the tomatoes to the mixing bowl with the corn. Toss in the chopped pepper to taste, keeping in mind that Scotch bonnet or

on top of spaghetti...

habanero peppers are very spicy. Add the olive oil, salt, and cilantro. Toss to combine.

4. Meanwhile, add a generous amount of salt to the pasta water and drop in the pappardelle. Cook at a full rolling boil, stirring often, until al dente. If desired, you may rest the stainless steel mixing bowl over the boiling water for a minute or two to warm the ingredients. When the pasta is cooked, drain it and transfer to the mixing bowl. Toss well and serve at once.

Spaghetti with Heirloom Tomatoes and Herbed Ricotta

Serves 6 to 8 as a first course or 4 to 6 as a main course

~~~~~~

This is a great pasta for a hot summer day. The heat of the steaming spaghetti is tempered by tossing it with a tomato salad. It chills just enough to keep the sweat off your brow.

A good, fresh, and creamy ricotta is essential here. If there is any hint of graininess in the cheese, whip it in a food processor until it is smooth.

A mixture of varied colored heirloom tomatoes makes a very attractive presentation. Be sure they are ripe and juicy, and haven't seen the inside of a refrigerator.

~~~~~~

1 cup fresh ricotta
¼ cup finely chopped fresh flat-leaf parsley
1 teaspoon sea salt
2 tablespoons finely minced shallot
2 tablespoons red wine vinegar
2 tablespoons sherry vinegar
5 to 6 large (2 pounds) fresh, juicy, ripe heirloom tomatoes
6 tablespoons extra virgin olive oil
¼ cup mixed chopped fresh herbs (basil, thyme, marjoram, chives)
1 pound dried spaghetti

1. Mix the ricotta, parsley, and a pinch of salt in a small bowl. Set aside.

2. In another small bowl, soften the shallots in the wine and sherry vinegars for at least 15 minutes.

3. Core and dice the tomatoes. Transfer them to a large pasta serving bowl. Toss with the olive oil, mixed herbs, and the remaining salt. Add the shallots with the vinegars and toss again.

4. Bring a large pot of water to a boil, generously salt the water, and drop in the spaghetti. Cook, stirring often, until the pasta is al dente. Drain and transfer the spaghetti to the bowl with the tomatoes. Toss to coat every strand of pasta. Spoon dollops of the herbed ricotta on top of the spaghetti and toss again just before serving.

on **top** of spaghetti...

◆ Spaghetti with Fresh Tomatoes and Mozzarella ◆

Serves 6 to 8 as a first course or 4 to 6 as a main course

The red, white, and green of this pasta reflect the colors of the Italian flag. And it is a flavor combination made in Italian heaven. Go to the effort of finding buffalo milk mozzarella. It has a creamier, softer texture than mozzarella made with cow's milk. When tossed with the juicy tomatoes, olive oil, and basil, the buffalo mozzarella weeps some of its milky whey into the mixture, creating a sauce that is more divine than the sum of its parts. Have a nice, crusty loaf of bread to dip into the pool of sauce left in the bowl after you have slurped up the last strand of spaghetti.

6 medium (about 2 pounds) fresh, ripe, and juicy tomatoes
2 small (4 to 6 ounces each) balls of fresh mozzarella (see Pasta Pantry), preferably buffalo
⅔ cup gently packed torn fresh basil leaves
⅔ cup extra virgin olive oil
1 teaspoon sea salt
1 pound dried spaghetti
Freshly grated Parmigiano-Reggiano

1. Core and dice the tomatoes. Transfer to a large pasta serving bowl.

2. Cut the mozzarella into cubes the same size as the tomato chunks and add to the tomatoes with the basil, olive oil, and salt. Toss together. Let stand at room temperature for 20 to 30 minutes, tossing the mixture every so often.

3. Bring a large pot of water to a boil, add a generous amount of salt, and drop in the spaghetti. Cook, stirring often, until al dente. Drain the pasta and toss into the bowl with the tomatoes and mozzarella. Serve right away with Parmigiano-Reggiano.

Spicy Pappardelle with Summer Tomatoes, Cucumbers, and Oregano

Serves 6 to 8 as a first course or 4 to 6 as a main course

This is about as close to pasta salad as we get. The pasta is cooked to order and bathed in a cool vinaigrette.

Sweet tomatoes and crunchy cucumbers pacify the fieriness of the spicy Scotch bonnet pepper sauce. The aromatic dried oregano boosts the flavor of its delicate fresh twin.

8 medium (about 3 pounds) fresh, ripe, and juicy garden tomatoes
2 small red onions
8 Kirby (pickling) cucumbers, skin on, coarsely chopped
2 to 4 teaspoons or more Scotch bonnet pepper sauce
⅔ cup extra virgin olive oil
4 teaspoons red wine vinegar
2 teaspoons good-quality fragrant dried oregano
2 tablespoons fresh oregano or marjoram leaves
1 to 2 teaspoons sea salt
1 pound dried pappardelle
½ cup chopped fresh flat-leaf parsley

1. Core the tomatoes, cut them in half vertically, then cut each half into 8 chunks. Transfer to a large serving bowl.

2. Peel the onions and cut in half vertically. Cut each half into very thin vertical slices. Add to the tomatoes in the bowl with the cucumbers, Scotch bonnet pepper sauce, olive oil, vinegar, dried and fresh oregano, and salt to taste. Set aside at room temperature for 30 minutes for the flavors to combine and for the taste of the raw onions, to soften and mellow in the vinaigrette.

3. Bring a large pot of water to a boil. Generously salt the water and drop in the pappardelle. Cook, stirring often, until al dente. Drain the pasta and toss in the bowl with the tomatoes and cucumbers. Add the parsley. Toss to combine and serve right away.

Pasta with Seafood

◆ Spaghetti Nizza ◆

Serves 6 to 8 as a first course or 4 to 6 as a main course

Is it Italian or French? Bilingual arguments abound concerning its provenance and the ingredients of the genuine article. Most likely all depended on what frugal cooks had on hand. After one taste of this spaghetti you can leave history and authenticity behind—at least until the bowls are empty.

2 tablespoons freshly squeezed lemon juice
½ cup extra virgin olive oil, plus more to toss with the pasta
1½ cups best-quality canned tuna packed in olive oil, drained
1 teaspoon dried oregano, crushed between your fingers to release its aroma
2 teaspoons finely chopped fresh oregano
1 to 2 fresh hot peppers, seeded and chopped, or ⅛ to ¼ teaspoon cayenne
1 teaspoon capers packed in salt, rinsed, dried, and finely chopped
16 black oil-cured olives, pitted and chopped
2 tablespoons finely chopped fresh flat-leaf parsley
4 small cooked and peeled potatoes, cut into ¼-inch dice (1 cup)
1 pound dried spaghetti
Lemon wedges (optional)

1. Whisk the lemon juice and olive oil together in a mixing bowl. Stir in the tuna, dried and fresh oregano, hot pepper, capers, olives, and parsley. Add the potatoes and toss to combine. Set aside.

2. Bring a large pot of water to a boil for the pasta. Generously salt the water and drop in the pasta. Cook, stirring often, until al dente. Drain the spaghetti, reserving a scant cup of cooking water.

3. Toss the spaghetti in a large, warmed bowl with 1 to 2 tablespoons olive oil. Add enough pasta water, a tablespoon at a time, to moisten and coat the spaghetti. Add the potato-tuna mixture and toss well. Serve right away in warmed bowls. Pass lemon wedges at the table to spritz more juice over the spaghetti if you like.

  on top of spaghetti...

◆ Linguine with Canned Tuna ◆

Serves 4 as a first course or 2 as a main course

This is one of George's all-time favorites. On the rare occasions we're apart, George either eats take-out Chinese food or linguine with tuna for dinner. He uses light tuna packed in olive oil because of its rich, full flavor and silky texture. The lemon zest is Johanne's addition because she thinks it brightens the flavors. George adds it only when Johanne is there to enjoy it with him.

4 (about 2 pounds) vine-ripened tomatoes, cored, or 1 cup chopped canned tomatoes
¼ cup extra virgin olive oil
2 teaspoons minced fresh garlic
½ teaspoon crushed red pepper flakes
½ teaspoon fennel seeds, lightly crushed with the back of a spoon on a cutting board
1 small (5-ounce) can solid light tuna packed in olive oil, drained
½ teaspoon sea salt
½ teaspoon finely minced lemon zest (optional)
8 ounces imported dried linguine
2 tablespoons chopped fresh flat-leaf parsley

1. Bring a large pot of water to a boil.

2. Drop the tomatoes in the boiling water for 30 seconds. With tongs, transfer the tomatoes to a cutting board, peel, and halve them horizontally. To remove the seeds, squeeze the tomatoes into a sieve or strainer suspended over a bowl. Discard the seeds, chop the remaining tomato pulp, and add it to the juices collected in the bowl. Set aside.

3. Heat the olive oil in a large sauté pan and add the garlic, red pepper flakes, and fennel seeds. Cook gently over medium heat until the garlic becomes golden. Add the tuna and ½ teaspoon salt, raise the heat, and sauté a few minutes until the tuna begins to sizzle and hop in the oil. Add the tomato pulp and juice, bring to a boil, reduce the heat, and simmer 4 minutes, or until the tomatoes have softened and released a bit more of their juice. Add the lemon zest, if you like, and set aside over low heat. Taste and add more salt if necessary.

4. Add a generous amount of salt to the boiling water and drop in the pasta. Cook at a full rolling boil, stirring often, until al dente. Drain, reserving some of the cooking water, and toss the pasta in the sauté pan with the tuna sauce. Add a little pasta water if the sauce seems too thick. Toss the pasta 1 minute in the sauce to absorb flavors, garnish with the parsley, and serve immediately.

◆ Linguine with Tuna "Meatballs" ◆

Serves 6 to 8 as a first course or 4 to 6 as a main course

Tuna meatballs? Why not? They're succulent, a nice change from polpettine made with ground beef, and would have been welcome on the meatless Friday nights of our youth.

In Italy, cheese is rarely combined with seafood. Exceptions exist in Calabria, Sicily, Sardinia, and other regions touching the sea. Here, a judicious amount of salty Pecorino Romano lifts the blandness of the tuna, giving it more body and vibrancy.

Leftovers? These tuna polpettine can be served cold, scooped out of the sauce with a slotted spoon, and drizzled with a little fresh lemon juice. Pass them around with toothpicks as an hors d'oeuvre. If you have extra sauce, reheat it and toss with fusilli and some freshly grated Pecorino Romano.

Tuna Polpettine
1 cup fresh bread crumbs
¼ cup milk
1 pound fresh tuna
1 tablespoon grated lemon zest
2 tablespoons minced fresh flat-leaf parsley
2 tablespoons minced fresh mint leaves
½ cup freshly grated Pecorino Romano
1 egg, lightly beaten
¼ teaspoon ground fennel seeds
1 teaspoon sea salt
Freshly ground black pepper

Tomato Sauce and Pasta
4 cups canned tomatoes and their juice (see Note)
⅓ cup chopped onions
½ teaspoon sea salt
⅓ cup extra virgin olive oil
Cayenne
½ cup dry white wine
3 tablespoons currants
1 pound dried linguine or spaghettini
Crushed red pepper flakes (optional)

1. In a small mixing bowl, toss the bread crumbs and milk together. Set aside until almost all the milk has been absorbed, about 5 minutes.

2. Meanwhile, coarsely chop the tuna—you will have about 2 cups. Transfer to a food processor and pulse on and off until it is finely chopped, but don't make a purée. Transfer to a large mixing bowl.

3. Add the lemon zest, parsley, mint, Pecorino Romano, egg, fennel seeds, salt, and some black pepper. Mix gently with a fork or wooden spoon. Fold in the soaked bread crumbs and any remaining milk. Gently mix to combine.

4. Form small polpettine, or balls, of the tuna mixture with the moistened palms of your hands. Each ball should take about 1 tablespoon of the tuna mixture and be just over an inch in diameter. As they're done, place the balls on wax paper on a sheet pan. When you've used all the tuna, you should have about 40 balls. Place in the refrigerator for about an hour to firm up while you make the tomato sauce.

5. Put the tomatoes, onions, salt, olive oil, a pinch of cayenne, wine, and 1 cup water in a large saucepan. Cover, bring to a boil, lower the heat, and simmer until the onions are soft and completely cooked through, about 45 minutes. Add the currants and continue to simmer an additional 15 minutes. Purée the sauce—the currants will be chopped into little bits. Return to the stove and bring back to a boil over moderately high heat. Lower the heat and drop in the tuna balls, one by one. Poach them for about 15 minutes—as they cook they will flavor the sauce.

6. Bring a large pot of water to a boil. Add a generous amount of salt and drop in the linguine. Cook, stirring often, until al dente. Drain the pasta and transfer to a heated serving bowl. Nap with enough of the sauce to coat each strand of linguine. Arrange the tuna polpettine around the pasta and serve right away with any extra sauce passed at the table. Serve with crushed red pepper if you like it hot.

Note: The sauce is puréed, so you can use crushed or whole canned tomatoes.

Spaghettini with Chopped Shrimp and Scallops in Rich Broth

Serves 6 to 8 as a first course or 4 to 6 as a main course

This spaghettini dish always gets rave reviews. Its success depends on the quality and freshness of the seafood. Give the shrimp and scallops a good sniff and trust your nose: You should smell the sea.

Be sure to buy "dry" scallops. Those labeled "wet" have been bathed in STP (sodium tripolyphosphate) to extend their shelf life. The solution dulls both the appearance and delicate flavor of the scallops. Dry scallops have an opalescent shine, a slightly tacky feel, and a sweet ocean scent.

3 ounces medium shrimp in their shells
5 ounces fresh scallops
½ cup extra virgin olive oil
¼ cup finely chopped onions
1 teaspoon finely minced fresh garlic
1 small fresh hot pepper
1 cup dry white wine
1 tomato, peeled, seeded, and finely chopped
½ teaspoon sea salt
1 pound dried spaghettini
2 tablespoons unsalted butter, softened
4 tablespoons finely chopped fresh flat-leaf parsley

1. Peel the shrimp, reserving the shells. Carefully devein the shrimp and coarsely chop them. Coarsely chop the scallops and combine them with the shrimp and ¼ cup water in the bowl of a food processor fitted with the steel blade. Pulse on and off to finely chop but don't create a purée. Add another tablespoon of water if the mixture becomes sticky. Cover, and set aside in the refrigerator while you make the broth.

2. Start the broth, or fumet, by heating the olive oil in a large straight-sided sauté pan. Add the reserved shrimp shells, onions, garlic, and hot

pepper. Sauté over moderate heat for about 10 minutes until the onions have softened and the shells have turned deep pink. Add the wine and reduce until you have ¼ to ⅓ cup left in the pan. Add 4 cups water and boil vigorously to reduce until you have about 3 cups of liquid left. Strain the fumet through a fine sieve into another large sauté pan. Add the tomato and bring to a boil. Taste and add salt if necessary. Set aside over very low heat and simmer gently while you cook the pasta.

3. Bring at least 5 quarts of water to a boil in a large pot. Generously salt the water and drop in the spaghettini. Cook, stirring often, until the pasta is almost al dente, about 4 minutes. Drain the pasta and transfer to the fumet. Fold in the chopped shrimp and scallops along with the butter and parsley. Simmer just until the spaghettini is al dente and the seafood is cooked through, 1 to 2 minutes. Serve right away.

◆ Spaghettini with Littleneck Clams "Macchiato" ◆

Serves 6 to 8 as a first course or 4 to 6 as a main course

Since clams are plentiful and delicious in Rhode Island, our menu at Al Forno always offers an appetizer, pasta, or main course featuring littleneck clams. For this spaghettini dish, the clams are cooked in a wine sauce stained—*macchiato* in Italian—with fresh tomato. The flavors remain light and bright, nicely enhancing the brininess of the clams.

3 tablespoons extra virgin olive oil
1 plump garlic clove, peeled and thinly
    sliced
3 tablespoons finely minced onions
1½ cups dry white wine
1 cup peeled, seeded, chopped, and
    drained fresh plum tomatoes
24 small littleneck clams, scrubbed clean
1 pound dried spaghettini or linguine

1. Bring a large pot of water to a boil.

2. Heat the olive oil in a large straight-sided sauté pan with a tight-fitting lid. Add the garlic and onions and sauté over moderate heat until the garlic becomes golden. Add the wine, increase the heat to moderately high, and bring to a boil. Continue to cook to reduce the liquid to 2 to 3 tablespoons. Add the tomatoes and clams, cover, and cook, shaking the pan now and then, over moderate heat until the clams open. All of the clams will not open at the same time. Check them after about 5 minutes and transfer any that have opened to a heated serving bowl. Every few minutes continue to check and transfer opened clams to the bowl until all the clams are cooked. Set the dish aside in a warm place. Keep the clam broth hot over very low heat while you cook the pasta.

3. Generously salt the boiling water and drop in the spaghettini. Cook, stirring often, until it is firm and underdone—about 2 minutes before it becomes al dente. Drain the pasta and toss into the broth in the sauté pan. Cook for 1 to 2 minutes to soften the pasta and allow it to absorb some of the liquid. Transfer the spaghettini to the serving bowl with the clams and serve right away.

on top of spaghetti...

◆ Linguine with Clam "Bolognese" ◆

Serves 8 as a first course or 4 to 6 as a main course

We playfully call this clam sauce "Bolognese" though it contains none of the meats used in a traditional Bolognese ragù. Instead, we borrow the technique and use clams and vegetables to make the sauce. This impostor is light and elegant with a "meaty" character from the minced clams. Chop all the vegetables finely so they will melt into the sauce, giving it the texture of a chunky purée.

There is no salt in this ragù as fresh clams contain an abundant amount naturally. Taste the sauce before adding the pasta to be sure it is seasoned well enough for your palate.

In Italy, it is rare to find cheese grated atop any seafood sauce. Instead, sautéed or toasted homemade, unflavored bread crumbs are used as an optional garnish.

¼ cup extra virgin olive oil
⅓ cup finely chopped onions
⅓ cup finely chopped carrots
⅓ cup finely chopped celery
2 teaspoons finely minced fresh garlic
1 tablespoon finely chopped fresh flat-leaf parsley
½ cup dry white wine
1 cup finely minced fresh clams with their juice
1⅔ cups puréed canned tomatoes
1 chopped fresh hot pepper or ¼ teaspoon cayenne
Freshly ground black pepper
1 pound dried linguine
4 to 6 tablespoons unsalted butter, at room temperature
Homemade sautéed or toasted bread crumbs (optional)

1. Put the olive oil, onions, carrots, celery, garlic, and parsley in a large straight-sided sauté pan. Cook the vegetables over moderate heat until soft without browning, about 10 minutes.

2. Add the wine, raise the heat, and cook at a brisk boil until most of the wine is evaporated, about 3 minutes.

pasta with seafood

3. Add the clams, tomatoes, hot pepper, and a generous grinding of black pepper. Bring to a boil, reduce the heat, and simmer gently for 15 minutes.

4. Bring a large pot of water to a boil for the pasta. When the sauce is nearly finished, generously salt the pasta water and drop in the linguine. Cook at a rapid boil, stirring frequently, until al dente. Drain the pasta and add to the sauté pan. Toss with 4 tablespoons of the butter or more to taste. The sauce should be glossy and clinging to the strands of linguine. Serve right away with the bread crumbs if you like.

◆ Linguine with Clams and Paprika ◆

Serves 6 to 8 as a first course or 4 to 6 as a main course

In Italy, especially near the sea, clams are almost ubiquitous in a sauce for pasta. There are two common versions: *al pomodoro*—red sauce with tomato, and *in bianco*—white sauce without tomato. This recipe defies classification as it contains no tomato but is red from the paprika that imparts a gorgeous crimson hue to the broth. Made from mild, sweet ground peppers, paprika has little in common with its Italian look-alike, peperoncino, which is made from fiery, blazingly spicy ground chile peppers.

⅔ cup extra virgin olive oil
⅔ cup finely chopped onions
4 tablespoons finely chopped fresh flat-leaf parsley
2 teaspoons finely minced fresh garlic
½ cup finely chopped leek
1 teaspoon fennel seeds, chopped or ground
4 teaspoons sweet Hungarian paprika
24 littleneck clams
⅔ cup dry white wine
Sea salt
1 pound dried linguine or spaghetti

1. Bring a large pot of water to a boil for the pasta.

2. Combine the olive oil, onions, parsley, garlic, leek, fennel seeds, and paprika in a large straight-sided sauté pan. Cook over moderate heat until the vegetables are soft and cooked through, about 10 minutes. Raise the heat and add the clams and wine. Cover and cook over moderate heat until all the clams open. Taste the broth and add some salt if necessary (often the clams provide enough).

3. Meanwhile, generously salt the boiling pasta water and drop in the linguine. Cook, stirring often, until al dente. Drain the pasta and add to the clam sauce. Toss together and serve right away.

Late Summer Linguine with Clams and Green Tomatoes

Serves 6 to 8 as a first course or 4 to 6 as a main course

~~~~~~

Make this in late summer when tomatoes are plentiful, or in the fall when frost threatens and the remaining green tomatoes are harvested.

4 small or 2 large green tomatoes (about 20 ounces)
½ cup extra virgin olive oil
1 heaping cup finely chopped onions
4 plump garlic cloves, peeled and finely minced
¼ to ½ teaspoon crushed red pepper flakes
24 littleneck clams, scrubbed clean under cold running water
Pinch of saffron threads
1 pound dried linguine

1. Bring 6 quarts of water to a boil in a large pot.

2. Cut the tomatoes in half horizontally, scoop out and discard the seeds, and chop up the pulp. Set aside.

3. Heat the olive oil in a 10- to 12-inch skillet with a tight-fitting lid. Add the onions and garlic and cook over high heat until the garlic becomes golden, about 2 minutes. Add the red pepper flakes, clams, tomatoes, and saffron. Cover, reduce the heat to medium-low, and cook until the clams open, about 7 minutes.

4. Meanwhile, add salt to the boiling water and drop in the linguine. Cook at a full rolling boil, stirring often, until the pasta is al dente. Drain, reserving about 1 cup of the pasta water. Toss the linguine in the skillet with the clams and sauce. Ladle in some of the pasta water, a little at a time, until the sauce is a bit soupy but still clings to the strands of linguine. Toss the pasta for 1 more minute so it can absorb the flavors of the sauce. Serve immediately.

on top of spaghetti...

◆ Shell-Shaped Pasta with Cuttlefish Sauce ◆

Serves 6 to 8 as a first course or 4 to 6 as a main course

Cuttlefish are fine-textured inkfish. Like squid, they have dense flesh that responds well to hard-and-fast cooking (deep-frying or grilling) or slow-and-easy-does-it cooking (braising or stewing). The technique here is a slow simmer that makes the cuttlefish meltingly tender. Squid, which are less supple, may need longer cooking.

This may seem like an enormous quantity of cuttlefish, but they shrink to a very manageable amount. If using squid instead, cut the bodies into rings and keep the tentacles whole.

> 2 pounds small, cleaned cuttlefish or squid
> 1 cup chopped onions
> 1 tablespoon finely chopped fresh garlic
> ¼ cup extra virgin olive oil
> 2 fresh hot peppers (about 4 inches each) or 2 to 4 dried hot peppers
> ¼ teaspoon sea salt
> 2 cups dry red wine
> 2½ cups fresh tomato pulp/purée (about 1½ pounds fresh plum tomatoes)
> 1 pound dried pipe rigate, lumache, or pasta shells

1. Pat the cuttlefish dry on paper towels. Set aside.

2. Combine the onions, garlic, olive oil, peppers, and salt in a large straight-sided sauté pan. Sauté over moderate heat until the onions are very soft and beginning to brown. Add the wine, raise the heat, and cook briskly to reduce the wine by half. Add the cuttlefish and continue to cook for 10 minutes. Add the tomato, cover, and bring to a boil. Lower the heat to maintain a gentle simmer. Cook for about 1 hour, or until the cuttlefish are very tender and the sauce has thickened.

3. Bring a large pot of water to a boil. Generously salt the water and drop in the pasta. Cook, stirring often, until al dente. Drain the pasta and transfer to the sauté pan with the cuttlefish. Toss together so that the pasta is coated and its little crevices are filled with sauce. Serve right away.

◆ Cappellini with Pan-Grilled Squid ◆

Serves 6 as a first course or 2 as a generous main course

We both love squid, so when they're on the menu at Al Forno, we set aside a few to take home for dinner. Although we are avid fans of grilling, there are some nights we are so hungry we can't wait the extra minutes for the coals to catch. Instead, we fire up our cast-iron skillet. This quick, high-heat method works extremely well, giving the squid a little crust without taking away any of their subtle taste.

Fresh jalapeño or cherry peppers give a little zing to this dish. The last-minute splash of vinegar provides balance and vivacity.

1 pound cleaned squid, cut into rings, with the tentacles halved lengthwise

2 tablespoons extra virgin olive oil

1 small fresh red jalapeño or cherry pepper, seeded and chopped

3 plump garlic cloves, peeled and finely minced

2 cups boiling water

4 anchovy fillets (see Pasta Pantry)

8 ounces dried cappellini

1 tablespoon best-quality red wine vinegar

¼ cup chopped fresh flat-leaf parsley

1. Bring a large pot of water to a boil for the pasta.

2. Thoroughly dry the squid on paper towels. Any moisture left on will prevent the squid from browning and developing a nicely caramelized exterior.

3. Heat a large cast-iron or heavy-bottomed skillet over high heat. Add the olive oil and swirl to coat the pan. Add the squid, searing just until opaque, 30 seconds to 1 minute per side. Add the jalapeño and cook over high heat until it softens and browns, about 2 minutes. Add the garlic and continue to cook, stirring for another minute or two, until the garlic turns golden. Off the heat, add the water, being careful not to burn yourself as the oil may splatter. Bring to a boil, add the anchovies, and simmer for 5 minutes, breaking up the anchovies with the back of a wooden spoon.

4. Add a generous amount of salt to the pasta water and drop in the cappellini. Cook the pasta at a full rolling boil, stirring often until al dente, 1 to 2 minutes. Drain the cappellini and toss into the skillet with the squid and broth. Add the vinegar and parsley, and toss again. Serve immediately.

◆ Gently Spiced Crab Spaghettini ◆

Serves 6 to 8 as a first course or 4 to 6 as a main course

When fresh crabs are at the fish market, we can't resist them and buy more than we can eat. Poached in an aromatic mixture of water, garlic, jalapeño, onion, and white wine, they make a succulent supper. We save the cooking broth for pasta as there is always a mound of leftover crabmeat to turn into another meal. Sometimes we take the easy way out and purchase ready-to-use lump crabmeat and bottled clam juice. (Clam juice can be salty, so taste it and dilute it to your preference to make this spaghettini.) Use a light-flavored olive oil—Ligurian would be ideal—as you want to enhance the sweet, delicate flavor of the crab without overwhelming it.

Add some spice by using ground Espelette pepper or hot paprika. For a more subtly spiced dish, choose sweet Hungarian paprika.

1 cup bottled clam juice, diluted with 1 cup water, or 2 cups leftover cooking broth
1 pound dried spaghettini
1 plump garlic clove, peeled and trimmed
¾ cup extra virgin olive oil
1½ to 2 teaspoons powdered Espelette pepper or hot or sweet Hungarian paprika
Large pinch of best-quality dried oregano
Freshly ground black pepper
Pinch of sea salt
2 cups cooked and picked-over crabmeat

1. Bring a large pot of water to a boil for the pasta.

2. Bring the diluted clam juice or broth to a simmer in a large straight-sided sauté pan.

3. Add salt to the pasta water and drop in the spaghettini. Cook at a full rolling boil, stirring often.

4. While the pasta is cooking, rub the garlic clove all over the bottom of a large, heated pasta serving bowl. Pour in the olive oil and sprinkle over the Espelette pepper and oregano. Grind black pepper over the spices. Add salt. The mix-

pasta with seafood 103

ture should be quite aromatic with overtones of garlic.

5. When the spaghettini is nearly cooked—about 2 minutes before it is al dente—drain it and toss in the simmering clam juice. Add the crabmeat, toss, and cook for 1 to 2 minutes, or until the pasta is al dente and most of the liquid has been absorbed by the spaghettini (it should be moist, not dry). Transfer to the pasta bowl, toss well, and serve immediately.

on top of spaghetti...

◆ Linguine with Mussels and Fresh Tomatoes ◆

Serves 4 as a first course or 2 to 3 as a main course

The combination of sweet, ocean-fresh mussels and juicy garden tomatoes is ambrosia. Summer-by-the-sea on a plate, this is a cinch to prepare and perfect for breezy, carefree vacation days (or nights).

A lightly flavored olive oil—like Ligurian—would be appropriate.

1½ cups peeled, seeded, and chopped plum tomatoes
6 tablespoons extra virgin olive oil
1 quart cleaned mussels
8 ounces dried linguine

1. Bring a large pot of water to a boil for the pasta.

2. Heat the tomatoes and half the olive oil in a large straight-sided sauté pan with a tight-fitting lid. Bring to a boil, toss in the mussels, cover, and cook over moderate heat, shaking the pan every so often, until the mussels open.

3. Meanwhile, generously salt the boiling water and drop in the linguine. Cook, stirring often, until al dente. Drain the pasta, reserving about ½ cup of the water, and transfer the linguine to the sauté pan. Drizzle with the rest of the olive oil and toss together with the mussels and tomatoes. If it seems dry, add some of the pasta water, a tablespoon at a time, until each strand of linguine is nicely coated, with some liquid surrounding the pasta and mussels. Serve right away in heated bowls.

◆ Linguine with Mussels, Garlic, and Fennel Seeds ◆

Serves 3 to 4 as a first course or 2 to 3 as a main course

In Italy, the seeds, bulbs, and fronds of cultivated Florentine fennel are all used in cooking. Wild fennel is also prized and harvested for its feathery tops and the flowers, which are painstakingly dried and crumbled into fennel pollen to flavor meat or fish.

Fennel is often paired with pork, as in the Tuscan sausage finocchiona, and fish, where it is an essential flavor component in Sicilian sardine sauce for pasta. It mates equally well with shellfish like mussels. Here, the fennel seeds are toasted to enhance their anise fragrance.

¼ teaspoon fennel seeds
4 tablespoons extra virgin olive oil
1 plump garlic clove, peeled and finely chopped
1 small fresh hot pepper or ⅛ to ¼ teaspoon crushed red pepper flakes (optional)
1 quart mussels
⅓ cup dry white wine
8 ounces dried linguine

1. Bring a large pot of water to a boil.

2. Toast the fennel seeds in a large straight-sided sauté pan over moderate heat, stirring constantly until you can smell their aroma. Add the olive oil, garlic, and hot pepper if you wish. Cook, stirring often, until the garlic becomes a rich golden color. Add the mussels. Cover the pan and raise the heat to moderately high, shaking the pan to evenly distribute the mussels. After 30 seconds, uncover the pan and add the wine and ⅓ cup water. Cover and cook, shaking the pan every few minutes, until all the mussels have opened.

3. Meanwhile, add a generous amount of salt to the boiling water and drop in the pasta. Cook, stirring often, until al dente. Drain the linguine and transfer to a heated serving bowl. Pour over the mussels and broth and serve right away.

◆ Linguine with Bottarga, Cherry Tomatoes, and Garlic ◆

Serves 6 to 8 as a first course or 4 to 6 as a main course

Bottarga is the pressed, salted, and dried roe of gray mullet or tuna. When you purchase it whole, or in slab form, it is packed in a lozenge shape with a protective skin that must be removed before using. Bottarga can vary in quality, so be sure to buy it from a good purveyor.

Salt the pasta water sparingly as it is used in the sauce. With the bottarga adding its own salt, it is best to have too little rather than too much. You can pass a saltshaker at the table.

1 pound dried linguine

8 ounces cherry tomatoes (if small, cut in half; if large, cut into quarters)

4 to 5 tablespoons extra virgin olive oil

1 to 2 small fresh hot peppers, finely chopped

1 garlic clove, peeled and finely minced

3 tablespoons powdered bottarga or ⅓ cup loosely packed shaved bottarga from a slab

4 tablespoons unsalted butter, softened

3 tablespoons finely chopped fresh flat-leaf parsley

1. Bring a large pot of water to a boil. Stir some salt into the water and drop in the pasta. Cook, stirring often, until al dente.

2. At the same time, heat the tomatoes, olive oil, and hot peppers in a large straight-sided sauté pan over moderately high heat. After 2 minutes, add ¼ cup of the pasta water, raise the heat, and allow the oil and water to emulsify.

3. When the linguine is al dente, drain it, reserving 1 cup of the pasta water. Transfer the pasta to the sauté pan and toss with the tomatoes. Add the garlic, bottarga, and half the butter. Toss with as much pasta water as necessary to create a creamy sauce. Add the remaining butter and parsley and toss again. Serve right away.

◆ Rigatoni with Anchovy and Fennel-Scented Tomato Purée ◆

Serves 6 to 8 as a first course or 4 to 6 as a main course

This sauce combines roasted fennel and onion in a savory blend with anchovy, garlic, tomato, and raisins. Roasting the fennel concentrates its flavor considerably. Its unmistakable aroma permeates the kitchen and transports us to Sicily's country roads lined with wild fennel.

Here is one of the rare fish-based sauces that work well with cheese. Serve it with sharp, salty Pecorino if you like.

½ cup raisins
1 fennel bulb, trimmed
2 large onions (8 ounces), peeled
3 tablespoons extra virgin olive oil
1 tablespoon ground fennel seeds
6 anchovy fillets (see Pasta Pantry), rinsed and patted dry on paper towels
2 plump garlic cloves, peeled and finely minced
1 cup tomato purée
1 pound dried rigatoni
Freshly grated Pecorino Romano (optional)

1. Heat the oven to 400 degrees.

2. Plump the raisins in warm water to cover for 5 minutes, drain, and set aside.

3. Cut the fennel bulb and onions vertically into sixths through the root ends, lay them out in a baking dish, and brush all over with 1 tablespoon of the olive oil. Cover and roast until the vegetables are soft, about 15 minutes. When the vegetables are cool enough to handle, finely chop them and set aside (this may be done in a food processor).

4. Heat the remaining olive oil in a large straight-sided sauté pan. Add the ground fennel seeds, anchovies, and garlic. Sauté over moderate heat, breaking up the anchovies with the back of a wooden spoon. Cook until the garlic is golden and the anchovies have dissolved into the oil, about 5 minutes. Add the reserved vegetables, tomato purée, and raisins. Simmer for 10 minutes.

5. Bring a large pot of water to a boil. Generously salt the water and drop in the rigatoni. Boil the pasta, stirring often, until done. Rigatoni should be a little softer than al dente. Drain the pasta and add to the sauce. Toss well and serve right away with freshly grated Pecorino Romano if desired.

Christmas Eve (or Anytime) Anchovy Aglio-Olio

Serves 6 to 8 as a first course or 4 to 6 as a main course

Every Christmas Eve, George and his family enjoyed a traditional Italian all-seafood dinner to observe the Catholic meatless fast. George's favorite course was the *primo*, or pasta—spaghetti aglio-olio, flavored with anchovies. His mom, Mary, had a light hand with seasoning and used anchovies to add depth rather than an explicit taste to her aglio-olio—an interesting salty note.

Mary used canned anchovy fillets packed in oil when she made this, but we prefer salt-cured anchovies. Although they are fractionally more trouble to prepare, their taste is pure and uncorrupted.

If you love anchovies, we encourage you to double or triple the amount listed below.

4 to 6 anchovy fillets (see Pasta Pantry)
½ cup extra virgin olive oil
2 tablespoons minced fresh garlic
Fine sea salt
1 pound dried spaghettini

1. Bring a large pot of water to a boil for the pasta.

2. Finely chop the anchovy fillets and put them in a large straight-sided skillet with the olive oil and garlic. Sauté over moderate heat, stirring often, until the garlic becomes golden and the anchovies break down and melt into the oil. Put your eyes on high alert as the garlic will be tinted beige by the anchovies, making it harder to see it turn color. As soon as the garlic is golden, immediately add 2 cups water. Be careful not to burn yourself as the oil has a tendency to spatter. Raise the heat and boil vigorously until the garlic is soft and the liquid has reduced by half. Taste the sauce and add salt if necessary.

3. Add some salt to the boiling pasta water and drop in the spaghettini. Cook, stirring often, until al dente. Drain and transfer the pasta to the skillet. Over moderately high heat, toss the spaghettini in the aglio-olio until it is nicely coated. Serve right away in heated bowls.

◆ Linguine with Anchovies, Red Bliss Potatoes, and Lemon ◆

Serves 6 to 8 as a first course or 4 to 6 as a main course

Anchovies, used in recipes from every region of Italy, are a great pantry staple. They are flavor boosters and bring out the best in less aggressive, soothing foods such as pasta or potatoes.

Anchovies, linguine, and Red Bliss potatoes make a nice trinity. Enhanced by fruity olive oil, verdant green parsley, crunchy bits of celery, and bracing lemon juice, this dish is alive with taste. Increase or decrease the number of anchovy fillets according to your preference. Be sure to chop the celery into very fine bits.

The suggested optional ingredients—crushed red pepper and/or garlic—are small additions with big impact. Serve them on the side if you like, so you can decide which version you like best.

6 small (12 ounces total) Red Bliss potatoes, peeled and cut into a small dice
20 or more anchovy fillets (see Pasta Pantry), finely chopped
1 cup extra virgin olive oil
1 cup finely minced celery
1 tablespoon finely chopped fresh flat-leaf parsley
Sea salt
Freshly ground black pepper
2 lemons
1 pound dried linguine
Crushed red pepper flakes (optional)
1 small garlic clove, peeled and finely minced (optional)

1. Bring a large pot of water to a boil for the pasta.

2. In a saucepan, cook the potatoes in boiling salted water to cover until tender when pierced with the point of a knife. Drain and transfer to a mixing bowl. Add the anchovy fillets, olive oil, celery, and parsley. Season with a little salt and ample pepper. Squeeze 1 lemon and add the juice to the bowl. Toss well and set aside to keep warm.

3. Generously salt the boiling pasta water and drop in the linguine. Cook, stirring often, until al dente. Drain (without shaking the linguine bone-dry) and transfer the pasta to the bowl with the anchovy and oil mixture. Toss to coat each strand of linguine and serve right away in warm bowls. Cut the remaining lemon into wedges to spritz each serving at the table. Add red pepper flakes and a touch of garlic if you like.

◆ Spaghettini with Anchovy and Mozzarella ◆

Serves 6 to 8 as a first course or 4 to 6 as a main course

This is Naples on a plate: The ingredients are standard-bearers of that vibrant city. Stroll past any Neapolitan restaurant or grocery store and you will see pure white orbs of fresh mozzarella bobbing in liquid. Fish markets boast fresh anchovies, while salted ones are available just about anywhere. Hot peppers and garlic, too, reflect the spicy, lusty temperament of Naples—always exciting and sometimes feeling a bit dangerous.

Fresh mozzarella is essential in this pasta dish. Use one made from buffalo milk, if possible. The cheese slumps into the hot linguine, melting into unctuous strands. There are few more sensual pleasures in a dish.

¼ cup extra virgin olive oil
2 teaspoons minced fresh garlic
Pinch or up to ½ teaspoon crushed red pepper flakes
6 anchovy fillets (see Pasta Pantry), chopped
1 pound dried spaghettini
½ teaspoon best-quality dried oregano
½ to 1 teaspoon chopped fresh thyme leaves (do not substitute dried thyme)
1 tablespoon chopped fresh flat-leaf parsley
2 (3 ounces each) balls of fresh mozzarella (see Pasta Pantry), cut into a small dice

1. Bring a large pot of water to a boil for the pasta.

2. Heat the olive oil, garlic, and as much red pepper flakes as you wish in a large sauté pan over moderately high heat. When the garlic becomes golden, lower the heat, add the anchovy fillets, and stir them into the oil. Within a minute or two, the anchovies will sizzle in the oil and begin to fall apart. Add 2 cups water, raise the heat, and bring to a rapid boil to reduce the liquid by half. Set aside over very low heat.

3. Stir a generous amount of salt into the boiling pasta water and toss in the spaghettini. Cook at a full rolling boil, stirring often, until al dente.

  on top of spaghetti...

Drain the pasta, reserving about 1 cup of the cooking water, and toss the spaghettini into the sauté pan. Over low heat, toss the pasta in the sauce to absorb the flavor for 1 minute. Add some of the pasta water, if necessary, to keep the spaghettini bathed in sauce. Off the heat, fold in the herbs and mozzarella. The hot pasta will soften and partially melt the mozzarella, causing the cheese to stretch into strings as you toss. Serve immediately.

Inspiration from Lunch in Liguria

The idea for this recipe and the one that follows was sparked by the antipasto, or appetizer, of a spectacular meal we enjoyed in San Rocco, high above Camogli and the Mediterranean Sea. Told by the concierge that the walk to the restaurant would be an easy thirty minutes, we set off for lunch. The walk was a hike and it was up 725 feet of stairs on a vertical path. By the time we reached the top, we were thirsty and famished.

At the lovely Trattoria Nonna Nina, our first course restored us. The antipasto was a plate of white anchovies bathed in fruity olive oil and sprinkled with a fine powder of dried oregano. It tasted like sea heaven. We were both surprised by the compatibility of the fish with such a pungent herb and thought it would make a great flavor combination for a pasta sauce (or two). Washed down with a light, barely sparkling local wine, we were happy indeed. The rest of our lunch was equally dynamic, and we were positively giddy (no doubt from the bubbly wine) on the way down the mountain.

You don't have to build up an appetite to enjoy these pastas, but everything does seem to taste better when you have worked for it. The following two recipes share the same quantities of anchovy and oregano. George's is gutsy and spirited; its robust taste is a credit to the fine olive oil and an ample amount of garlic. The second pasta sauce, Jo's, is soft and smooth, with the richness of butter rounding out the flavors and smoothing the edges. Try both!

on top of spaghetti...

George's Fedelini with Anchovy, Oregano, Garlic, and Olive Oil

Serves 6 to 8 as a first course or 4 to 6 as a main course

6 plump garlic cloves, peeled and finely
   chopped
¾ cup extra virgin olive oil
24 anchovy fillets (see Pasta Pantry),
   chopped
1 tablespoon best-quality dried oregano
1½ cups dry white wine
1 pound dried fedelini

1. Bring a large pot of water to a boil for the pasta.

2. Cook the garlic in olive oil in a large straight-sided sauté pan over moderate heat. As soon as the garlic is a rich golden color, lower the heat and add the anchovies, swirling them in the oil. Rub the oregano between your fingers to release the aroma and add to the sauté pan. Stir together, breaking up the anchovies with the back of a wooden spoon. After a minute or two add the wine and 1½ cups water, being careful not to spatter yourself with the hot oil. Bring to a boil and reduce by half. Keep warm over low heat while you cook the pasta.

3. Salt the pasta water and drop in the fedelini. Cook, stirring often, until the pasta is quite firm and a bit undercooked (about 2 minutes before al dente). Drain the pasta, reserving about 1 cup of the water. Transfer the fedelini to the sauté pan. If the sauce seems too soupy, boil over high heat to reduce. If it seems too thick, add some of the pasta water, a tablespoon at a time, until the sauce generously coats each strand of fedelini. Toss with the sauce until the pasta is al dente and has absorbed some of the flavors. Serve right away in heated bowls.

◆ Jo's Linguine with Anchovy, Oregano, and Butter ◆

Serves 6 to 8 as a first course or 4 to 6 as a main course

1½ cups dry white wine
24 anchovy fillets (see Pasta Pantry),
   chopped
¼ heaping cup chopped fresh flat-leaf
   parsley
1 tablespoon best-quality dried oregano
1 pound dried linguine or spaghettini
12 tablespoons (1½ sticks) unsalted butter,
   cut into tablespoon-sized chunks

1. Bring a large pot of water to a boil for the pasta.

2. Combine the wine, 1½ cups water, anchovy fillets, and parsley in a large straight-sided sauté pan. Rub the oregano between your fingers to release its aroma and add to the pan. Bring to a boil and cook over moderately high heat to reduce by half. Keep warm over low heat while you cook the pasta.

3. Salt the pasta water and drop in the linguine. Cook, stirring often, until the linguine is quite stiff, about 2 minutes before it is al dente. Just before draining the pasta, swirl the butter into the anchovy sauce in the sauté pan. Drain the linguine, reserving about 1 cup of the pasta water. Transfer the linguine to the sauté pan and cook, tossing all the while, for about 2 minutes, or until the pasta is al dente. If the sauce seems too thick, add enough of the pasta water to coat each strand of linguine generously. Serve right away in heated bowls.

on top of spaghetti...

Pasta with Poultry, Meat, and Rabbit

◆ Pappardelle with Duck Ragù ◆

Serves 6 to 8 as a first course or 4 to 6 as a main course

~~~~~~

Duck is widely available and makes a ragù special enough for an occasion. To mimic the leaner ducks of Italy (more like our wild ducks), we roast legs only at high heat and then remove the duck fat before adding the cooked and boned meat to the sauce. The rendered fat can be discarded (a terrible shame) or saved (an excellent idea) to make delicious fried potatoes.

This recipe makes about 6 cups of sauce—more than you need for a pound of pasta. Left-over sauce can be frozen for an impromptu get-together, or refrigerated for a few days. The leftover ragù also makes a great topping for crostini.

2 pounds duck legs
½ to 1 teaspoon sea salt
Freshly ground black pepper
2 cups dry red wine
½ cup extra virgin olive oil
3 cups finely chopped onions
½ cup finely chopped carrots
1 cup finely chopped celery
Two 10-inch sprigs rosemary, spiky leaves
   only, finely chopped
3 juniper berries
3 cups homemade duck or chicken stock,
   heated to a boil
1 cup chopped canned tomatoes
1 pound dried pappardelle or rigatoni, or
   1 batch George's Fresh Pasta (page 212),
   cut into pappardelle or hankies
Freshly grated Parmigiano-Reggiano

1. Heat the oven to 400 degrees.

2. Lay out the duck legs in one layer in a baking pan—a 9 × 12-inch baking sheet is perfect. Sprinkle with ½ teaspoon salt and some pepper. Roast for 40 minutes, or until completely cooked through. Set the duck legs aside on a cutting board and discard or reserve the duck fat for another use. Add ½ cup of the wine to the baking sheet and set over moderately low heat. Deglaze

the pan, scraping up any bits left behind by the duck. Set aside.

3. Meanwhile, heat the olive oil, onions, carrots, celery, rosemary, and juniper berries in a heavy pot or enamel-coated cast-iron Dutch oven. Season with the remaining salt and some pepper. Sauté over moderate heat until the vegetables are very soft, about 20 minutes. Raise the heat, add the remaining wine and the deglazing wine with the duck bits from the baking sheet. Bring to a rapid boil. Allow the wine to boil for about 5 minutes until almost completely evaporated. Add the hot stock and tomatoes, bring to a boil, and reduce the heat to maintain a gentle simmer.

4. When cool enough to handle, remove and discard the skin from the duck legs. Remove and reserve the bones and finely chop the meat. Transfer the bones (they will add more depth to the sauce) and chopped duck to the sauce simmering on the stove. Cook an additional 30 minutes, remove the bones, and set the sauce on the lowest possible heat. Taste for salt and add more if necessary.

5. Bring a large pot of water to a boil for the pasta. Generously salt the water and drop in the pappardelle. Cook, stirring often, until al dente. Drain the pasta and transfer to a heated serving platter or very shallow bowl. Toss with enough sauce to nicely coat the noodles without drowning them. Serve right away with Parmigiano Reggiano and extra sauce passed at the table.

◆ Fettuccine with Venetian Chicken Sauce ◆

Serves 6 to 8 as a first course or 4 to 6 as a main course

In Venice, water is everywhere. With the canals and the lagoon spilling into the Adriatic, one associates Venetian cooking with fish and seafood. It's true you can eat delectable local sea creatures in a select group of impeccable restaurants. We have feasted on razor clams, scallops, feisty mantis shrimp, inky cuttlefish, and octopus—the list goes on. But there is more to this *cucina*. You could be regaled by grilled radicchio from nearby Treviso; steamed white asparagus from Bassano; wild mushrooms prepared in every imaginable guise; criminally rich Venetian calves' liver; risotto with vegetables, meats, or white truffles; silky, homemade pastas; and some very impressive desserts. One dish we have found inspirational is a delicate vegetable sauce made with tiny pieces of diced chicken tossed with ribbon noodles. We took this food souvenir of Venezia home with us and created a sauce and pasta that evoke happy memories of that magic city. Our elegant, suave sauce is made with carrots. Its striking yellow-orange color is food for the eyes.

2 cups homemade chicken stock (see Pasta Pantry)
8 ounces skinned and boned chicken breasts
6 tablespoons unsalted butter
1 small garlic clove, peeled and finely chopped
1 cup finely chopped carrots
¼ teaspoon sea salt
1 cup tomato juice, preferably organic
1 pound dried fettuccine or fresh fettuccine (see page 214)
Freshly grated Parmigiano-Reggiano

1. Bring the chicken stock to a boil in a saucepan.

2. Cut the chicken breasts into lengthwise strips about the width of a finger. Drop the strips into the boiling stock. Cover and bring to a boil. Lower the heat and simmer for 4 minutes. Remove the cover and set aside, allowing the chicken to cool in the liquid. When cool, transfer the chicken to a cutting board and reheat the stock.

3. Meanwhile, melt 1 tablespoon of the butter in another large saucepan. Stir in the garlic and cook over low heat until the garlic becomes golden. Add 1 cup water to prevent the garlic from browning. Stir to combine. Add the carrots and salt and cook over moderate heat, stirring often,

on top of spaghetti...

until the mixture is nearly dry with just a bit of water left. Be vigilant and stir constantly toward the end of this step to be sure the carrots do not brown at all. Add the hot stock and tomato juice. Cover and bring to a boil. Lower the heat, set the cover ajar, and simmer gently for 35 minutes, or until the carrots are very soft. Purée with an immersion blender until you have a smooth purée. Set aside.

4. Cut the chicken strips lengthwise into ⅛-inch-thick slices, then cut across to make ⅛-inch dice. Add the chicken to the sauce and reheat gently.

5. Bring a large pot of water to a boil. Generously salt the water and drop in the fettuccine. Cook, stirring often, until al dente. Drain the pasta and transfer to a heated platter or shallow gratin dish. Toss with the remaining butter and fold in enough sauce to coat the noodles generously. Sprinkle with Parmigiano-Reggiano and serve at once. Pass more cheese at the table.

♦ Spaghettini with Sautéed Chicken Livers ♦

Serves 4 as a first course or 2 to 3 as a main course

Chicken livers are much appreciated all over Italy—and at Al Forno, too. We spread them on crostini the way the Tuscans like them; fold them into risotto as the Venetians do; or enjoy them in this much-loved pasta unique to our restaurant.

Buy very fresh, plump, rosy-colored livers and be diligent in cleaning away any green spots as they cause the livers to be bitter.

4 ounces chicken livers
Sea salt
3 tablespoons unsalted butter
1 tablespoon finely chopped shallots
½ cup dry white wine
1 cup homemade chicken stock (see Pasta Pantry)
8 ounces dried spaghettini
¼ cup heavy cream
Freshly ground black pepper
Pinch of cayenne
1 tablespoon finely chopped fresh flat-leaf parsley
1 tablespoon finely chopped fresh sage (do not substitute dried sage)
Freshly grated Parmigiano-Reggiano

1. Bring a large pot of water to a boil for the pasta.

2. Dry the livers completely on paper towels. Trim away and discard any green spots or connective tissue. Cut each lobe in half and sprinkle with salt.

3. Heat the butter over moderately high heat in a large straight-sided sauté pan. When the foam subsides and the butter begins to brown, add the livers and sauté quickly to brown all over. Scoop out the livers with a slotted spoon and transfer them to a platter. Keep warm.

4. Return the sauté pan to a moderate flame and toss in the shallots. Cook until golden. Pour in the wine to prevent the shallots from browning and cook, scraping up any bits of liver left behind. Let the wine bubble away until the mixture becomes syrupy. Add the chicken stock and bring to a boil. Reduce the heat and simmer for 3 minutes. Set aside off the heat.

5. Generously salt the pasta water and drop in the spaghettini. Cook, stirring often, until al dente. While the pasta is cooking, finish the sauce.

6. Return the sauté pan to moderate heat. Add the cream, pepper, and cayenne. Bring to a boil but do not let it reduce. Add the chicken livers.

  on top of spaghetti...

7. Remove the spaghettini from the boiling water about 2 minutes before it is al dente. Transfer to the sauté pan and toss with the sauce and livers. Cook for 2 minutes, or until the pasta is al dente and it has absorbed some of the sauce. Fold in the parsley and sage and toss again. Sprinkle with an ample amount of Parmigiano-Reggiano, toss, and serve right away.

◆ Rigatoni with Lamb Sauce ◆

Serves 6 to 8 as a first course or 4 to 6 as a main course

Nothing flatters the taste of lamb or lightens its richness like mint. It adds a sweet, refreshing flavor to this sauce.

We often prepare this recipe with leftover cooked lamb. If you have leftovers from a roast, remove and discard the bones. Chop the meat in a food processor until the bits are quite small but well before it is reduced to a purée. If your roast was well seasoned with salt, you may need less than the amount specified here.

1½ cups finely diced onions
5 plump garlic cloves, smashed, peeled, and finely minced
¼ cup extra virgin olive oil, plus a few tablespoons for the cherry tomatoes
1 jalapeño or other hot pepper
1 heaping cup chopped carrots
½ cup chopped celery
One 1-inch piece peeled fresh ginger
1 teaspoon sea salt
1 to 1½ pounds raw or cooked ground lamb
¼ cup chopped fresh flat-leaf parsley
2 tablespoons dried mint, crushed with your fingers
2 cups dry white wine
½ cup fresh cherry tomatoes, cut in half
2 to 3 tablespoons fresh mint leaves, cut into a chiffonade
1 pound dried rigatoni
Freshly grated Pecorino Romano

1. Put the onions and garlic in a large heavy-bottomed saucepan with ¼ cup olive oil. Sauté over low heat for 10 minutes.

2. While the onions and garlic are sautéing, chop the hot pepper, carrots, celery, and ginger in a food processor until they are finely minced but not reduced to a mush. Transfer to the saucepan and stir into the onions and garlic. Add ½ teaspoon salt. Continue to sauté, stirring often, un-

  on top of spaghetti...

til all the vegetables are soft and cooked through. This could take another 10 to 15 minutes.

3. Add the lamb, raise the heat to moderately high, and stir until the meat is no longer pink. If you are using cooked ground lamb, stir it into the vegetable mixture until it is well incorporated and moistened by the olive oil and vegetable juices. Add the parsley, dried mint, and wine. Bring to a boil. Reduce the heat and simmer vigorously until most of the wine has evaporated. Taste and add more salt if necessary.

4. Bring a large pot of water to a boil.

5. Toss the cherry tomatoes with the fresh mint and enough olive oil to coat them. Add salt to taste and set aside.

6. Add a generous amount of salt to the boiling water. Drop in the rigatoni and cook, stirring often, until al dente (the pasta tubes should collapse a bit). Drain and transfer the pasta to a large, heated serving bowl. Toss with enough of the sauce to coat the pasta generously. Top with the tomatoes and serve right away with extra sauce passed at the table with the Pecorino Romano.

Sunday Gravy with Sausages and Meatballs

Serves 6 to 8 as a first course or 4 to 6 as a main course

The way to George's heart is definitely through his stomach. The E-Z Pass is with spaghetti and meatballs. We make several different sauces for our meatballs, but none is better than the recipe we learned from George's mom, Mary Germon. Like most Italian Americans, she called her sauce "gravy," and it was part of every holiday feast and any Sunday dinner. She sauced spaghetti or homemade ricotta ravioli with this gravy. It is also the first step to making Mary's Lasagne (page 253), another of her specialties.

Mom had her own business and worked more than forty hours a week. She was one of the original multitaskers, often doing the week's laundry and ironing at the same time as preparing a meal for the family. She had this gravy put together and bubbling on the stove in no time flat—something George always reminds Johanne when she frets and fusses over it.

This recipe makes a large amount of sauce, but it takes no longer than a small batch and it freezes well. Save what you don't use for Mary's Lasagne or Ricotta Ravioli (page 228), or keep it as insurance in the freezer for an impromptu meal.

¼ cup extra virgin olive oil
3 center-cut pork chops (total weight, 1 to 1¼ pounds)
1¼ pounds Italian sweet sausage, halved horizontally
1 cup chopped onions
2 plump garlic cloves, peeled and finely minced
¼ teaspoon fennel seeds
½ teaspoon fine sea salt
3½ cups puréed canned tomatoes
One 6-ounce can (¾ cup) tomato paste
Cheese rinds from Parmigiano-Reggiano or end bits of Pecorino Romano (optional)
Mary's Meatballs (recipe follows)
1 pound dried spaghetti or rigatoni
Freshly grated Pecorino Romano

1. Heat the olive oil in a heavy-bottomed stockpot. Add the pork chops and sausages and brown on all sides. Transfer the pork chops to a plate to make room for the onions. Toss the onions into the pot with the garlic, fennel seeds, and salt. Sauté over moderate heat, stirring frequently and scraping up any bits left behind by the pork and sausages, until the onions are soft and golden.

2. Put the pork chops back in the pot with any juices on the plate. Add the tomatoes, 4½ cups water, and tomato paste. Drop in a few cheese rinds or ends if you have any. They are completely optional but give a nice flavor to the sauce. Cover the pot, bring to a boil, lower the heat, and simmer for 30 minutes. Gently drop in the meatballs, 1 at a time, shaking the pot a bit to encourage them to nestle in with the pork and sausage and to make room for the addition of more meatballs. After all the meatballs have been added, continue to simmer, covered, for an hour longer, or until the pork chops are very tender.

3. To finish the gravy, transfer the pork chops to a cutting board. Remove and discard the bones, chop up the meat, and return it to the sauce. Keep warm over low heat while you cook the pasta.

4. Bring a large pot of water to a boil. Generously salt the water and drop in the spaghetti. Cook, stirring often, until al dente.

5. To eat as you would at Mary's table, follow her method of saucing either cooked and drained spaghetti or ravioli. Start with a large, heated deep platter or pasta bowl. Cover the bottom with a ladleful of gravy and a good sprinkling of Pecorino Romano. Top with half the pasta. Add more gravy and cheese, the remaining pasta, and another layer of gravy and cheese. Serve right away with more grated cheese. Pass the meatballs, sausage, pork, and additional gravy in a bowl at the table.

Mary's Meatballs

12 ounces ground beef

4 slices white sandwich bread, crusts removed and discarded, cut into tiny cubes

¾ cup milk

¾ to 1 cup freshly grated Pecorino Romano

3 fresh basil leaves, torn into small pieces (optional)

1 tablespoon chopped fresh flat-leaf parsley

1 egg, lightly beaten

½ teaspoon fine sea salt

In a large mixing bowl, combine the beef, bread, and milk. Add the cheese, basil, parsley, egg, and salt. Mix gently but thoroughly. Form into small meatballs, no more than 1½ inches in diameter.

Makes 26 to 28 meatballs

Macaroni with Hidden Asset Meat Sauce

Serves 12 to 16 as a first course or 8 to 12 as a main course

~~~~~~

Italian women—and some men, too—are legendary for seeing the hidden assets in leftovers. They are kitchen wizards who can transform the surplus of yesterday into an exquisite sauce, crostini topping, antipasto, risotto, or filling for pasta. Nothing edible is ever thrown away: Something appetizing can always be made from a leftover roast, a piece of chicken, or some vegetables.

After a few days of entertaining guests at home, our refrigerator is filled with odds and ends of braises and roasts—mementos of delicious meals we have shared—presenting an opportunity to be as creative as our Italian friends.

This recipe makes a large quantity, but it can be halved or quartered according to the cache of goodies you have. If you have a small amount of meat, chop it by hand. We use a food processor for larger quantities by pulsing on and off until the meat is in little pieces. This should be done in small batches so the morsels are not reduced to a paste. Food processors do their work so quickly it is easy to blink an eye and end up with mush.

We use one of several treasured terra-cotta casseroles (from George's previous life as a production potter) for ragù making. Kept on moderate heat with a flame tamer, the ceramic pots are unparalleled for even heat distribution and slow cooking. An enamel-coated cast-iron casserole, Dutch oven, or a good, sturdy heavy-bottomed pot will do a fine job, too.

Although spaghetti (thick or thin) and macaroni (rigatoni or penne) work equally well with this sauce, we suggest the sturdier macaroni if you are cooking more than a pound of pasta. It is easier to manage and is more forgiving. Large quantities of spaghetti can become too soft in the time it takes to sauce and serve them to a crowd.

~~~~~~

on top of spaghetti...

2 tablespoons extra virgin olive oil
⅔ cup chopped onions
¼ cup chopped celery
½ teaspoon sea salt
3 cups chopped cooked meat
¾ cup dry red wine
¾ cup braising liquid from the meat or
   homemade chicken stock (see Pasta
   Pantry)
1 cup tomato juice, preferably organic
4 cups chopped canned tomatoes and their
   juice
2 pounds dried rigatoni, penne, or fusilli
8 tablespoons (1 stick) unsalted butter, cut
   into tablespoon-sized chunks
Freshly grated nutmeg
Freshly grated Parmigiano-Reggiano

1. Put the olive oil, onions, celery, and salt in a large pot. Cook over low to moderate heat until the vegetables are translucent and soft without browning, about 20 minutes.

2. Add the meat and continue to cook, stirring often, until steaming hot, 5 to 10 minutes.

3. Add the wine, bring to a boil, lower the heat, and simmer for 40 to 50 minutes, stirring every so often, until most of the alcohol evaporates and the taste of the wine mellows.

4. Add the braising liquid or chicken stock and tomato juice, bring to a boil, lower the heat, and simmer for 15 minutes.

5. Add the chopped tomatoes and juice, bring to a boil, and simmer for 5 minutes.

6. To serve, bring a large pot of water to a boil. Generously salt the water and drop in the pasta. Cook, stirring often, until al dente. Drain the pasta and transfer to a heated serving bowl or individual heated bowls. Ladle on some of the sauce, dot with butter, grate some nutmeg on top, and serve right away with Parmigiano-Reggiano and more sauce passed at the table.

◆ Penne with Sunday Pork Ragù ◆

Serves 6 to 8 as a first course or 4 to 6 as a main course

Sunday is our favorite day of the week. The restaurant is closed, the pressure is off (for twenty-four hours anyway), and we can have a leisurely day to ourselves. We're usually up early and thinking about food. Off we go to the farmers' markets—or supermarkets—looking for something to make for lunch. We rarely go with a preconceived idea, but often end up with the makings of a ragù for pasta—just the right thing for a Sunday treat.

Slow cooking a ragù is perfect for a laid-back day. After the prep is done, and the pork browned, the rest of the cooking requires only intermittent attention.

This recipe calls for a small amount of spareribs—more for flavoring the sauce than being a substantial part of the meal. Don't be afraid to pick up the ribs and eat them with your fingers. It's a shame to miss even a morsel of the succulent meat.

½ cup extra virgin olive oil
¾ pound pork spareribs
½ cup finely chopped onions
½ cup finely chopped carrots
½ cup finely chopped celery
½ cup finely chopped fennel bulb
1 tablespoon fennel seeds
½ teaspoon sea salt
Freshly ground black pepper
½ cup dry white or red wine
1¾ cups chopped canned tomatoes
1 cup tomato juice, preferably organic
1 pound dried penne or spaghetti
Freshly grated Parmigiano-Reggiano

1. Heat 2 tablespoons of the oil in a large terracotta or heavy-bottomed pot with a lid. Add the pork and brown on all sides. Transfer the pork to a plate and discard the fat. Toss the onions, carrots, celery, fennel bulb and seeds, salt, pepper, and remaining olive oil into the pot. Cook, covered, over low heat, stirring occasionally, until the vegetables are very soft without browning, about 30 minutes.

2. Add the wine and cook, uncovered, until it is almost completely reduced. Return the pork to the pot and add the chopped tomatoes and tomato juice. Bring to a boil, cover, and cook

for 45 minutes to an hour, or until the pork is falling-apart tender. Keep warm over low heat while you cook the pasta.

3. Bring a large pot of water to a boil. Generously salt the water and drop in the penne. Cook, stirring often, until al dente. Drain the pasta and transfer to a heated serving bowl. Add enough of the sauce to coat each morsel generously. Arrange the spareribs around the penne. Serve right away with extra sauce and Parmigiano-Reggiano passed at the table.

Pork Ragù with Horseradish

At George's house, spaghetti with pork ragù was also a popular choice for Sunday dinner. His mom, Mary Germon, made the ragù just the way her mom did before her. At the table, Mary added an unusual condiment—traditional in her mother's house—that never failed to delight the children: freshly grated horseradish. George and his sisters competed to see who could eat the most. The dining room was filled with the strong, pungent aroma of horseradish flecks flying off the grater. It was hard to tell if the tears streaming down everyone's faces were caused by laughing so hard, or from the nose-clearing, eye-watering volatile oils of the root. George's dad, Demetri, grew the horseradish in his backyard garden but would never touch the stuff himself. A Greek with a refined palate and appreciation for subtlety in cooking, he just shook his head and called the rest of the family crazy. Meanwhile, Mary and the kids happily enjoyed the wow taste and creamy appearance the horseradish gave the pasta.

Horseradish is sneaky. The whole, unblemished roots have no scent until they are bruised, cut, or grated. The roots are sold with some soil clinging to them—just scrub and peel away the outside skin.

For Mary's Sunday ragù, prepare the preceding recipe. Omit the Parmigiano-Reggiano and substitute Pecorino Romano. At the table, provide a good hunk of cleaned and peeled horseradish with a grater to pass along with the cheese. Serve the pasta in individual heated bowls. Add as much cheese and horseradish as you like and toss with the pasta. Take a deep breath and eat.

George's Rigatoni with Sausage and Ricotta

Serves 6 to 8 as a first course or 4 to 6 as a main course

We met Sandro Fabris, the former food and beverage manager of the Hotel Cipriani in Venice, when we taught cooking classes there. Like us, Sandro likes nothing better than to discuss food after hours over a soothing glass of wine. He regaled us nightly with stories of his mother's cooking—descriptions that made our mouths water even though we were sated by the dinner we had just finished.

Sandro shared with us his mother's trick for her sausage-based sauces. She removes the meat from its casing and breaks it up in a bowl with cold water, then stores it, covered, in the refrigerator overnight. The cold water helps break up and separate the meat. It cooks in the soaking liquid without clumping up. We have adopted Signora Fabris' method for this pasta and sausage recipe and for Jo's Spaghetti with Sausage and Wine (page 134).

3 hot or sweet Italian pork sausages (about 12 ounces)
½ teaspoon sea salt
1 pound dried rigatoni or penne
1 cup fresh ricotta
Freshly ground black pepper
Freshly grated Pecorino Romano

1. Remove the casings from the sausage and break up the meat into small bits in a bowl. Add 6 cups cold water and stir well to combine. Cover and refrigerate for at least 2 hours or up to 24 hours.

2. Bring a large pot of water to a boil for the pasta.

3. Transfer the sausage and the water in which it has been soaking to a large straight-sided sauté pan. Sprinkle with salt. Bring to a boil and cook, stirring often, until half the water has evaporated and the sausage is completely cooked. The bits of meat should be well bathed in liquid. Be careful not to reduce it too much. Taste and add salt if necessary. Set aside over very low heat to keep warm.

4. Generously salt the pasta water and drop in the rigatoni. Boil the pasta, stirring frequently, until it is al dente. Drain and toss into the sauté

  on top of spaghetti...

pan with the sausage mixture. Cook, stirring frequently, over low heat for 2 minutes to allow the pasta to absorb some of the flavor from the sausage. Off the heat, fold in ½ cup of the ricotta and a good sprinkling of pepper (we like a generous amount). Spoon the pasta into warmed individual bowls or a heated serving bowl. Dot with the remaining ricotta and serve right away with Pecorino Romano. Pass the peppermill at the table for a little more spice.

◆ Jo's Spaghetti with Sausage and Wine ◆

Serves 6 to 8 as a first course or 4 to 6 as a main course

Most Italian sweet sausage is flavored with fennel. If you cannot find it, buy unflavored pork sausage or sausage meat and season it with whole or ground fennel seeds—½ teaspoon will perk up 8 ounces of sausage meat.

The wine in this pasta sauce adds a sharp note that cuts through the richness of the sausage.

2 sweet fennel-flavored Italian sausages (8 ounces), casings removed
2 cups dry white wine
½ cup firmly packed fresh flat-leaf parsley, leaves only
2 teaspoons fennel seeds (optional)
2 large garlic cloves, peeled and trimmed
½ teaspoon sea salt
½ cup extra virgin olive oil
Freshly ground black pepper
1 pound dried spaghetti
4 tablespoons freshly grated Pecorino Romano, plus more to pass at the table

1. Put the sausages, wine, and 2 cups cold water in a mixing bowl. Break up the sausage with your fingers or two forks. Cover and refrigerate for at least 30 minutes or up to several hours.

2. Bring a large pot of water to a boil for the pasta.

3. Finely chop the parsley, fennel seeds (if you wish), garlic, and salt together on a cutting board. Transfer to a large straight-sided sauté pan. Add the olive oil and cook over moderately high heat until the garlic is golden. Add the soaked sausage meat with the wine and water. Bring to a boil and reduce the liquid by half. Grind in as much black pepper as you like. Set aside over very low heat.

4. Generously salt the pasta water and drop in the spaghetti. Cook, stirring often, until al dente. Drain the pasta, reserving about 1 cup of the pasta water.

5. Transfer the spaghetti to the sauté pan and toss. If it seems dry, add some of the reserved pasta water, a tablespoon at a time, until the spaghetti is well coated and moist. Add the Pecorino Romano; toss again. Serve right away in heated bowls. Pass extra cheese at the table.

on top of spaghetti…

◆ Pasta Shells with Spicy Sausage Red Sauce ◆

Serves 6 to 8 as a first course or 4 to 6 as a main course

This versatile sauce works with many different cuts of string pasta as well as macaroni shapes. It is the type of effortless recipe that George categorizes as "boy food," since he thinks the direct approach appeals to guys who hate to fuss in the kitchen but who like to eat well. In reality, this sauce will beguile anyone—from dainty to macho.

This sausage sauce is also ideal for George's Toss-and-Tumble "Cheater's" Lasagne (page 255)—another "boy" recipe.

8 ounces sausage meat or 2 hot Italian sausages (8 ounces), casings removed
1 cup finely chopped onions
1 plump garlic clove, peeled and finely minced
½ teaspoon fennel seeds
Pinch of cayenne (optional)
1 teaspoon sea salt
¼ cup extra virgin olive oil
4 cups tomato juice, preferably organic
1 pound dried pasta shells, rigatoni, or spaghetti
1 cup freshly grated Parmigiano-Reggiano, plus more to pass at the table

1. Combine the sausage meat, onions, garlic, and fennel seeds in a bowl with 1½ cups cold water. Break up the meat with your fingers or two forks, combining it with the other ingredients. Cover and refrigerate for at least 30 minutes or up to several hours.

2. Transfer the sausage mixture to a large, heavy saucepan with a lid—an enamel-coated cast-iron pot is ideal. Stir in the cayenne (if you would like it more spicy) and salt, and pour over the olive oil. Bring to a boil and cook, stirring often, over moderate heat until all the water has cooked away and only the oil remains to moisten the ingredients.

3. Add the tomato juice, cover, and bring to a boil. Reduce the heat and gently simmer for 30 minutes with the lid slightly ajar.

4. Bring a large pot of water to a boil. Add a generous amount of salt and drop in the pasta. Cook, stirring often, until al dente. Drain the pasta and transfer to a heated serving bowl. Ladle on enough sauce to generously coat the pasta with a little puddle on the bottom. Sprinkle over the Parmigiano-Reggiano and toss. The cheese will thicken the sauce. If it seems dry, add more sauce. Serve right away with extra sauce and cheese passed at the table.

◆ Midnight Meat Sauce for Spaghetti ◆

Serves 3 to 4 as a first course or 2 to 3 as a main course

When you crave Bolognese sauce but are short on time, try this sauce. It has the intensity of a long, slow-cooked ragù, but is ready in minutes. It's perfect for a late-night romantic dinner for two followed by a crunchy salad of mixed greens. Or you can double the recipe to share with friends at any time of the day.

The nutmeg creates a lovely liaison between the beef and Parmigiano-Reggiano. Be sure to grate fresh whole nutmeg; do not use the preground stuff.

4 ounces ground beef

1 cup milk

2 tablespoons extra virgin olive oil

1 plump garlic clove, peeled and finely minced

1 anchovy fillet (see Pasta Pantry), coarsely chopped

2 tablespoons tomato paste

½ teaspoon fine sea salt

8 ounces dried spaghetti

Scant ⅛ teaspoon freshly grated nutmeg

¼ to ½ cup freshly grated Parmigiano-Reggiano

1 tablespoon unsalted butter

1. Bring a large pot of water to a boil.

2. Put the beef in a mixing bowl and pour over the milk. With your fingers or two forks, break up the beef into tiny bits and completely incorporate it into the milk. Soaking the meat in milk—even for a short time—will allow the lactic acid in the milk to tenderize the meat and give the sauce a more velvety texture.

3. Heat the olive oil in a 10- to 12-inch sauté pan over moderately high heat. Add the garlic and cook, swirling the pan often, until the garlic becomes golden. Lower the heat and add the anchovy and tomato paste. Cook, stirring frequently, over moderate heat for 2 to 3 minutes until the tomato paste darkens a shade and the mixture becomes fragrant. Off the heat, slowly add the beef-milk mixture, being careful not to burn yourself as the oil may splatter. Stir in the salt.

4. Return the sauté pan to high heat, bring the mixture to a rapid boil, lower the heat, and simmer until the meat is thoroughly cooked, about 5 minutes. At this point, you will still have liquid in the pan, but the beef will darken and almost dissolve into the sauce. Taste for seasoning, adding more salt if necessary, and set aside over very low heat while you cook the pasta.

  on top of spaghetti...

5. Add a generous amount of salt to the boiling water and drop in the spaghetti. Cook at a full rolling boil, stirring frequently, until the pasta is al dente. Drain the spaghetti, reserving about ½ cup of the pasta cooking water, and toss the pasta into the sauté pan with the sauce. At this point, the sauce should have the consistency of heavy cream. If the sauce has reduced too much, add some of the pasta water, a tablespoon at a time. Continue to toss the spaghetti in the sauce for 1 minute to absorb flavor. Add the nutmeg and toss again to thoroughly incorporate the spice.

6. Divide the pasta into heated serving bowls, sprinkle over the Parmigiano-Reggiano, and dot with butter. Serve immediately.

◆ Rigatoni in Bianco ◆

Serves 6 to 8 as a first course or 4 to 6 as a main course

In bianco, or "in white," is a phrase used in Italian cooking to describe a pasta sauce made without tomatoes. No matter if there is green parsley or red hot peppers to tint the dish, it is still called white. The absence of color in no way means absence of taste. In fact, recipes for pasta in bianco are prized for their clear flavors, lightness, and delicacy.

The white cloud of fluffy ricotta on top reinforces the theme.

1 cup finely chopped onions
2 plump garlic cloves, peeled and finely minced
¾ cup finely chopped fennel bulb
2 to 3 tablespoons finely chopped fresh flat-leaf parsley
½ teaspoon sea salt
½ cup extra virgin olive oil
4 cups finely minced white mushrooms
1 pound ground beef
1½ cups chicken or beef stock, preferably homemade, or water
1 pound dried rigatoni or spaghetti
3 tablespoons loosely packed fresh mint leaves
½ cup fresh ricotta

1. Heat the onions, garlic, fennel, half the parsley, salt, and olive oil in a large straight-sided sauté pan over moderately low heat. Cook, stirring often, for about 20 minutes, or until the vegetables are very soft and beginning to brown.

2. Raise the heat until the vegetables are sizzling and add the mushrooms. Cook for 3 minutes over moderately high heat. Add the beef and cook, stirring often, until the beef loses any pink color and is completely cooked. Add the stock or water, cover, bring to a boil, lower the heat, and simmer for 10 minutes. Taste and add more salt if necessary. Set aside over low heat while you cook the pasta.

3. Bring a large pot of water to a boil. Generously salt the water and drop in the rigatoni. Cook, stirring often, until al dente. Drain the pasta and transfer to the sauté pan with the sauce. If the sauce seems too soupy, reduce it by raising the heat and cooking briskly for 1 to 2 minutes. The pasta should be generously bathed in sauce.

4. Finely chop the mint and add to the pasta with the remaining parsley. Toss and serve right away. Pass a bowl of ricotta at the table to dollop on each portion.

  on top of spaghetti...

◆ Garganelli with Veal Ragù ◆

Serves 6 to 8 as a first course or 4 to 6 as a main course

This versatile sauce works well with many pasta shapes, both dried and homemade. Try it with garganelli, penne, or rigatoni, or use it in the recipe for Jo's Fast "Cheater's" Lasagne (page 257).

If you have leftover veal from a roast, use it in place of the stewing veal. Cut the veal roast into tiny cubes and fold them into the vegetables in step 2. Toss for a few minutes, add the wine, and proceed with the rest of the recipe.

¼ cup extra virgin olive oil
5 tablespoons unsalted butter
1 cup finely chopped onions
½ cup finely chopped carrots
½ cup finely chopped celery
½ teaspoon ground fennel seeds
½ to 1 teaspoon sea salt
1 pound stewing veal or leftover cooked veal roast, cut into ¼- to ⅜-inch cubes
½ cup dry white wine
½ cup milk
1 cup chopped canned tomatoes in heavy purée
1 cup homemade chicken stock (see Pasta Pantry)
1 pound dried garganelli, penne, or rigatoni (Rustichella d'Abruzzo makes a great garganelli)
Freshly grated Parmigiano-Reggiano

1. Heat the olive oil and 2 tablespoons of the butter in a heavy-bottomed saucepan (about 8-inch diameter and at least 4 inches deep) or flameproof terra-cotta casserole (with a lid). Add the onions, carrots, and celery. Sauté the vegetables over low heat, stirring occasionally, until they are very soft and have almost melted into a purée. This can take about 30 minutes and requires patience. The vegetables must be soft before proceeding with the recipe or they will not soften further.

2. Add the fennel seeds and salt. Sauté for 2 minutes until the fennel is fragrant. Raise the heat and add the veal. Cook, stirring, until the meat is no longer pink. Add the wine, reduce the heat, and cook gently, stirring often, until almost all the wine has evaporated, about 30 minutes. Add the milk, raise the heat, and cook until the milk has evaporated. Stir in the tomatoes and stock, and simmer, covered, until the veal is tender, an additional 30 minutes or more.

3. Bring a large pot of water to a boil. Generously salt the water and drop in the pasta. Cook, stirring often, until al dente. Drain the garganelli and transfer to a heated serving bowl. Cut up the remaining butter and toss with the pasta. Divide among heated bowls and top with a ladle of ragù. Pass extra sauce and Parmigiano-Reggiano at the table.

on top of spaghetti...

Pennone with Easter Sunday Ragù

Serves 6 to 8 as a first course or 4 to 6 as a main course

Growing up in Catholic households, Easter Sunday was a big deal for both of us—a holy day of celebratory food, family, and friends gathered at the table after Mass. Johanne's kitchen was filled with whiffs of traditional Polish foods, like cabbage and potato pierogi, garlicky kielbasa, head-clearing homemade horseradish tinted magenta with grated beets, and sweet babka with pastel-colored eggs nestled in its braids.

The aromas in George's house reflected his dad's Greek background and his mom's Italian roots. Scents of Dad's unctuous feta pita and his baklava cooling on the counter competed with Mom's memorable tomato sauce bubbling gently on the stove. Steam from the pasta pot waiting for homemade ravioli made the atmosphere in the kitchen moist and heady with oregano and basil. There were typical American things to eat, too, like roast turkey at George's or fresh ham at Johanne's, but it was the ethnic food that mattered most and to this day is compelling.

Now, we celebrate Easter with a gaggle of dishes echoing our families' traditions.

We discuss what we will cook weeks ahead. One thing is for sure—pasta is always on the menu as the *primo*, or first course. This is one of our holiday favorites as the sauce must be prepared several hours ahead or better yet, the day before, leaving us more time on Sunday to relax and enjoy being with our loved ones.

Use either brisket or short ribs for this sauce. These particular cuts of beef are well marbled, but most of the fat melts in the cooking, floats to the surface, and solidifies when chilled for easy removal. This recipe makes more sauce than you will need for a pound of pasta. Leftovers will keep well in the freezer or in the fridge for a few days, ready to heat up for another celebration.

2½ pounds beef brisket or short ribs
1½ cups finely chopped onions
1 cup finely chopped carrots
⅓ cup finely chopped celery
¾ cup finely chopped fennel bulb
3 plump garlic cloves, peeled and finely
  minced
1 to 2 tablespoons extra virgin olive oil
Sea salt
1 cup dry red wine
4 cups tomato juice, preferably organic
1 pound dried pennone or rigatoni
Freshly grated Parmigiano-Reggiano

1. Brown the meat on all sides, starting with the fattiest surfaces first, in a large nonstick or well-seasoned pot. The fat will melt and help color and caramelize the leaner sides. If the meat is too lean and sticks to the pan, add a few drops of olive oil. Transfer the browned beef to a plate. Pour off and discard the fat.

2. Toss the onions, carrots, celery, fennel, and garlic into the pot. Moisten with a tablespoon of the olive oil. Cook over moderate heat, scraping up any crusty bits left behind by the beef. Add some salt and more olive oil if necessary. Sauté over low heat, stirring from time to time, until the vegetables are very soft. This could take 20 to 30 minutes.

3. Return the beef to the pot. Add the wine, raise the heat, and cook, stirring often, until the wine evaporates. Add the tomato juice and 1 cup water. Cover and bring to a boil. Lower the heat and simmer gently until the meat is very tender, about 2 hours or more.

4. Remove the meat from the sauce. Refrigerate the meat and sauce separately. Chill several hours or overnight, long enough for the fat to rise to the surface of the sauce and solidify.

5. To finish the sauce, remove and discard all the fat on the surface. Remove the bones and/or any visible fat from the beef. Cut the meat up into small pieces and combine with the sauce. Reheat the sauce, covered, over low heat. Stir it up every so often, and check to be sure it is not sticking to the bottom of the pot. When the sauce is bubbling hot, lower the heat to maintain a gentle simmer, and bring a large pot of water to a boil to cook the pasta.

6. Generously salt the pasta water and drop in the pennone. Cook, stirring often, until al dente. Drain the pasta and transfer to a heated serving bowl. Toss with enough of the sauce to coat each noodle generously but without the pasta swimming in sauce. Serve right away with extra sauce passed at the table along with the Parmigiano-Reggiano.

◆ Pappardelle with Rabbit ◆

Serves 6 to 8 as a first course or 4 to 6 as a main course

Pappardelle con la Lepre, or long, flat fresh noodles with wild hare sauce, is one of the glories of the Tuscan kitchen. It is not easy to find hare unless you cozy up to a hunter, so we make our sauce with rabbit. Marinating the meat in red wine with herbs and spices for a day enhances its taste and makes a sauce with lingering depth and rich complexity.

We serve the rabbit sauce with fresh, hand-cut homemade ribbon noodles or, in a pinch, we use an excellent-quality dried pappardelle, available in well-stocked markets. Buy ribbon pasta packaged in nests rather than flat. The flat ones annoyingly cement themselves together when boiled no matter how much you stir them.

The juniper berries lend this sauce a unique taste. Give the ones in your cupboard a good sniff. They should have a strong scent reminiscent of gin. If they are not fragrant, they're past their prime and you need a new jar.

You will have more sauce than you need for a pound of pasta. Leftovers can be frozen, refrigerated for a few days, or used as a topping for crostini.

The Marinade
1½ cups chopped carrots
1½ cups chopped onions
½ cup chopped celery, including any tender leaves
2 plump garlic cloves, gently crushed, with root ends and peel removed
5 juniper berries
3 cloves
½ teaspoon black peppercorns
4 cups dry red wine
2 fresh bay leaves or 1 dried bay leaf
One 10-inch sprig fresh rosemary, spiky leaves only
1 sprig fresh marjoram
3 to 4 large fresh sage leaves (do not substitute dried sage)
¼ teaspoon crushed fennel seeds
1 fresh rabbit (about 2 pounds), cut into 6 to 8 pieces
1 rabbit liver or 4 ounces chicken livers
½ to 1 teaspoon sea salt

The Sauce
½ cup extra virgin olive oil
½ cup finely diced prosciutto
½ cup red wine vinegar
2 cups tomato juice, preferably organic
3½ cups homemade rabbit or chicken stock, brought to the boiling point

The Pasta

1 pound dried pappardelle or fresh pappardelle, hand-cut into long ¾-inch-wide strips (page 214)

Extra virgin olive oil, for anointing the pasta

Freshly grated Parmigiano-Reggiano

Cayenne

1. Combine all the marinade ingredients, including the rabbit pieces and liver, in a large nonreactive bowl or in a heavy-duty Ziploc bag nestled in a bowl. Cover and refrigerate for 24 hours. If the rabbit is not completely submerged, turn the pieces in the marinade every so often.

2. When you are ready to prepare the sauce, remove the rabbit and liver from the marinade and set aside to drain. Pour the vegetables, herbs, spices, and wine into a colander over a bowl to catch and reserve all the liquid. Let the vegetables dry in the colander for 30 minutes, pressing down on them or shaking the colander every so often to eliminate as much moisture as possible.

3. Transfer the veggies, herbs, and spices to a large, unheated heavy-bottomed pot with a lid—an enamel-coated cast-iron pot is ideal. Stir in the olive oil and set the pot over moderately high heat. Sauté, stirring often, until the vegetables are cooked through and have turned a rich brown; this will take about 20 minutes. Be patient as this step is important to the depth of the final sauce. Keep in mind that the red wine will have tinted the vegetables, so you must taste them to determine if they are fully cooked.

4. Add the prosciutto and cook for 3 minutes. Add 1 cup of the reserved wine. This will loosen any browned bits of vegetables on the bottom of the pan. Scrape them up with a wooden spoon and stir into the mixture. Raise the heat and allow the wine to evaporate completely. Repeat with 1 more cup of wine. Repeat with ½ cup wine and the vinegar. Add the rabbit pieces, the liver, and ½ cup wine. Cook, basting the rabbit a few times, until the liquid has boiled away. Repeat the process of glazing and deglazing the rabbit with the remaining wine in ½-cup increments. Add the tomato juice and cook for 5 to 7 minutes. Add the hot stock, cover, and bring to a boil. Reduce the heat to maintain a gentle simmer, set the lid slightly ajar, and cook until the rabbit is very tender, about 1 hour.

5. Scoop out the rabbit pieces and transfer to a cutting board. Set aside to cool.

6. Remove the bay leaves and purée the sauce with the liver. The mixture will not be completely smooth. An immersion blender is the perfect tool for this. If you don't have one, you may use a conventional blender. In that case, either let the sauce cool or be extremely careful puréeing the hot liquid as the steam can pop the container top off and spew the sauce over you and the kitchen.

7. Return the puréed sauce to a clean pot.

8. Remove the bones from the cooled rabbit pieces. Watch out for the tiny, elusive ones that can easily be overlooked. With a sharp knife, chop the meat into small pieces (about ⅛ inch square) and return the rabbit to the sauce. Taste and add

on top of spaghetti...

more salt if necessary. Reheat over a very low flame—you may want to use a flame tamer.

9. Bring a large pot of water to a boil for the pasta. Generously salt the water and drop in the pappardelle. Cook, stirring often, until al dente. Drain the pasta without shaking all the water off and return the pappardelle to the pasta pot. Toss with just enough olive oil to keep the noodles loose and slippery (a little pasta water clinging to the noodles helps). Divide the pappardelle onto heated flat plates, top each portion with a ladleful of sauce (about ½ cup sauce for each first-course portion or 1 cup sauce for each main-course portion), and serve at once. Pass the Parmigiano-Reggiano, cayenne, and extra sauce at the table.

Primo-Secondo, or Two for One

Eating a meal in Italy is a ritual consisting of many courses. The basic meal starts with a *primo*, or first course, of pasta, risotto, or soup followed by a *secondo*, or main course of fish, meat, or poultry (eggs or an elaborate preparation of the vegetable of the moment also make a fine main course). A crisp salad or simply prepared vegetables come next. Dessert finishes the feast—most often with a bowl of fresh fruit or fruit salad, but it could be cheese instead. Variables on this formula abound: Sometimes there is an antipasto before the primo; sometimes there is a *dolce*, or elaborate sweet, at the end of the meal.

Eating like this in a restaurant is one thing, but who has time to prepare all those courses at home every day? Our solution is to cook one recipe served in two parts—slow-cooked braised meat, for example, whose cooking juices are generous enough to sauce a first course of pasta. Any number of stews work well for this two-for-one mode of eating. Savvy Italians have been preparing meals like this for many generations. Busy mamas (or papas) can give their families a steaming bowl of spaghetti or macaroni plus a protein course with just a bit more effort than for a single dish. Followed by a simple green salad—and, perhaps, fresh fruit for dessert—it is a satisfying meal. This is a great way to eat at home and an easy way to entertain, too.

The remaining recipes in this chapter will give you a pasta and main course. Like the food in Italy, the preparations are unpretentious and call for modest but tasty cuts of meat. Some require long cooking to tenderize and bring out their succulence, but none require constant supervision. The meats used in this group of primo and secondo—chicken, beef, veal, pork, or lamb—can bubble away gently with a periodic check-in while you occupy yourself with other tasks nearby.

on top of spaghetti...

◆ Spaghetti and Summer Chicken Cacciatore ◆

Serves 8

This hunter's-style chicken is so chockful of onions, celery, and tomatoes that you could call it a vegetable ragù with chicken. Ripe, juicy tomatoes are essential for the fresh taste of this light version of an Italian classic. Be diligent in removing all the pesky seeds from the tomatoes as they have a tendency to lend a disagreeable bitterness to the sauce if left in.

The pasta *primo*, or first course, is bathed in the cacciatore stewing juices with the addition of sautéed mushrooms—an ingredient often associated with hunter's style or game cooking. Parmigiano-Reggiano folded into the spaghetti thickens and enriches the sauce. That leaves the chicken and vegetables needing only a crusty loaf of bread to be sure every drop of broth is savored.

This recipe can easily be doubled. In fact, the chicken is so good cold, you may want to make extra. In that case, brown the thighs in batches, adding the pancetta to the last batch.

8 medium (2½ to 3 pounds) ripe, juicy garden tomatoes
8 chicken thighs (about 3 pounds)
2 tablespoons extra virgin olive oil
2 ounces pancetta, finely chopped (4 tablespoons)
4 cups chopped onions
3 cups chopped celery, including the tender inner leaves
1 jalapeño pepper, finely minced
⅛ teaspoon crushed red pepper flakes
1 to 2 teaspoons sea salt
1 sprig fresh rosemary
2 fresh bay leaves or 1 dried bay leaf
¼ cup coarsely chopped fresh flat-leaf parsley
½ cup dry white wine
1 pound dried spaghetti or spaghettini
4 tablespoons unsalted butter
2 cups (about 5 ounces) thinly sliced mushrooms
Freshly grated Parmigiano-Reggiano

1. Bring a small pot of water to a boil. Drop in the tomatoes, a few at a time, and cook each batch for 30 seconds. With tongs, transfer the tomatoes to a cutting board. Remove the cores, skin the tomatoes, and cut them in half horizontally. Gently squeeze the tomato halves over a strainer suspended above a bowl so that the seed pockets fall into the strainer. Scoop out any stubborn seeds from the tomato cavities with your forefinger. Set aside the tomato pulp on the cutting board. Rub the tomato seeds in the strainer with the back of a spoon or rubber spatula to push all the tasty tomato bits and juice into the bowl below. Discard the seeds. Coarsely chop the tomato pulp and add to the collected juices and bits of tomato in the bowl. You should have about 5 cups of pulp and juice. Set aside.

2. Remove and discard the skin and any excess fat from the chicken thighs. Dry them thoroughly on paper towels.

3. Heat the olive oil in a large Dutch oven or heavy-bottomed pot with a lid. Add the chicken thighs and sauté over brisk heat for 4 to 6 minutes to brown the first side. Turn the thighs, sauté for 2 minutes, add the pancetta, and continue to cook until the second side browns, an additional 2 to 4 minutes. Transfer the chicken pieces to a plate and keep warm. If the pancetta has not begun to brown by this time, allow it to cook another minute or two.

4. Stir the onions, celery, jalapeño, red pepper flakes, half the salt, rosemary, bay leaves, and parsley into the pot with the pancetta. Lower the heat, stirring the vegetables and scraping up any browned bits left behind by the chicken.

Sauté the vegetables gently, stirring every now and then, for about 10 minutes until they have softened. Add the wine, raise the heat, and cook, stirring until the wine has evaporated.

5. Return the chicken and any juices that have collected on the plate to the pot with the vegetables. Add the chopped tomatoes and their juices, cover the pot, and bring to a boil over moderately high heat. Lower the heat and simmer gently, stirring occasionally, for 40 minutes, or until the chicken is cooked through. During the last few minutes of cooking, taste the sauce, adding more salt if necessary. Remove the rosemary sprig and bay leaves. Keep warm over low heat.

6. To serve the first course, bring plenty of water to a boil in a large pot. Generously salt the water and drop in the pasta. Stir often to prevent the strands from sticking together.

7. Meanwhile, heat the butter in a large straight-sided sauté pan. Add the mushrooms and cook, tossing frequently, until the mushrooms are cooked through.

8. As soon as the pasta is cooked al dente, drain it and add to the mushrooms in the sauté pan. Toss to combine. Transfer to a large heated serving bowl. Nudge the chicken to one side of the pot and ladle enough of the sauce onto the pasta to coat each strand. Toss again with Parmigiano-Reggiano and serve the pasta at once for your first course.

9. For the main course, serve the chicken, vegetables, and some sauce with a crusty loaf of bread.

◆ Pappardelle and Saffron-Scented Milk-Braised Chicken ◆

Serves 6

Braising chicken in milk results in meltingly tender and silky-textured meat. Don't be alarmed when you remove the lid and see milk curds bobbing around the surface. A quick whir with an immersion blender at the end of cooking will result in a creamy emulsion for the pasta first course, with plenty of sauce left to nap the second course of chicken.

Saffron's lovely color combines with the onions and tomatoes to give the sauce a Titian tint.

5 tablespoons extra virgin olive oil
1 large (4½ pounds) chicken, cut into 10 to 12 pieces
2 cups finely chopped onions
½ teaspoon sea salt
1 heaping cup chopped green or red tomatoes
1 cup dry white wine
4 cups milk
½ teaspoon saffron threads
8 ounces (½ batch) George's Fresh Pasta (page 212), cut into pappardelle, or 12 ounces dried pappardelle
Freshly grated Parmigiano-Reggiano (optional)

1. Heat 3 tablespoons of the olive oil in a large, heavy pot with a lid—an enamel-covered cast-iron Dutch oven is ideal. Brown the chicken pieces on all sides.

2. Transfer the chicken to a platter and discard most of the oil. Put the remaining olive oil in the pot with the onions and salt. Cook over moderately low heat, scraping up any browned bits of chicken left behind. Continue to cook, stirring often, until the onions are very soft and are browning a little. This could take 20 to 30 min-

utes. Add the tomatoes and cook an additional 5 minutes. Add the wine, raise the heat, and cook until the wine evaporates.

3. Meanwhile, heat the milk with the saffron in a saucepan until it scalds and tiny bubbles appear around the edge of the pan. Set aside and keep warm.

4. Return the chicken pieces and any juices to the pot with the onions and tomatoes. Pour over the saffron-infused milk. Cover and bring to a boil. Lower the heat and simmer gently, stirring every so often, until the chicken is tender, about 45 minutes. Transfer the chicken to a platter and blend the sauce in the pot. Taste and add more salt if necessary. Return the chicken pieces to the pot and keep warm over the lowest possible heat.

5. To serve the first course, bring a large pot of water to a boil for the pasta. Generously salt the water and drop in the pappardelle. Cook, stirring often, until the pasta is tender with a silky, soft texture and a little bite. Drain the pasta and transfer to a heated serving bowl. Ladle over enough of the braising liquid to coat each ribbon noodle nicely without allowing it to swim in sauce. Serve right away with Parmigiano-Reggiano if you like.

6. Follow the pasta with a second course of chicken napped with sauce. A nice loaf of country-style bread would be a good accompaniment to sponge up the juices.

on top of spaghetti...

◆ Pasta Hankies and Brasato al Barolo ◆

Serves 6

Barolo is a big, powerful, and opulent red wine made from the nebbiolo grape. It is unique to Piemonte, the northwestern region of Italy that borders France, where it is called the "king of wine and the wine of kings." The same region of Italy produces beef of unparalleled excellence. It is no wonder the two have been combined in the regal Brasato al Barolo, or beef braised in Barolo wine. Traditionally served on Sunday, it is a slow-cooked classic dish prepared with boneless beef that is moist, juicy, and fork-tender. To achieve the same juiciness with American beef, which is less fatty, we use a combination of boneless stewing beef and short ribs. The fat in the short ribs dissolves in the simmering broth, rises to the surface, and is carefully skimmed off before serving, leaving behind only its succulent taste.

Often, the brasato broth is served with pasta as a *primo,* or first course, as we suggest here. Inventive Piemontese cooks use any leftover brasato beef bits as a filling for the next day's agnolotti—the minuscule local ravioli—as a filling for cabbage leaves in the winter, or for stuffed zucchini flowers in the summer.

Our pasta choice for the broth is homemade sheets cut into hanky-size squares. You can substitute dried pasta if you wish—pappardelle, fettuccine, or penne would all work well. Since dried pasta is less rich than homemade, increase the amount to 12 ounces to serve 6 people.

After the pasta, serve the brasato meats moistened with their cooking juices. Pass a good loaf of country bread around the table, if you like, to enjoy every last drop. Finish the meal with a mix of lettuces and bitter greens, dressed with olive oil and freshly squeezed lemon.

This dish usually disappears in seconds, but if you happen to have any leftovers, you can use the beef to make a delicious filling for ravioli (page 236).

5 tablespoons extra virgin olive oil

2 pounds short ribs

2 pounds stewing beef, cut into large chunks

2¼ cups diced onions

½ cup finely chopped carrots

½ cup finely chopped celery

1 teaspoon sea salt

4 plump garlic cloves, trimmed and peeled

9 cups dry red wine, preferably Barolo

2 cups beef or chicken broth

2 cloves

1 fresh bay leaf or 1 dried bay leaf

3 tablespoons unsalted butter

2½ to 3 cups thickly sliced white mushrooms

8 ounces (½ batch) George's Fresh Pasta (page 212), rolled and cut into hankies

Freshly grated Parmigiano-Reggiano

1 tablespoon tomato paste

1 cup blanched fresh or frozen peas

1. Heat 2 tablespoons of the olive oil in a large, heavy casserole. We like to use an enamel-covered cast-iron Dutch oven. Add the short ribs and as many pieces of stewing beef as will fit in the pot in one layer without crowding. Brown the beef on all sides over moderately high heat. Transfer the browned pieces to a large plate and continue to brown the remaining pieces of beef. Set aside.

2. Drain off any fat left in the casserole. Add the remaining olive oil and the onions and cook over moderate heat for 5 minutes, stirring often. Add the carrots and celery; sprinkle with salt and sauté the vegetables slowly until they are soft and just beginning to brown. This could take about 20 minutes.

3. Drop in the garlic and pour in the wine. Bring to a boil and boil rapidly for 5 minutes. Return the beef to the casserole and add the broth, cloves, and bay leaf. Cover and bring to a boil. Lower the heat to maintain a very gentle simmer. If on the lowest heat you have more than a gentle simmer, set the cover askew a bit and/or use a heat diffuser. In the first hour of cooking, skim off any scum that floats to the surface. Thereafter, spoon off the fat on the surface every 15 minutes or so. Cook until the beef is fork-tender. It could take 2 to 2½ hours for the short ribs. Remove any chunks of stewing beef from the pot if they become tender before the ribs. Keep the pieces moistened with some of the cooking juices and return them to the pot when the ribs are done. At this point, you can leave the casserole on the lowest possible heat with a diffuser, or turn off the heat until you are ready to serve the second course.

4. To serve the first course, bring a large pot of water to a boil for the pasta. Use a pasta cooker with a built-in strainer if you have one.

5. Ladle 1½ cups broth from the beef in the casserole into a heatproof measuring cup. Let stand for a few minutes, and then spoon off the fat that floats to the surface. Or you can use one of those handy pitchers that pour from the bottom, leaving the fat behind. Set aside.

6. In a large straight-sided skillet, heat 2 tablespoons butter over high heat. When the foam subsides, add the mushrooms and stir and toss

Penne with Easy Norma
(page 24)

Spaghetti with Fresh Spinach and Gorgonzola
(page 30)

Farfalle with Zucchini, Zucchini
Flowers, and Broth (page 33)

Orecchiette with Cool Chickpeas
(page 30)

Spaghetti Aglio-Olio

(page 51)

Linguini with Frenched Green Beans and Parsley "Pesto"
(page 58)

Mostaccioli with Tomato "Pesto"

(page 61)

Tagliatelle or Spaghetti with Little Girl's Tomato Sauce

(page 75)

Salina-Style Spaghettini with Cherry Tomatoes

(page 81)

Pappardelle and Saffron-Scented Milk-Braised Chicken

(page 149)

Linguini with Mussels and Fresh Tomatoes

(page 105)

Pasta Baked with Radicchio, Gorgonzola, and Pancetta
(page 205)

Fettuccine with Venetian Chicken Sauce

(page 120)

Sunday Gravy with Sausages
and Meatballs (page 126)

Shells Baked with Tomato, Cream,
Corn, and Five Cheeses (page 191)

Jo's Fast Cheater's Lasagne
(page 257)

Roasted Asparagus Lasagne
(page 251)

them in the butter. Sauté until the mushrooms are cooked through and beginning to brown. If they absorb all the butter and seem dry, lower the heat until they release some of their juices, then raise the heat again to brown. Add the reserved broth to the mushrooms and bring to a boil. Reduce to the lowest heat.

7. Salt the boiling water in the pasta pot and drop in the noodles. Cook until al dente. Do not undercook; you want the pasta to have a silky, almost slippery texture. Drain the pasta and slide into the skillet with the mushrooms. Add the remaining butter and toss gently. Serve immediately with Parmigiano-Reggiano.

8. To serve the *secondo*, or second course, purée some of the broth. If you have an immersion blender, stack the meat on one side of the casserole so you have a pool of broth to purée. Otherwise, transfer about half of the liquid to a blender and blend, taking care not to burn yourself, as the hot liquid and steam have a tendency to expand and pop off the lid. Return the puréed broth to the casserole.

9. Stir the tomato paste thoroughly into the broth and add the peas. Reheat gently until the peas are cooked through and serve the brasato with a crusty loaf of bread to sop up the juices. As this is a rich dish, follow the brasato with a salad of lettuces and bitter greens.

◆ Spaghetti and Beef-Stuffed Peppers ◆

Serves 6

Pale green finger peppers or Hungarian peppers are much more subtle in flavor than the bell variety and work well with a delicate stuffing of beef and ricotta. Sautéing the peppers before filling them imbues the oil with their essence and gives a more pronounced pepper taste to the finished sauce.

We have found that the best peppers come from local farmers' markets. It seems when we ask for sweet peppers they give us hot ones and vice versa. As a result, we have had experience with both kinds when preparing this recipe. If you are as enthusiastic about spicy food as we are, try using hot peppers—taste a seed beforehand to determine their strength. Otherwise, you may find an unsuspecting guest at your table turning crimson and reaching for something to put out the fire.

This recipe produces a generous pasta course, followed by a smaller-scaled main course. A nice green salad and chunk of aged Parmigiano-Reggiano round out the meal.

6 ounces ground beef
¼ cup plus 2 tablespoons fresh ricotta
⅓ cup freshly grated Parmigiano-Reggiano
⅓ cup freshly grated Pecorino Romano
1 egg, lightly beaten
2 tablespoons chopped fresh flat-leaf parsley
¼ teaspoon sea salt
6 large (7 to 8 inches long) light green finger, Hungarian, or hot, spicy peppers
2 tablespoons extra virgin olive oil
5 tablespoons unsalted butter
¾ cup finely chopped onions
3½ cups tomato juice, preferably organic
1 pound imported dried spaghetti or spaghettini
Freshly grated Parmigiano-Reggiano or Pecorino Romano

on top of spaghetti...

1. In a bowl, gently mix together the beef, ricotta, Parmigiano-Reggiano, Pecorino Romano, egg, parsley, and salt until well combined. Cover and refrigerate the filling for 30 minutes.

2. Slice off the top of the peppers at the stem end and gently pull out and discard the seeds.

3. Heat the olive oil in a skillet large enough to accommodate the peppers in one layer. Add the peppers and their tops and sauté gently, turning every so often for even cooking. When the peppers have softened and browned in spots—this will take 10 minutes or less—transfer them to a platter to cool.

4. Add 1 tablespoon of the butter to the skillet with the chopped onions. Sauté over moderate heat until the onions are translucent and soft. Add the tomato juice and ½ cup water; cover and bring to a boil, reduce the heat, and keep the sauce at a bare simmer.

5. Meanwhile, stuff the cold filling into the cooled peppers, gently pushing the mixture into the peppers with a small spoon. Be careful not to rip the peppers. Attach the tops of the peppers to their bottoms with toothpicks to encourage the filling to stay in place. If you have extra filling after all the peppers are stuffed, make tiny meatballs—about ¼-inch diameter—to cook with the peppers.

6. Put the stuffed peppers into the simmering tomato sauce. Gently drop in the meatballs if you have any. Cover the skillet, adjust the heat to maintain a simmer, and cook for 40 to 50 minutes. Don't worry if some of the filling escapes into the sauce. It will still be delicious.

7. To serve, bring a large pot of water to a boil. Generously salt the water and drop in the pasta. Cook, stirring often, until al dente. Drain the pasta and transfer to a heated serving bowl. Toss with the remaining butter. Nudge the peppers to one side of the skillet and spoon enough of the sauce on the pasta to coat every strand. Top with the meatballs if you have any. Serve right away as a first course with freshly grated cheese passed at the table. Keep the peppers covered on the lowest flame until you are ready for the main course.

8. Serve the peppers napped with some of the remaining sauce on heated plates, along with a crusty loaf of bread, followed by an ample salad.

◆ Spaghetti and Braised Polpettone ◆

Serves 6

These moist and savory polpettone, or big meatballs, are like individual poached meat loaves. The sauce is super on spaghetti, or on homemade pasta cut into hanky shapes, fettuccine, or pappardelle.

Serve the main course with a green vegetable—sautéed spinach is especially nice. Or follow the polpettone with a seasonal salad.

The Polpettone
5-ounce chunk mortadella, cut into ½-inch cubes
6 slices white sandwich bread, crust removed, cut into ½-inch cubes
1½ cups freshly grated Grana Padano or Parmigiano-Reggiano
1 tablespoon finely chopped fresh flat-leaf parsley
1 teaspoon sea salt
10 turns of the pepper mill
1 egg, lightly beaten
¾ cup milk
8 ounces ground beef

The Braising Liquid
1 cup finely chopped onions
1 plump garlic clove, peeled and finely chopped
¼ cup extra virgin olive oil
1 teaspoon sea salt
6 cups tomato juice, preferably organic, heated

The Pasta
12 ounces dried spaghetti or ½ batch George's Fresh Pasta (page 212), cut into hankies
Freshly grated Grana Padano or Parmigiano-Reggiano
Crushed red pepper flakes (optional)

1. Make the polpettone by combining the mortadella, bread, cheese, parsley, salt, and pepper in the bowl of a food processor (if your processor is small, you can do this in two batches). Pulse on and off until you have a fine, crumbly mixture. Transfer to a large mixing bowl. Add the egg, milk, and beef. Mix the ingredients together thoroughly, being careful not to overmix or the polpettone will be tough. Shape the mixture into 6 equal-sized oval patties, about 6 ounces each, measuring 5 inches long, 2 inches wide, and 1½ inches thick. Refrigerate the polpettone while you make the sauce.

2. Combine the onions, garlic, olive oil, salt, and 1 cup water in a 12-inch straight-sided skillet (with a tight-fitting lid). Bring to a boil, uncovered, stirring occasionally. Cook over moderate heat until the water has boiled away, leaving only the oil in the pan to moisten the onions, about 15 minutes. Keep a close eye on the pan and stir more frequently as the water evaporates (stir constantly toward the end of this process). Lower the heat if necessary to prevent the onions from sticking to the pan and browning. The onions will be softened but not completely cooked.

3. Add the hot tomato juice, cover the pan, and bring to a boil. Uncover and gently place the polpettone in the sauce. Cover and simmer over low heat for 1 hour and 15 minutes. Keep the pan on the lowest possible heat on a flame tamer while you prepare the first course.

4. Bring a large pot of water to a boil for the pasta. Generously salt the water and drop in the spaghetti. Cook, stirring often, until al dente. Drain the pasta and transfer to a heated serving bowl. Ladle on enough of the braising liquid to coat every strand of spaghetti. Sprinkle with an ample amount of cheese, toss, and serve right away. Pass more cheese and the red pepper flakes, if you like, at the table.

5. For the second course, serve the polpettone moistened with sauce on heated plates. You can accompany the beef with a green vegetable or follow with a crisp green salad.

◆ Saffron-Sauced Pasta and Osso Buco ◆

Serves 6

Osso buco is always a sellout at Al Forno, and it's an equally popular choice at home. Cooked slowly and carefully, it is one of the most tender and succulent cuts of veal. Ask the butcher for center-cut osso buco so each piece has an ample proportion of meat to bone. End pieces often yield very little veal.

For the first course, silky homemade noodles or excellent-quality dried pappardelle or tagliatelle are bathed in veal juices enhanced by the tenacious scent of saffron.

The main-course veal can be served sprinkled with gremolata or grated lemon zest.

6 tablespoons unsalted butter
4 tablespoons extra virgin olive oil
6 center-cut (about 4 pounds) veal shanks, each about 1½ inches thick
2 cups chopped onions
1 heaping cup chopped carrots
1 heaping cup chopped celery
¾ cup finely diced prosciutto
½ teaspoon or more sea salt
3 cups dry white wine
4 to 6 cups homemade chicken stock (see Pasta Pantry), heated to the boiling point
1 teaspoon saffron threads
¼ cup heavy cream
1 to 2 tablespoons tomato paste
12 ounces fresh pappardelle (page 214) or dried pappardelle, or tagliatelle
Freshly grated Parmigiano-Reggiano
Gremolata (recipe follows) or grated zest of 1 lemon (optional)

1. Heat 2 tablespoons of the butter and 2 tablespoons of the olive oil in a Dutch oven or enamel-covered cast-iron pot large enough to accommodate the shanks in one snug layer. When the butter foam has subsided, add the veal and brown on all sides. Be patient here and allow the shanks to achieve a deep, rich, burnished color. Transfer the veal to a large plate and discard the fat in the pot.

 on **top** of spaghetti...

2. Add the remaining olive oil to the pot with the onions, carrots, celery, ½ cup of the prosciutto, and salt. Cook over moderate heat, stirring often and scraping up all the bits of browned veal sticking to the pot. After 10 minutes or so, when the onions have softened, add 1 cup of the wine. Raise the heat and cook, stirring often, until most of the wine has evaporated. Repeat this process one more time. Return the veal to the pot with the vegetables and moisten with the last cup of wine. Baste the meat continually with the liquid until most of it has evaporated and you are left with vegetables that are soft and glossy with wine glaze. Add 4 cups of the hot stock, cover, and bring to a boil. Reduce the heat to maintain the gentlest of simmers. Cook, basting the veal often, until tender, 1½ to 2 hours (if at any time there seems to be too little broth, add more hot stock, ¼ cup at a time, to keep the shanks bathed in liquid). Set aside off the heat.

3. Bring a large pot of water to a boil for the pasta.

4. Transfer 1½ cups of the veal broth (leaving behind the vegetables) to a large straight-sided sauté pan. Add the saffron threads and set aside for 10 minutes. Reheat the broth and saffron over moderate heat. Add the remaining ¼ cup prosciutto, heavy cream, and tomato paste. Bring to a boil, then lower the heat to simmer while the pasta cooks.

5. Generously salt the boiling water and drop in the pasta. Cook, stirring often, until al dente. Drain the pasta, saving about 1 cup water.

6. Swirl the remaining butter into the pasta sauce in the sauté pan. Add the noodles and toss so that the pasta is nicely coated. Add some of the pasta water (or remaining stock), tablespoon by tablespoon, if the sauce is too thick. The noodles should be moist with some broth around them. Serve right away in heated bowls with Parmigiano-Reggiano passed at the table.

7. To serve the main course, transfer the veal pieces to a heated plate and keep warm. Purée the veal broth and vegetables with an immersion blender or food mill. (This can also be done in a conventional blender or food processor; be extremely careful not to burn yourself as the steam in the hot liquid has a tendency to expand and pop the top off the blender or escape from the bowl of the food processor.) Reheat the puréed broth and veal shanks gently over moderately low heat, stirring often.

8. Serve the osso buco on heated plates moistened generously with the puréed broth. Be sure to offer a marrow spoon or a small espresso spoon to scoop out the marrow in the middle of the bone. It is a rich indulgence to savor every so often. Serve with gremolata or grated lemon zest if you wish.

◆ Gremolata ◆

~~~~~~~~~~~~~~~~~~~~~~~~~~~~~~~~~~~~

The traditional aromatic garnish for osso buco, gremolata is a fine chop of parsley, lemon zest, and garlic. It is a tasty embellishment when you are in the mood for the punchy taste of raw garlic.

~~~~~~~~~~~~~~~~~~~~~~~~~~

¼ cup fresh flat-leaf parsley leaves
Grated zest of 1 lemon, preferably organic
1 garlic clove, trimmed and peeled
Pinch of sea salt

Make the gremolata by finely chopping together the parsley, lemon zest, garlic, and salt. You can stir this into the puréed broth a few minutes before serving to tone down the taste of the garlic, or sprinkle it on the veal shanks just before you bring them to the table.

◆ Fettuccine and Braised Veal Shoulder with Pancetta ◆

Serves 4

This recipe started out as a main course but when we spied, then tasted, the mouthwatering juices around the roast, we thought: Hmm…pasta opportunity!

The first course works well with fresh ribbon noodles or dried fettuccine packaged in nests.

Accompany the sliced veal roast with a cooked leafy green vegetable like broccoli rabe, spinach, collards, turnip tops, dandelions, or escarole. Follow with a green salad.

Leftover roast can be used for Garganelli with Veal Ragù (page 139) or for sandwiches.

One 2-pound rolled and tied boneless veal shoulder roast
2 to 3 tablespoons extra virgin olive oil, plus more to drizzle on the veal
Heaping ¼ cup (2 ounces) finely chopped pancetta
1¾ cups finely chopped onions
½ teaspoon sea salt
1 cup dry white wine
1 fresh bay leaf or dried bay leaf
1 cup veal, beef, or chicken stock
½ cup canned tomato purée
½ batch George's Fresh Pasta (page 212), cut into fettuccine, or 8 ounces dried fettuccine
3 tablespoons unsalted butter
Freshly grated Parmigiano-Reggiano

1. Dry the roast thoroughly on paper towels. (It will not brown properly if there is any moisture on the surface.)

2. Heat 1 tablespoon olive oil in a heavy casserole. We like to use an oval enamel-covered cast-iron Dutch oven a few inches larger on all sides than the veal roast. Brown the roast over moderately high heat to sear it on all sides. Transfer the

veal to a platter and keep warm. Discard the fat left in the pan.

3. Toss the pancetta into the pan (it will sizzle immediately from the residual heat). Stir in 1 tablespoon olive oil and place over moderate heat. Sauté, stirring often, until the pancetta browns. Add the onions and salt. Stir with a wooden spoon, scraping up any browned bits left behind from the veal and pancetta. The onions will quickly take on a light caramel color from the meat residue. Cook, stirring often, until the onions are soft and lightly browned on the edges, about 12 minutes. Moderate the heat and/or add additional oil if the onions seem too dry and begin to stick to the pan.

4. Return the veal to the casserole with any juices that have collected on the platter. Add half the wine and the bay leaf. Bring to a boil and cook, uncovered, for 3 minutes, turning the veal every so often. Add the remaining wine and continue to cook (and turn the veal) until almost all the liquid has evaporated and the onions have a shiny glazed look. Add the stock and tomato purée. Cover, bring to a boil, and lower the heat to maintain a gentle simmer. You may need a heat diffuser. Be sure to check the roast periodically to be sure it is just barely bubbling rather than boiling. Cook the veal, turning every 15 minutes, for 45 minutes to 1 hour, or until an instant-read thermometer registers 145 to 150 degrees. Transfer the roast to a cutting board and cover loosely with foil.

5. Bring a large pot of water to a boil for the pasta.

6. Transfer 1 to 1½ cups of the veal cooking juices (with some of the onions and pancetta) to a large straight-sided sauté pan over moderate heat. Cook, stirring often, until the pan juices have lost the watery look and have reduced by half. Keep warm over the lowest possible flame.

7. Generously salt the boiling water and drop in the pasta. Cook, stirring often, until al dente. Reserve 1 cup of the cooking water and set aside. Drain the pasta and transfer to the sauté pan with the cooking juices. Add the butter and toss, over moderate heat, to coat the noodles. If it seems dry, add some pasta water, a tablespoon at a time, until the sauce clings to the strands with a little extra liquid surrounding them. Transfer the pasta to 4 heated bowls and top with a sprinkle of Parmigiano-Reggiano. Serve right away with additional cheese passed at the table.

8. To serve the main course, purée the remaining veal juices in the pot with an immersion blender and reheat. Cut the veal into thin slices and nap with the sauce. Drizzle each portion with a little olive oil. Serve with the vegetable of your choice and follow the veal with a crisp green salad.

on top of spaghetti...

◆ Rigatoni and Spareribs ◆

Serves 4 to 6

Slow, gentle, moist cooking makes these spareribs mouthwatering and juicy. To make them especially tender, remove and discard the thin membrane on the inside of the ribs.

The rib sauce works well with different cuts of pasta. Given a choice, George will always insist on spaghetti while Johanne fancies a sturdy rigatoni.

Serve a crusty loaf of bread with the ribs as a main course. Follow with a bitter green salad like arugula or watercress.

1 teaspoon sea salt
1 teaspoon fennel seeds
3 pounds baby back spareribs, divided into 3-rib pieces cut between the bones
2 tablespoons extra virgin olive oil
2 plump garlic cloves, peeled and finely minced
2 cups finely chopped onions
2 cups dry white wine
4 cups tomato juice, preferably organic
1 fresh bay leaf or dried bay leaf
1 pound imported dried rigatoni, spaghetti, or tagliatelle
Freshly grated Pecorino Romano

1. In a small bowl, mix together the salt and fennel seeds.

2. Dry the spareribs thouroughly on paper towels, then rub them all over with the salt and fennel mixture. Transfer the ribs to a sturdy Ziploc bag and refrigerate for 12 to 24 hours so the flavor of the fennel has a chance to penetrate the pork. The salt in the spice mixture will draw out some of the moisture from the ribs. Pat them dry with paper towels before proceeding with the recipe.

3. Heat the olive oil in a Dutch oven or heavy-bottomed pot. Brown the ribs on both sides and transfer to a platter. Toss the garlic and onions into the pot, scraping up any browned bits left by the ribs. Sauté over moderate heat for 5 minutes, or until the onions have softened. Add the wine, raise the heat, and boil over brisk heat for 5 minutes to evaporate some of the wine and soften its taste. Add the tomato juice, ¼ cup water, and bay leaf. Return the ribs to the pot with any juices that have collected on the plate. Cover, bring to a boil, lower the heat, and maintain a gentle simmer for 1 hour and 15 minutes, or until the ribs are tender. Check the consistency of the sauce. If it seems to be thin, remove the ribs to a platter and keep warm. Reduce the sauce over moderately high heat for 5 to 10 minutes. Return the ribs to the pot and keep them hot over a very low flame while you cook the pasta.

4. Bring plenty of water to a boil in a large pot. Generously salt the water and drop in the rigatoni. Cook, stirring often, until al dente (for rigatoni, the pasta tubes should collapse a bit). Drain and transfer the pasta to a heated serving bowl. Toss with enough of the sparerib sauce to coat the pasta. Sprinkle with Pecorino Romano, toss again, and serve right away as a first course.

5. For the main course, serve the spareribs with some of their sauce on heated plates accompanied by a crusty loaf of bread. Follow with a salad of bitter greens, like arugula or watercress.

◆ Mostaccioli and Sage-Scented Braised Pork ◆

Serves 6

The wine in this sauce creates a meltingly tender roast and imparts a lovely red-burnished umber color to it. Choose a roast covered with a thin layer of fat. Most of the fat melts in the cooking, but keeps the pork nice and juicy. Don't skimp on the sage. It may seem like a lot, but its intense flavor is curiously tempered in the slow braise.

2 to 3 tablespoons extra virgin olive oil
One 2- to 3-pound boneless pork loin roast
1 cup chopped onions
¼ to ½ teaspoon sea salt
4 plump garlic cloves, peeled, gently
   smashed and trimmed
¼ cup loosely packed fresh sage leaves
   (do not substitute dried)
1½ cups dry red wine
3 cups chopped canned tomatoes and
   their juice
1 cup chicken stock
12 ounces dried mostaccioli
Freshly grated Pecorino Romano

1. Choose a deep, heavy pot or Dutch oven, with a tight-fitting lid that is just a little bit larger than the roast. In it, heat half the olive oil over moderately high heat and brown the pork on all sides. Transfer the pork to a platter and discard the excess oil and rendered fat in the pot without disturbing any of the browned bits on the bottom. Stir in the onions, salt, garlic, and sage. This will immediately cool down the pan and loosen the pork pieces left behind. Add the remaining olive oil and cook the vegetables over moderate heat, scraping up the browned bits and stirring often, until the onions are soft and beginning to brown. Add the wine and bring to a boil over brisk heat. Cook for about 6 minutes, or until the wine has greatly reduced and has a glossy look. Add the tomatoes and stock and bring to a boil. Return the pork to the pan with any juices on the platter. Cover and simmer gently for about 1 hour, or until the meat registers 145 degrees on an instant-read thermometer. Transfer the pork to a cutting board (it will continue to cook as it rests), tent it loosely with a piece of foil, set aside, and keep warm while you prepare the pasta for the first course. Taste the sauce and add more salt if necessary. Keep the sauce simmering, covered, on the lowest possible heat.

2. Meanwhile, bring a large pot of water to a boil. Add a generous amount of salt and drop in the mostaccioli. Cook, stirring often, until al dente. Drain the pasta and transfer to a heated serving

bowl. Ladle a generous amount of sauce over the mostaccioli. Sprinkle with Pecorino Romano and toss again. Serve right away with extra cheese passed at the table.

3. For the main course, slice the pork and transfer to a heated platter. Nap with some of the remaining sauce and serve with or without a vegetable accompaniment.

on top of spaghetti...

Penne and Country-Style Spareribs Braised in Milk

Serves 4

Photographs of food have always influenced our cooking. Our shelves are lined with cookbooks and coffee-table books filled with pictures from every region of Italy. Our trips end with luggage weighted down by books we cannot resist. If we can't be in Italy enjoying a meal at a trattoria, ristorante, or in a friend's kitchen, we can at least daydream with the images.

In one of our favorite books on Tuscan cooking, the food looks so compelling, the diners look so jovial and satisfied, it's hard to resist the temptation to hop on a plane that very minute. One picture has a gray-haired smiling woman, dressed in a colorful cotton housedress and apron, in the Chianti countryside, offering a crusty casserole to the camera. It is filled with an enormous pork roast cooked in milk with rosemary branches spiked into it. Who wouldn't want to eat that?

Sadly, there was no recipe to accompany the picture. That didn't stop us from trying to duplicate it. We knew the recipe included pork, milk, and herbs. We experimented with

pork roasts of every sort—loins and shoulders (both butt and picnic)—hocks, and then spareribs and pork belly. One of our favorites is made with meaty country spareribs. Ask your butcher to chop each rib into three pieces for easy cooking. You could also use St. Louis–style spareribs—or baby-backs, but you'll need an additional pound as most of their weight is bone.

The milk in the sauce reduces and becomes curdlike and nut colored from the caramelization of the pork and vegetables. Blended after cooking, the liquid will have a creamy consistency perfect for saucing pasta. Try it with dried penne or rigatoni. If you feel like making fresh pasta, fettuccine is ideal.

1½ pounds country-style spareribs, each
   one cut into 3 pieces
2 tablespoons extra virgin olive oil
2 sprigs fresh rosemary
1½ cups finely chopped onions
1 cup finely chopped celery
1 plump garlic clove, peeled and finely
   minced
2 sprigs fresh sage
2 fresh bay leaves or 1 dried bay leaf
½ teaspoon sea salt
Freshly ground white pepper
3 cups milk, heated
8 ounces dried penne or rigatoni
Freshly grated Parmigiano-Reggiano

1. Dry the meat well on paper towels.

2. Heat the olive oil in a large, heavy pot with a lid—an enamel-coated cast-iron Dutch oven is best. Add the rosemary and spareribs. Brown the ribs thoroughly on all sides. Transfer to a platter. Discard the rosemary if it has browned too much. Otherwise keep it in the pot.

3. Toss the onions, celery, garlic, sage, bay leaves, salt, and a generous amount of pepper into the pot. Cook over moderate heat, scraping up any bits left by the browned pork. Continue to cook until the vegetables are very soft and beginning to brown, about 20 minutes. Return the pork and any juices on the platter to the pot. Add the hot milk, cover, and bring to a boil. Lower the heat and simmer gently, turning the pork now and then, until it is falling-apart tender, 1 to 1½ hours. Transfer the pork to a platter with a slotted spoon. Remove and discard the bay leaves and the rosemary and sage twigs (keep the rosemary and sage leaves). Whir the sauce with an immersion blender to a creamy consistency. Put the pork back in the pot and keep warm over the lowest possible heat.

4. To serve the first course, bring a large pot of water to a boil for the pasta. Generously salt the water and drop in the penne. Cook, stirring often, until al dente. Drain and transfer the pasta to a heated serving bowl. Nap with enough sauce to coat the pasta well. Toss and serve right away with Parmigiano-Reggiano passed at the table.

5. As the second course, serve the spareribs moistened with the remaining sauce.

Penne and Tomato-Lemon–Braised Lamb Shoulder

Serves 8

The idea for this recipe came from our friend Wendy Suntay—a terrific cook. One Sunday, she prepared a Turkish lunch for us with a main course of lamb legs roasted for hours in a tomato-lemon mixture until it was falling-off-the-bone tender. When we made it some time later, there was so much sauce—much more than a loaf of bread could sop up. Inhaling the fragrant broth, we remembered a lamb ragù we enjoyed in Sicily that had a similar taste. Why not use the lamb sauce on pasta for a first course? Often there is surplus lamb and extra juice after everyone has been sufficiently satisfied. So chop up any remaining lamb, combine it with the leftover liquid, and enjoy it served over pasta the next day.

If your butcher cannot provide you with a lamb shoulder (this delectable cut is often sold boned or cut up to use as stew meat), substitute a bone-in leg of lamb.

1 lemon
⅔ cup freshly squeezed lemon juice
1½ cups tomato paste, preferably organic (two 6-ounce cans)
½ teaspoon sea salt
One 5- to 6-pound bone-in lamb shoulder
5 to 6 sprigs fresh thyme
Freshly ground black pepper
1 pound dried penne
Freshly grated Pecorino Romano

1. Heat the oven to 350 degrees.

2. Remove the yellow zest from the lemon with a sharp vegetable peeler, being careful to leave the bitter white pith behind. Set aside. (You can squeeze the peeled lemon as part of the volume of the juice.)

3. Stir together the lemon juice, tomato paste, salt, and 2 cups water; add the lemon zest.

4. Place the lamb in a roaster with a tight-fitting lid that is just large enough to hold the meat snugly. Pour the tomato and lemon mixture over the meat. Add the thyme and a liberal amount of black pepper. Drape a piece of moistened parchment paper directly over the lamb and liquid.

Cover the roaster and bake for 1 hour. Lower the oven temperature to 325 degrees and roast an additional hour, or until the lamb is very tender—almost falling off the bone. Taste the sauce and add more salt if necessary. Keep the lamb warm while you prepare the pasta course.

5. Bring a large pot of water to a boil. Generously salt the water and drop in the penne. Cook, stirring often, until al dente. Drain the pasta and transfer it to a heated serving bowl. Nudge the lamb to one side of the roaster and tip the pan a bit to ladle enough of the tomato-lemon sauce over the penne to coat it nicely. There should be a little puddle of sauce on the bottom of the bowl. Sprinkle a liberal amount of Pecorino Romano over the pasta and toss. Serve right away with extra cheese passed at the table.

6. For the main course, slice the lamb, place it on a heated platter, and nap it with some of the remaining sauce. Serve with or without a vegetable accompaniment.

on top of spaghetti...

Pasta with Egg and Cheese

◆ Linguine with Mozzarella, Egg, and Capocollo ◆

Serves 6 to 8 as a first course or 4 to 6 as a main course

Fresh mozzarella is just the right complement to the capocollo in this dish. The delicate flavor of the smooth, creamy cheese gives balance to the gutsy sauce.

You can substitute an equal amount of prosciutto or Italian salami for the capocollo for a slightly different-tasting dish. Be sure to have extra grated cheese to pass at the table.

> 3 large eggs, at room temperature
> ½ cup freshly grated Parmigiano-Reggiano
> Pinch of salt
> 4 tablespoons extra virgin olive oil
> 3 ounces (½ to ⅔ cup) finely chopped capocollo
> 2 teaspoons coarsely chopped fresh sage (do not substitute dried sage)
> 1 pound dried linguine
> 2 balls of fresh mozzarella (6 ounces total), cut into a small dice (see Pasta Pantry)

1. Bring a large pot of water to a boil.

2. Mix the eggs, Parmigiano-Reggiano, and salt together in a small bowl. Set aside.

3. Heat the olive oil, capocollo, and sage in a large straight-sided sauté pan over moderate heat. Cook, stirring from time to time, until the capocollo gives off some of its fat and begins to crisp up. Ladle ½ cup boiling water from the pasta pot into the sauté pan and cook until most of the liquid has evaporated. Set aside over the lowest possible heat. If the mixture becomes dry, add a tablespoon or two of additional boiling water.

4. Stir a generous amount of salt into the boiling water and toss in the linguine. Cook at a full rolling boil, stirring often, until al dente. Just before draining the pasta, scatter the mozzarella over the bottom of the sauté pan to soften.

5. Drain the pasta, reserving ½ cup of the cooking water, and toss the linguine into the sauté pan. Over low heat, toss the pasta in the sauce until combined with the mozzarella. If the pasta seems too dry, add some reserved pasta water, a tablespoon at a time, to moisten. The cheese will stretch into strings as you toss. Off the heat, fold in the egg and Parmigiano mixture and toss until every strand of linguine is coated. The sauce should be creamy. If the eggs have not thickened, stir over very low heat until the eggs cling to the pasta. Serve immediately with extra grated Parmigiano passed at the table.

Fettuccine with Mascarpone and Parmigiano-Reggiano

Serves 6 to 8 as a first course or 4 to 6 as a main course

For us, this sauce brings together the fundamentals of Italian cooking: quality, simplicity, clarity, and balance. By itself, the recipe defines our style. There are no extraneous components. Each ingredient is essential.

This is a delicate dish with a silky sauce that clings to the pasta. Buy fettuccine packaged in nests rather than flat. The flat strands tend to stick together in the boiling water no matter how much you stir them.

4 large eggs
6 tablespoons mascarpone
1 teaspoon sea salt
24 turns of the pepper mill
1 pound dried fettuccine
1 cup freshly grated Parmigiano-Reggiano, plus extra to pass at the table

1. Bring a large pot of water to a boil.

2. Whisk the eggs, mascarpone, salt, and pepper in a heatproof mixing bowl that is large enough to sit on top of your pasta pot. Set aside.

3. Add a generous amount of salt to the boiling water, drop in the fettuccine, and cook at a full rolling boil, stirring frequently, until al dente. While the pasta is cooking, rest the mixing bowl above the boiling water to warm the mixture, stirring frequently, to prevent the eggs from curdling. When the fettuccine is al dente, drain it and toss the pasta into the mascarpone mixture. Fold in the Parmigiano-Reggiano, toss, and serve immediately. Pass extra cheese and the pepper mill at the table.

Spaghetti with Creamy Egg, Prosciutto, and Spicy Arugula

Serves 3 to 4 as a first course

Arugula is a peppery green that adds spice to salads, soups, pasta, and risotto. Here it adds pizzazz to this pasta sauce rich with eggs, prosciutto, and cheese.

Arugula becomes more assertive as it matures. If baby leaves are unavailable, use a smaller amount of large leaves. Cut the big ones up into a fine chiffonade by stacking the leaves on top of one another, rolling them up lengthwise, and slicing the roll crosswise to make fine, thin strips so they wilt quickly into the sauce.

If your prosciutto is particularly salty, you may need no additional salt in the recipe.

> 2 large eggs, at room temperature
> Pinch of sea salt (optional)
> ¼ cup freshly grated Parmigiano-Reggiano
> ¼ cup freshly grated Pecorino Romano
> ⅓ cup finely chopped prosciutto
> 1½ teaspoons finely chopped fresh hot pepper
> 1 plump garlic clove, peeled and finely minced
> ¼ cup extra virgin olive oil
> 3 cups loosely packed baby arugula leaves
> 8 ounces dried spaghetti
> 1 tablespoon unsalted butter

1. Bring a large pot of water to a boil for the pasta.

2. Mix together the eggs, optional salt, Parmigiano-Reggiano, and Pecorino Romano in a small mixing bowl. Set aside.

3. Heat the prosciutto, hot pepper, garlic, and olive oil in a large straight-sided sauté pan over moderate heat. Cook, stirring often, until the garlic is golden. Add the arugula and ⅓ cup boiling pasta water to the pan, taking care not to burn yourself as the oil may spatter. Toss together to wilt the arugula. Most of the water will evaporate. Set aside off the heat.

4. Generously salt the pasta water and drop in the spaghetti. Cook, stirring often, until al dente. Drain the pasta, reserving about ½ cup of the cooking water. Transfer the pasta to the sauté pan and toss over low heat. Add a few tablespoons of pasta water and the butter and toss again. Off the heat, quickly add the egg and cheese mixture and toss constantly until the strands of spaghetti are coated. The eggs should remain creamy without curdling. Serve right away in warmed bowls.

◆ Spaghetti with Tripe-No-Tripe Tomato Sauce ◆

Serves 6 to 8 as a first course or 4 to 6 as a main course

George loves the tripe in tomato sauce served at one of our favorite restaurants, Mike's Kitchen in Cranston, Rhode Island. Johanne prefers eggs *disguised* as tripe, a specialty of Rome for fast days and meatless meals.

Beaten eggs are made into a thin *frittata*, or omelet, and cut it into strips that look like tripe. The egg strips are then stewed in the same kind of tomato sauce one would prepare for real tripe. Lavishly showered with Pecorino Romano, it makes a satisfying meal. We turn the Roman dish into a meatless, robust sauce for pasta. Be sure to have a chewy, country bread on hand so none of the sauce goes to waste.

¼ cup plus 1 tablespoon extra virgin olive oil
¾ cup finely chopped onions
2 sprigs fresh flat-leaf parsley, leaves only, finely chopped
Rounded ½ cup finely chopped carrots
½ cup finely chopped celery
1 plump garlic clove, peeled and finely chopped
¼ teaspoon crushed red pepper flakes, plus more to pass at the table
1 teaspoon sea salt
½ cup dry white wine
3½ cups chopped canned tomato pulp and juice
12 to 15 large fresh mint leaves
1 bay leaf, preferably fresh
One 1-inch by 3-inch piece Parmigiano-Reggiano rind (optional)
3 large eggs
¼ cup freshly grated Parmigiano-Reggiano
1 pound dried spaghetti
Freshly grated Pecorino Romano

on top of spaghetti...

1. Heat ¼ cup olive oil in an earthenware pot or heavy-bottomed saucepan with the onions, parsley, carrots, celery, garlic, red pepper flakes, and ½ teaspoon salt. Sauté over moderate heat until the vegetables are very soft without allowing them to brown, 20 to 25 minutes. Add the wine, raise the heat, and allow the wine to all but evaporate, stirring often. Add the tomatoes and 2 cups water. Tear half the mint leaves into bits and add to the sauce with the bay leaf and cheese rind if you wish. Cover, bring to a boil, and lower the heat to maintain a gentle simmer. Cook for 30 minutes. Taste the sauce and add more salt if necessary.

2. Meanwhile, make the fake tripe: Whisk the eggs until just combined. Stir in the grated Parmigiano-Reggiano. Finely mince the remaining mint leaves and add to the eggs with ¼ teaspoon salt. Heat the remaining tablespoon olive oil in a large nonstick sauté pan with sloping sides. Pour in the egg mixture all at once. Tilt the pan and swirl the eggs to cover the bottom of the pan—like making a crepe—so that you have a thin *frittata*, or omelet. Cook until set, about 2 minutes. Loosen the frittata and flip over to cook the other side for an additional minute. Transfer to a cutting board. When cool enough to handle, roll up the frittata and cut it into ½-inch-wide strips of fake tripe. Set aside.

3. After the tomato sauce has cooked for 30 minutes, remove the bay leaf and cheese rinds, if you have used any, and purée the sauce with an immersion blender. Bring back to a simmer, drop in the egg strips, and simmer gently, covered, for an additional 30 minutes over very low heat.

4. Bring a large pot of water to a boil. Generously salt the water and drop in the spaghetti. Cook, stirring often, until al dente. Drain the pasta and transfer to a heated serving bowl. Nudge the fake tripe to one side of the pot and ladle enough of the sauce onto the spaghetti to coat each strand (don't worry if a few egg strips slip in, too). Top with fake tripe and any sauce clinging to it. Sprinkle with plenty of Pecorino Romano. Pass more cheese at the table along with additional crushed red pepper. Serve right away.

◆ Spaghetti with Egg, Pancetta, and Saffron ◆

Serves 4 as a first course and 2 to 3 as a main course

Saffron is the most valuable of spices. Although costly, a little bit goes a long way, giving this spaghetti its penetrating taste and lovely orange hue.

Choose saffron threads rather than ground saffron. The ground spice can be easily adulterated with less costly powders of similar color, like turmeric or safflower.

⅛ teaspoon saffron threads
2 large eggs, at room temperature
½ cup freshly grated Pecorino Romano
½ cup freshly grated Parmigiano-Reggiano
Sea salt
⅓ cup (1½ ounces) finely diced pancetta
Crushed red pepper flakes
1 to 2 tablespoons extra virgin olive oil
8 ounces dried spaghetti

1. Bring a large pot of water to a boil for the pasta.

2. Soak the saffron in ¼ cup warm water for about 10 minutes.

3. Whisk the eggs in a bowl until just combined. Stir in the cheeses. Add a few pinches of salt. Set aside.

4. Over moderate heat, sauté the pancetta in a large skillet with a pinch of red pepper flakes and 1 tablespoon of the olive oil. Cook until the pancetta has released some of its fat and begins to brown. Add the saffron and water and stir with a wooden spoon to scrape up any bits of pancetta that may have stuck to the pan. Set aside on a flame tamer over the lowest possible heat.

5. Generously salt the pasta water and drop in the spaghetti. Cook, stirring often, until al dente. Drain the spaghetti and toss with the pancetta and remaining olive oil in the skillet. Over low heat, toss and fold over the pasta to be sure each strand is coated with the pancetta and oil. Remove from the heat.

6. Working quickly, pour the egg mixture over the spaghetti and toss to combine. The eggs should thicken on the strands of the hot spaghetti and become smooth and creamy without curdling. If the sauce remains too thin, return the skillet to the lowest possible heat, tossing the pasta constantly until you have the proper consistency. Serve right away.

◆ Spaghetti with Scrambled Eggs, Asparagus, and Mushrooms ◆

Serves 4 as a first course and 2 to 3 as a main course

Fresh asparagus and mushrooms make a lovely pairing in this pasta dish, and the scrambled eggs bring everything together in a satisfying jumble.

Purchase asparagus that are firm with tightly closed tips. Mushrooms should be firm, too, with unblemished caps that have not splayed open.

2 tablespoons unsalted butter
2 tablespoons extra virgin olive oil
½ cup finely chopped onions
8 ounces fresh asparagus, trimmed and cleaned
6 to 8 medium (3 ounces) fresh mushrooms, trimmed, cleaned, and finely chopped
3 large eggs, at room temperature
¼ teaspoon sea salt
½ cup freshly grated Parmigiano-Reggiano
8 ounces dried spaghetti
Freshly grated Pecorino Romano

1. Bring a large pot of water to a boil for the pasta.

2. Heat the butter, olive oil, and onions in a large straight-sided sauté pan over moderate heat. Cook, stirring often, until the onions are very soft and completely cooked through without browning.

3. Slice off the tips of the asparagus and cut them in half vertically. Coarsely chop the remaining stalks.

4. When the onions are cooked, add the asparagus and mushrooms to the sauté pan. Cook over moderately high heat, stirring often, until the vegetables are soft, about 8 minutes. Set aside and keep warm.

5. Break the eggs into a mixing bowl and beat them with a fork until the whites and yolks are just combined. Stir in a few pinches of salt and Parmigiano-Reggiano. Set aside.

6. Generously salt the pasta water and drop in the spaghetti. Cook, stirring often, until al dente. Drain the pasta, reserving about 1 cup of the cooking water. Transfer the spaghetti to the sauté pan with the vegetables. Toss over moderately low heat until every strand of spaghetti is coat-

ed. If it seems dry, add some of the pasta water, a tablespoon at a time. Pour in the egg mixture and stir and toss just until the eggs begin to develop soft curds. Remove from the heat when the eggs are a little underdone as they retain heat and will continue to cook. Serve right away in heated bowls. Pass the Pecorino Romano at the table.

◆ Penne with Anna's Idea ◆

Serves 6 to 8 as a first course or 4 to 6 as a main course

Talking about food in Italy is a hoot. Everyone has an opinion about everything they eat. Discussions often include verbal recipe swapping or tales of something wonderful feasted upon at a family gathering, at a friend's house, or in a restaurant.

Our friend Anna Tasca Lanza, a great Sicilian cook and culinary expert, always has more than food to pass around her lively table. She loves to share her latest edible discovery as much as an anecdote about a nearly extinct fruit she is protecting in her garden, or a forgotten traditional recipe she has ferreted out and made new again. She gave us the idea for this penne made with cheese and pasta water. The exact details of the conversation are long gone—was it ricotta mixed with local melting cheeses? Did it come from Palermo, or Catania, or somewhere else in Italy? Its provenance may be unknown, but the visual impression of cheese and water whipped into a creamy emulsion stayed with us. This is how we have reinvented it.

1 pound dried penne
1 cup fresh ricotta
¼ cup mascarpone
⅔ cup freshly grated Parmigiano-Reggiano
⅔ cup freshly grated Pecorino Romano
1 heaping cup finely diced fresh mozzarella
Freshly ground black pepper
Sea salt

1. Bring a large pot of water to a boil. Generously salt the water and drop in the penne. Cook, stirring often, at a full rolling boil.

2. Mix the ricotta, mascarpone, Parmigiano-Reggiano, and Pecorino Romano together in a large mixing bowl. Fold in the mozzarella. Drizzle in ½ cup of the boiling pasta water while whipping the ingredients together with a wooden spoon. Beat the cheeses together until you have a creamy emulsion with lumps of mozzarella. Add a generous amount of pepper and stir it in. Season with salt.

3. When the penne is al dente, drain it, reserving about ½ cup of the pasta water. Transfer the penne to the mixing bowl and toss in the sauce. The pasta should be nicely coated. If it seems dry, add some pasta water, a tablespoon at a time, until you have a loose consistency without the

noodles clumping together. Serve right away in heated bowls.

Fresh Herb Lovers' Idea

Add ¼ cup finely chopped parsley, 1 teaspoon finely chopped rosemary, and 1 teaspoon finely chopped sage to the cheese mixture after seasoning with pepper and salt in step 2. Fold in 10 roughly torn basil leaves and 10 roughly torn mint leaves. Proceed with the recipe.

Gorgonzola Lovers' Idea

For a sharper cheese flavor, beat ⅓ cup diced Gorgonzola into the ricotta, mascarpone, Parmigiano, and Pecorino in step 2. Fold in the mozzarella and proceed with the recipe.

on top of spaghetti...

Fettuccine with Eggs, Cheese, and Tomatoes

Serves 4 as a first course or 2 to 3 as a main course

The success of this dish depends entirely on the taste of the tomatoes. They should be full of flavor with a hint of acidity. Fresh plum tomatoes work best. Off-season, when no good tomatoes are to be found, substitute an equal amount of chopped canned tomatoes in heavy purée.

The tomato-egg sauce is quite delicate. Spice lovers can opt for the pepper/cayenne addition.

---

2 large eggs, at room temperature
¼ cup freshly grated Parmigiano-Reggiano
¼ cup freshly grated Pecorino Romano
2 tablespoons unsalted butter, cut into small cubes
Sea salt
Freshly ground black pepper (optional)
Cayenne (optional)
½ to ⅔ cup peeled, seeded, and chopped fresh plum tomatoes
8 ounces dried fettuccine or fresh fettuccine (page 214)

---

1. Bring a large pot of water to a boil for the pasta.

2. Whisk the eggs in a small mixing bowl until just combined. Fold in the cheeses, half the butter, and a few pinches of salt. Add either (or both) black pepper or cayenne if you like. Set aside.

3. Heat the tomatoes in a large straight-sided sauté pan with the remaining butter. Season with salt. Keep warm over the lowest possible heat so the tomatoes cook through but do not reduce to a paste. They should be neither watery nor too thick.

4. Generously salt the boiling water and drop in the fettuccine. Cook, stirring often, at a full rolling boil until al dente. Drain, reserving ½ cup of the pasta water. Transfer the pasta to the sauté pan and toss to coat the pasta with the tomatoes. Off the heat, quickly pour in the egg mixture all at once, while stirring and tossing constantly to prevent the eggs from curdling. The sauce should cling to the fettuccine and nicely coat each ribbon of pasta. If the mixture seems dry, add some of the pasta water, a tablespoon at a time, until you have a velvety mixture with no evidence of curdled egg. Serve right away in warmed bowls. Pass extra cheese at the table.

◆ Spaghetti with Eggs, Sausage, Peppers, and Onions ◆

Serves 4 as a first course or 2 to 3 as a main course

～～～～～～～～～～～～～～～～～～～～～～～～～～

There is nothing quite like the fragrance of sweet peppers and onions frying in fruity olive oil. It's a great melding that evokes long-ago and recent memories: the aroma of Johanne's cousin Theresa's late-night fried-pepper sandwich wafting from the kitchen in Maine—so compelling it wakes you up with hunger pangs. Or breakfast at George's house—Dad at the stove, after an early-morning harvest in his backyard garden, cooking peppers and onions for scrambled eggs.

Anyone who has walked through the food stalls at an Italian-American street fair will recall the appealing wall of scent that hits you as you stroll past the sausage vendors.

The homey combination—peppers and onions—is hard to beat. Add the perfect consorts: eggs, sausage, and spaghetti, and you have the makings of a very comforting meal. Purchase mild, sweet peppers—pale green Italian or Hungarian finger peppers or yellow banana peppers.

～～～～～～～～～～～～

2 large eggs
Pinch of crushed red pepper flakes
¼ teaspoon sea salt
¼ cup plus 2 tablespoons freshly grated Pecorino Romano
1 tablespoon extra virgin olive oil
1 tablespoon unsalted butter
2 sweet Italian pork sausages (6 to 8 ounces), cut into ⅜-inch rounds
1½ cups thinly sliced sweet Italian or yellow banana peppers
¼ cup finely chopped onions
Scant tablespoon chopped fresh flat-leaf parsley
8 ounces dried spaghetti

1. Bring a large pot of water to a boil for the pasta.

2. Mix the eggs together with the crushed red pepper flakes, salt, and cheese. Set aside.

3. Heat the olive oil and butter in a large straight-sided sauté pan. Add the sausages and brown on all sides (the butter may turn a nutty brown; that's okay). Add the peppers, onions, and parsley and sauté over moderately high heat to cook

on top of spaghetti…

the vegetables. When the onions brown, stir in ¼ cup of the pasta water, scrape up any sausage bits sticking to the pan, and lower the heat so the mixture is just barely simmering.

4. Generously salt the pasta water and drop in the spaghetti. Cook, stirring often, until al dente. Drain the pasta, reserving about 1 cup water. Transfer the spaghetti to the sauté pan. Toss over low heat until every strand is coated with the cooking juices. If it seems dry, add more pasta water, a tablespoon at a time. The spaghetti should move freely without clumping together. Off the heat, add the egg and cheese mixture. Toss constantly until the spaghetti is generously coated with the creamy eggs. If the mixture doesn't thicken enough to coat the spaghetti, return the pan to low heat and toss until it thickens around the strands without curdling. Serve right away in warmed bowls.

Baked Pasta

Baked pasta, or pasta al forno, has been a popular menu item from the day we opened our restaurant in January 1980. Since then, the repertoire has expanded, but the essential elements are the same—macaroni tossed with cream and/or tomato; a single cheese or a combination of two or more; a seasonal vegetable or some meat perhaps; and aromatics. Baked in the intense heat of deck (or wood-burning) ovens, the pasta emerges piping hot, bubbling, and tinged with the tip of a charred noodle here and there. The crunchy bits on top combined with the softer macaroni below make a simply irresistible dish.

When we began to compile the recipes of Al Forno Restaurant for our first cookbook, *Cucina Simpatica,* it was obvious we had to include some for baked pasta. To our delight, those recipes received the most enthusiastic raves from our friends, customers, and readers. They loved the ease of putting them together—especially for entertaining, but also for a simple family meal. It is the alchemy, too, the magic that occurs in the oven that beguiles anyone who tastes the pasta. The macaroni soaks up the flavor of the liquid surrounding it like a sponge. The elements don't just mingle; they band together and unify.

In this chapter, we offer a new collection of pasta al forno, with something appropriate for any time of the year.

Here are some tips for success: Choose a sturdy macaroni and parboil it to order—just before you are ready to mix it with the sauce and bake. The ingredients for the sauce can be put together ahead of time, combined in a mixing bowl, covered, and refrigerated for several hours. That leaves you with very little last-minute preparation—it takes a mere 4 to 5 minutes to parboil the pasta (a good rule of thumb is to parboil the pasta for 1 minute less than half the cooking time suggested on the package). Although there is some leeway in timing, keep in mind that pasta—even when it is only parboiled—continues to soften. Mixed with liquid, even cold liquid, the macaroni will absorb some or most of it and lose its firmness. For this reason, don't be tempted to cook the pasta, mix it with the sauce, put it into a baking dish, and leave it in the refrigerator for hours—or even 30 minutes—until dinnertime. If the pasta is soft before it hits the oven, it will be devoid of character and much less delectable. In other words, you will end up with a gummy mess. Baked macaroni is best when there is a combination of textures—soft portions of pasta on the bottom, al dente portions in the middle and toward the top, and crunchy bits poking out above the rest that are browned by the flash of oven heat. The whole should be moist, with sauce bathing the noodles.

Size and depth matter when choosing a baking dish. Small, individual shallow ones (1 to 1½ cups for appetizer portions; ones with a 2- to 3-cup capacity for main-course portions) are ideal. Transferred from the oven to napkin-lined plates, they can be brought to the table quickly while the pasta is still bubbling—filling the room with enticing aroma. You can use one large dish instead with a 10- to 12-cup capacity (or two smaller dishes with a 5- to 6-cup capacity each) for any of the recipes. Be sure the dish is shallow. Using a deep casserole will increase the baking time and soften the pasta too much. Shallow dishes create more surface area, allow the pasta to cook quickly, and afford the greatest opportunities for the crispy spots to develop on top.

For optimum crunchies, when you transfer the mixture to the baking vessels, don't try to smooth out the surface of the pasta or push the macaroni down into the sauce. The portions that are not submerged will be the ones to crisp up in the oven.

◆ Ziti Baked with Cream and Parmigiano-Reggiano ◆

Serves 6 to 8 as a first course or 4 to 6 as a main course

This deluxe pasta brims with the mellow, nutty taste of Parmigiano-Reggiano. The cheese is a vital ingredient in this dish, so it must be the real thing. Parmigiano's melting ability acts as a binding agent to create a sensual texture fit for the glitziest occasion or any day when a little luxury is warranted or needed.

2½ cups heavy cream
3 cups freshly grated Parmigiano-Reggiano
¼ teaspoon sea salt
Freshly ground white pepper
1 pound dried ziti
4 tablespoons unsalted butter

1. Preheat the oven to 500 degrees.

2. Bring a large pot of water to a boil for the pasta.

3. In a large mixing bowl, combine the cream with all but ¼ cup of the cheese. Add salt and pepper to taste. Set aside.

4. Generously salt the boiling water and drop in the ziti. Cook the pasta, stirring often, for 5 to 6 minutes. The ziti will be parboiled and too hard to eat; it cooks further in the oven. Drain in a colander, reserving about 1 cup water. Transfer the pasta to the cream mixture in the bowl. Toss to combine. There should be plenty of liquid surrounding the pasta. If it seems too dry or too thick, add some of the pasta water, a tablespoon at a time, until the pasta moves freely in the sauce. Divide the mixture among 6 to 8 small, individual shallow ceramic gratin dishes (1½- to 2-cup capacity) for a first course or 4 to 6 medium, individual gratin dishes for a main course. Sprinkle with the remaining cheese and dot with butter. Bake until the pasta is bubbly, hot, and lightly browned on top, about 10 minutes.

The Ultimate Macaroni and Cheese

On January 2, 2000, we celebrated the twentieth anniversary of Al Forno Restaurant—and the millennium. We prepared a feast for a small group of friends. No one remembers any course but the baked pasta! To the above recipe we added thick slices of fresh black truffle, nestled underneath the top layer of ziti, cream, and cheese.

Truffles come in colors: black and white (or mottled deep charcoal and beige). The best black ones come from France and the most prized whites are found in Piemonte, the northwestern corner of Italy. While black truffles take to heat and can be cooked briefly (as we did with our showstopper macaroni and cheese), the white ones are so delicate they must be shaved raw into paper-thin slices over the pasta just before s erving. There is much debate over which truffle is the most ambrosial. They are both heavenly, and incomparable. Either one will give you a treat—it might be a once-in-a-millennium extravagance—but it makes a splash no one will soon forget.

Shells Baked with Tomato, Cream, Corn, and Five Cheeses

Serves 6 to 8 as a first course or 4 to 6 as a main course

Rhode Island cannot boast about a long growing season like California or Florida, but our short, intensely hot spell in the summer months produces superb fruits and vegetables just the same. Our corn, for instance, is unparalleled—especially the crops grown near the ocean, where the moist salt air and fog contribute to its taste.

Corn arrived in Italy from the New World in the sixteenth century. Ground into cornmeal, it is the main ingredient for polenta and remains a staple of the Italian diet. Fresh, sweet corn on the cob, however, is yet to be appreciated and is largely unavailable, while insipid canned kernels are finding their way into inferior salads. We freely admit to being dilettantes using native corn in this pasta. If the wily Italians could crow about corn as good as ours, it would be as popular and prized as porcini mushrooms! We therefore offer this pasta without apologies.

2 cups heavy cream
1 cup chopped canned tomatoes
¾ cup freshly grated Pecorino Romano
¾ cup coarsely shredded fontina
4 tablespoons crumbled Gorgonzola
2 tablespoons fresh ricotta
2 small (4 ounces total) balls of fresh
    mozzarella (see Pasta Pantry), sliced
½ to ¾ teaspoon sea salt
2 cups fresh cooked corn kernels
6 fresh basil leaves, chopped
1 pound dried conchiglie rigate, or ridged
    pasta shells
4 tablespoons unsalted butter

1. Preheat the oven to 500 degrees. Bring a large pot of water to a boil for the pasta.

2. In a mixing bowl, combine all the ingredients except the pasta and butter. Stir well to combine.

3. Generously salt the boiling water and drop in the pasta. Parboil for 5 minutes, stirring often. Drain the pasta (it will be too hard to eat; it cooks further in the oven) and add to the ingredients in the mixing bowl. Toss to combine. Divide the

mixture among 6 to 8 small, individual shallow ceramic gratin dishes (1½- to 2-cup capacity) for a first course or 4 to 6 medium individual gratin dishes for a main course. Dot with butter and bake until bubbly and brown on top, about 10 minutes.

◆ Baked Shells with Cauliflower and Ricotta ◆

Serves 6 to 8 as a first course or 4 to 6 as a main course

In New England, we're used to cold weather and cold weather vegetables. For most of the winter, our markets are filled with sturdy choices from the cabbage family, or out-of-season produce from the South or West Coast. Coming up with a new way to prepare cauliflower is a challenge, but this pasta fits the bill. The humble vegetable is gussied up with cream, cheese, and the occasional sweet burst of dried currants.

3½ cups heavy cream
1½ cups (3 ounces) freshly grated Pecorino Romano
¼ teaspoon sea salt
¼ to ½ cup fresh ricotta
Freshly ground black pepper
6 cups cauliflower florets and stems, cut into small pieces (1 medium cauliflower)
1 pound dried conchiglie or penne
1 tablespoon currants
4 tablespoons unsalted butter

1. Heat the oven to 500 degrees.

2. Bring 6 quarts of water to a boil in a large pot.

3. In a large mixing bowl, combine the cream, Pecorino Romano, salt, ricotta, and as much pepper as you like. Mix well and set aside.

4. Generously salt the boiling water and drop in the cauliflower. As soon as the water returns to a boil, add the pasta. Cook, stirring often, for 5 to 6 minutes. The pasta will be parboiled and too hard to eat; it cooks further in the oven. Drain and transfer the pasta and vegetables to the mixing bowl with the cream and cheeses. Mix well. Sprinkle over the currants and incorporate them in the mixture, distributing evenly.

5. For a first course, divide the mixture among 6 to 8 individual shallow ceramic gratin dishes (1½- to 2-cup capacity). For a main course, divide the mixture among 4 to 6 larger gratin dishes. Dot with butter and bake until the pasta is bubbling, hot, and lightly browned on top, about 10 minutes.

Variation

For a touch of luxury, an element of mystery, and a flash of sunny yellow on gray, frosty days, try this recipe with saffron. Steep ½ to 1 teaspoon of saffron threads (depending on the intensity and quality of the saffron) in the cream for an hour before preparing the recipe. The color alone will bring cries of delight at the table.

◆ Ziti Baked with Mushrooms, Cream, and Parmigiano-Reggiano ◆

Serves 6 to 8 as a first course or 4 to 6 as a main course

We have made this pasta with all sorts of wild mushrooms—porcini, chanterelles, and morels. Cultivated ones—white, brown, portobello, or oyster—work just as well. There are so many interesting mushrooms available today in well-stocked supermarkets, it is worth experimenting with them as they each have their own allure.

4 tablespoons unsalted butter
4 tablespoons extra virgin olive oil
¼ cup finely chopped onions
¼ cup finely chopped shallots
5 to 6 cups finely chopped wild or cultivated mushrooms
Heaping ½ cup finely chopped fresh fennel bulb
¼ teaspoon sea salt
2 tablespoons chopped fresh flat-leaf parsley
2 tablespoons chopped fresh mint leaves
2 bay leaves, preferably fresh
½ teaspoon fresh thyme leaves
½ teaspoon chopped fresh marjoram
2½ cups heavy cream
1½ cups Parmigiano-Reggiano
Freshly ground white pepper
1 pound dried conchiglie rigate, or ridged pasta shells

1. Preheat the oven to 500 degrees. Bring 6 quarts of water to a boil in a large pot.

2. Heat the butter and olive oil in a large straight-sided sauté pan. Add the onions and shallots and sauté over moderate heat until they are translucent and tender, about 5 minutes. Raise the heat

and add the mushrooms, fennel, and salt. Stir in the parsley, mint, bay leaves, thyme, and marjoram. Cook, stirring often, until the mushrooms and fennel have cooked through and are very soft. Taste and add more salt if necessary. Transfer to a large mixing bowl. Add the heavy cream, 1 cup of the Parmigiano-Reggiano, and white pepper to taste.

3. Generously salt the boiling water and drop in the pasta. Parboil at a full rolling boil, stirring often, for 4 to 5 minutes. Drain the pasta, reserving about 1 cup water. Toss the pasta into the mixing bowl with the mushroom mixture. Stir together to combine. If the mixture seems too dry or too thick, add some of the reserved water, a tablespoon at a time, until the pasta moves freely with plenty of liquid around it.

4. Transfer to small or medium individual shallow baking dishes or one large shallow gratin dish. Bake for 8 to 10 minutes, until bubbly and browned on top. Serve right away, sprinkled with the remaining Parmigiano-Reggiano.

Penne Baked with Asparagus, Cream, and Pancetta

Serves 6 to 8 as a first course or 4 to 6 as a main course

Asparagus are one of the most welcome harbingers of spring. We like them hot, cold, roasted, steamed, or boiled. We eat them plain or lavishly garnished with eggs and Parmigiano-Reggiano. Their unique taste beautifully flavors this baked pasta. If you have a little more or a little less asparagus on hand, it's okay; the measurement doesn't have to be precise.

2½ cups heavy cream
¾ cup freshly grated Parmigiano-Reggiano
¾ cup freshly grated Pecorino Romano
1 pound cooked asparagus, cut on the diagonal into small pieces
Sea salt
1 pound dried penne or conchiglie shell pasta
¼ cup chopped pancetta

1. Heat the oven to 500 degrees. Bring a large pot of water to a boil.

2. In a large mixing bowl, combine the cream, cheeses, and asparagus. Season with a little salt, keeping in mind the pancetta will add saltiness, too. Set aside.

3. Add a generous amount of salt to the boiling water and drop in the pasta. Cook, stirring often, for 4 to 5 minutes. The pasta will be parboiled and too hard to eat; it cooks further in the oven. Drain, reserving about 1 cup water, and transfer the pasta to the mixing bowl with the cream and cheeses. Mix well. If the mixture seems too dry or too thick, add some of the pasta water, a tablespoon at a time, until the pasta moves freely with plenty of liquid surrounding it.

4. Transfer to a large shallow baking/serving dish or individual shallow baking dishes. Dot evenly with the pieces of pancetta and bake until the pasta is bubbling, hot, and lightly browned on top, about 10 minutes. Check the pasta about halfway through to be sure there is enough liquid in the dish. If it seems dry, add a few tablespoons of cream or reserved pasta water.

on top of spaghetti...

◆ Penne Baked with Eggplant, Tomato, and Mozzarella ◆

Serves 6 to 8 as a first course or 4 to 6 as a main course

Gooey and delicious, this pasta is addictive. Buffalo milk mozzarella will give you a creamier sauce, while cow's milk mozzarella will melt into supple strings to twirl around your fork.

4 cups diced eggplant
1 cup finely chopped onions
6 cups tomato juice, preferably organic
½ cup extra virgin olive oil
1 plump garlic clove, peeled and finely chopped
½ teaspoon sea salt
Pinch of cayenne
1 pound dried penne
2 cups (12 to 14 ounces total) diced fresh buffalo or cow's milk mozzarella
Freshly grated Parmigiano-Reggiano

1. Heat the oven to 500 degrees.

2. Combine the eggplant, onions, tomato juice, olive oil, garlic, salt, and cayenne in a small saucepan. Cover, bring to a boil, lower the heat, and simmer gently for about 20 minutes, or until the eggplant and onions are soft. Taste and add more salt if necessary. Set aside.

3. Bring a large pot of water to a boil for the pasta. Generously salt the water and drop in the penne. Cook, stirring often, for 4 to 5 minutes (the pasta will be parboiled and too hard to eat; it cooks further in the oven). Drain and transfer to a large mixing bowl. Top with the eggplant and tomato sauce. Fold in the mozzarella. Transfer to a large shallow baking dish or individual shallow baking dishes and bake until the pasta is bubbling hot and beginning to brown on top, 10 to 15 minutes. Serve right away with Parmigiano-Reggiano passed at the table.

◆ Shells Baked with Spinach, Herbs, and Walnuts ◆

Serves 6 to 8 as a first course or 4 to 6 as a main course

The flavors of *pansoti con salsa di noci*—herb- and cheese-filled ravioli with walnut sauce—inspire this unusual baked macaroni. A specialty of Liguria, the pansoti are traditionally made with two ingredients that never travel beyond the region—preboggion, an intensely flavored herb and plant mixture, and prescinsena, a slightly tart cow's milk cheese. A combination of spinach, arugula, and cultivated herbs replaces the indigenous preboggion, and the prescinsena is replaced with sour cream.

1¼ cups finely chopped onions
2 fresh bay leaves or 1 dried bay leaf
1 small garlic clove, peeled and finely minced
2 tablespoons unsalted butter
2 tablespoons extra virgin olive oil
½ teaspoon sea salt
2½ cups heavy cream
4 cups tightly packed baby spinach, borage, watercress, or chicory leaves
1 cup tightly packed baby arugula leaves
1 teaspoon finely chopped fresh sage
½ teaspoon finely chopped fresh basil
1 teaspoon finely chopped fresh marjoram
¼ teaspoon finely chopped fresh summer savory
2 teaspoons finely chopped chives
1 cup finely chopped walnuts
½ cup cubed fontina
½ cup freshly grated Pecorino Romano
1 cup freshly grated Parmigiano-Reggiano
Freshly grated nutmeg
1 pound dried conchiglie rigate, or ridged pasta shells
3 tablespoons sour cream or crème fraîche

1. Combine the onions, bay leaves, garlic, butter, olive oil, and salt in a small saucepan. Sauté over moderately low heat until the onions and garlic are very soft and completely cooked through, about 15 minutes. Add the cream and scald—heat just until little bubbles form around the outside edge. Set aside off the heat for 30 minutes to steep together.

2. Bring a large pot of water to a boil for the pasta. Heat the oven to 500 degrees.

3. In another saucepan, drop the spinach and arugula leaves in boiling salted water. Cook, stirring often, until the greens are wilted, about 2 minutes. Drain in a colander.

4. When the greens are cool enough to handle, squeeze out as much water as possible. Transfer to a cutting board and finely chop. Combine the chopped greens, sage, basil, marjoram, summer savory, and chives in a large mixing bowl. Add the walnuts, fontina, Pecorino Romano, Parmigiano-Reggiano, and a good scraping of nutmeg (a microplane is the ideal tool for this). Remove and discard the bay leaves and add the cooled cream and sour cream to the mixing bowl. Stir to combine. Taste and add salt if necessary. Set aside.

5. Generously salt the boiling water and drop in the pasta. Cook, stirring often, to parboil, 4 to 5 minutes (the pasta will be too hard to eat; it will continue to cook in the oven). Drain the shells, reserving about 1 cup of the water. Toss the pasta with the ingredients in the mixing bowl until well combined; you want the shells to capture some of the walnuts, herbs, and cheese in their crannies. Add ½ cup reserved pasta water and toss again. Transfer to individual shallow baking dishes or a large shallow gratin dish. There should be ample liquid surrounding the pasta. If not, nap with additional pasta water. Bake until bubbly and hot, with some of the pasta shells browning on top. Serve right away.

◆ Pasta Baked with Peas and Ham ◆

Serves 6 to 8 as a first course or 4 to 6 as a main course

Peas have been appreciated in Rome for a long time. Ancient Romans first ate them cooked from their dried form. In the sixteenth century, when fresh garden peas were cultivated in Italy, the Romans embraced them, too. Today, almost every springtime menu will include *piselli al prosciutto*, or peas cooked with prosciutto. They make fine playmates; pork mingles nicely with sweet peas. Here, they team up with cream and cheese to make a standout pasta.

Use fresh peas if you have a vegetable garden or live close to a farm stand. Peas turn starchy in the blink of an eye and can be disappointing—especially when you factor in the time it takes to shuck them. There is no better choice for this pasta than superfresh peas. If they are unavailable, substitute quality frozen peas.

4 ounces prosciutto cotto, or cooked ham
1 cup blanched fresh or frozen peas
½ cup freshly grated Pecorino Romano
¾ cup freshly grated Grana Padano or Parmigiano-Reggiano
2½ cups heavy cream
¼ teaspoon fine sea salt
Freshly grated nutmeg
1 pound dried pasta shells, pipe rigate, or penne

1. Bring a large pot of water to a boil for the pasta. Heat the oven to 500 degrees.

2. Cut the ham into long, ½-inch-wide strips, then cut across to make 1- to 1½-inch-long pieces (you should have about 1 cup). Toss in a large mixing bowl. Add the peas, Pecorino Romano, ½ cup of the Grana Padano, cream, and salt. Mix together. Add just enough grated nutmeg for a good whiff to reach your nose. You want to flavor the cream discreetly. Fold it into the mixture and add more salt if necessary.

3. Generously salt the boiling water and drop in the pasta. Cook, stirring often, for 4 minutes. The pasta will be parboiled and too hard to eat; it cooks further in the oven. Drain the macaroni, reserving 1 cup of the water, and transfer

the pasta to the mixing bowl. Add ½ cup pasta water and toss again. There should be abundant liquid surrounding the pasta. Add more water if it looks too dry or too thick.

4. Transfer the pasta and its sauce to individual shallow baking dishes or to 1 or 2 large shallow baking dishes. Bake for 8 to 10 minutes (check halfway through the baking time and drizzle with more pasta water if necessary), until bubbly hot with a few browned noodles on top. Serve right away with the remaining Grana Padano passed at the table.

Penne Baked with Sausage, Broccoli, and Tomatoes

Serves 6 to 8 as a first course or 4 to 6 as a main course

~~~~~~

Choose crisp, fresh broccoli for this recipe and don't discard the stems! Using a vegetable peeler, peel away the tough skin until you reach the pale green interior, then chop up the stems and use them with the florets.

For the tomato sauce, you can use Pomodoro—Al Forno's Tomato Sauce (page 70) or A Simple Tomato Sauce (page 72) in its blended version.

~~~~~~

2 sweet Italian pork sausages (about 8 ounces)
2 heaping cups small broccoli florets and chopped stems
1 cup freshly grated Pecorino Romano, plus more to pass at the table
Crushed red pepper flakes
3½ cups tomato sauce
Sea salt
1 pound dried penne rigate

1. Bring a large pot of water to a boil. Heat the oven to 500 degrees.

2. With a fork, prick the sausages in a few places. Parboil them in lightly salted boiling water for 6 to 8 minutes. Remove with a slotted spoon and set aside. In the same water, cook the broccoli for 2 minutes. Remove with a slotted spoon and transfer to a large mixing bowl. Reserve the water.

3. Cut the sausages into ¼-inch-thick rings and add to the broccoli. Add the cheese, a pinch or two of red pepper flakes, and the tomato sauce. Taste and add salt if necessary. Set aside.

4. Generously salt the boiling pasta water and drop in the penne. Cook, stirring often, for 4 to 5 minutes. The pasta will be parboiled and too hard to eat; it cooks further in the oven. Drain the pasta and mix with the ingredients in the bowl. Stir in ½ to ¾ cup reserved sausage water—make sure there is plenty of liquid surrounding the penne. Transfer to individual shallow baking dishes or to 1 to 2 large shallow baking dishes. Bake for 8 to 10 minutes, or until bubbly hot with a few browned pasta quills on top. Serve right away with extra cheese passed at the table.

◆ Penne Baked with Zucchini and Tomatoes ◆

Serves 6 to 8 as a first course or 4 to 6 as a main course

Fresh zucchini and windowsill pots of basil can be found in our markets almost year-round. Quality fresh tomatoes, on the other hand, are strictly a summertime pleasure. This pasta is first-rate when made with ripe, garden tomatoes but no less delicious in cooler months when only canned ones are available. You can prepare this recipe with an equal amount of Pomodoro—Al Forno's Tomato Sauce (page 70) or A Simple Tomato Sauce (page 72). For lazy days, an excellent-quality, plain chopped canned tomato will be fine. If you use any of these substitutions, you may need to thin the sauce with a little pasta water, tossed with the macaroni before baking.

> 2 tablespoons extra virgin olive oil
> 2 cups diced small zucchini
> ½ teaspoon or more sea salt
> 1½ cups heavy cream
> 1½ cups chopped fresh peeled and seeded plum tomatoes
> ½ cup freshly grated Grana Padano or Parmigiano-Reggiano
> ½ cup freshly grated Pecorino Romano
> ½ cup chopped mozzarella
> ½ cup gently packed fresh basil leaves
> 1 pound dried penne rigate or pasta shells

1. Heat the oven to 500 degrees. Bring a large pot of water to a boil.

2. Heat the oil in a large skillet over moderately high heat. Add the zucchini, sprinkle with ¼ teaspoon salt, and sauté, tossing often, until it is tender but still retains its shape. Transfer to a large mixing bowl. Use a slotted spoon for this if the oil seems excessive.

3. Add the cream, tomatoes, and cheeses to the zucchini. Tear up the basil leaves and stir into the mixture with the remaining salt. Taste and add more salt if necessary. Set the sauce mixture aside.

4. Generously salt the boiling water and drop in the pasta. Cook, stirring often, for 4 to 5 minutes. The pasta will be parboiled and too hard to eat; it cooks further in the oven. Drain the penne, reserving about 1 cup water if using tomato sauce or canned tomatoes. Transfer the pasta to the mixing bowl and combine thoroughly with the sauce mixture. If it seems too thick, add some of the reserved water, a tablespoon at a time, until the pasta moves freely and is surrounded by liquid.

5. Transfer to individual shallow baking dishes or to 1 to 2 large shallow baking dishes. Bake for 8 to 10 minutes, or until the pasta is bubbly hot, with bits of browned penne poking out on top. Serve right away.

on top of spaghetti...

Pasta Baked with Radicchio, Gorgonzola, and Pancetta

Serves 6 to 8 as a first course or 4 to 6 as a main course

In Italy, radicchio is commonly added to winter salads with other greens. It can also be served hot, grilled over a wood fire and drizzled with olive oil, or as the main ingredient in risotto. The taste of radicchio works well in this baked pasta when combined with sharp Gorgonzola and salty pancetta.

2½ cups heavy cream
½ cup homemade chicken stock (see Pasta Pantry)
2 cups finely shredded radicchio or Belgian endive
½ cup freshly grated Parmigiano-Reggiano
½ cup freshly grated Pecorino Romano
½ cup freshly grated fontina
¼ cup finely crumbled Gorgonzola
½ teaspoon or more fine sea salt
1 pound dried pasta shells or rotini
¼ cup finely chopped pancetta

1. Heat the oven to 500 degrees. Bring a large pot of water to a boil.

2. In a large mixing bowl, combine the cream, stock, radicchio, all the cheeses, and salt. Taste and add more salt if necessary. Set the sauce mixture aside.

3. Generously salt the boiling water and drop in the pasta. Cook, stirring often, for 4 to 5 minutes. The pasta will be parboiled and too hard to eat; it cooks further in the oven. Drain the pasta, reserving about 1 cup water. Transfer the macaroni to the mixing bowl and combine thoroughly with the sauce mixture. If the sauce seems too thick, add some of the reserved pasta water, a tablespoon at a time, until the pasta moves freely and is surrounded by liquid.

4. Transfer to individual shallow baking dishes or to 1 to 2 large shallow baking dishes. Evenly distribute the pancetta over the surface and bake for 8 to 10 minutes, or until the pasta is bubbly hot, with bits of browned pancetta and pasta poking out on top. Serve right away.

Baked Pasta "Bianca" with Cream and Five Cheeses

Serves 6 to 8 as a first course or 4 to 6 as a main course

More and more superb Italian cheeses are being imported to North America. You can use the ones suggested here or make substitutions according to what you can find locally. For instance, if stracchino—a slightly acid cow's milk cheese—is available, use it instead of the mascarpone. An excellent-quality Grana Padano can fill in for the Parmigiano-Reggiano. Mild, melting Italian fontina can swap places with the distinctive blue-veined bold Gorgonzola. Enjoy developing your own special blend of cheeses!

2½ cups heavy cream
½ to 1 cup homemade chicken stock
  (see Pasta Pantry)
¼ cup finely crumbled Gorgonzola
½ cup freshly grated Parmigiano-Reggiano
½ cup freshly grated Pecorino Romano
2 tablespoons mascarpone
½ cup chopped mozzarella
½ teaspoon or more sea salt
1 pound dried pasta shells or penne rigate

1. Preheat the oven to 500 degrees. Bring a large pot of water to a boil.

2. Combine the cream, ½ cup chicken stock, all the cheeses, and salt in a large mixing bowl. Mix well. Taste and add more salt if necessary. Set aside.

3. Generously salt the boiling water and drop in the pasta. Cook, stirring often, for 4 to 5 minutes. The pasta will be parboiled and too hard to eat; it cooks further in the oven. Drain the pasta and transfer the macaroni to the mixing bowl. Combine thoroughly with the sauce mixture. If it seems too thick, add some more chicken stock, a tablespoon at a time, until the pasta moves freely and is surrounded by liquid.

4. Transfer to individual shallow baking dishes or to 1 or 2 large shallow baking dishes. Bake for 8 to 10 minutes, or until the pasta is bubbly hot. Serve right away.

on top of spaghetti...

Rotini Baked with Tomatoes and Parmigiano-Reggiano

Serves 6 to 8 as a first course or 4 to 6 as a main course

This elegant little number will be at home at a smart dinner party or a Sunday family supper. Try using one cheese, Parmigiano-Reggiano, for its delicate, aristocratic qualities. For an edgier appeal, dust the pasta at the table with a sprinkle of some sharper, slightly salty, and piquant Pecorino Romano.

3 cups Simple Tomato Sauce (page 72), in its blended form
1½ cups homemade chicken stock (see Pasta Pantry)
1 cup freshly grated Parmigiano-Reggiano
Sea salt
1 pound dried rotini or penne rigate
2 tablespoons unsalted butter
Freshly grated Pecorino Romano or Parmigiano-Reggiano

1. Heat the oven to 500 degrees. Bring a large pot of water to a boil.

2. Mix together the tomato sauce, chicken stock, and Parmigiano-Reggiano in a large mixing bowl. Taste and add salt if necessary. Set aside.

3. Generously salt the boiling water and drop in the pasta. Cook, stirring often, for 5 to 6 minutes. The pasta will be parboiled and too hard to eat; it softens further in the oven. Drain, without shaking the noodles bone-dry, and transfer to the bowl with the sauce ingredients. Toss together thoroughly.

4. Transfer to small individual shallow baking dishes or to 1 or 2 large shallow baking dishes. Dot with butter and bake for 8 to 10 minutes, or until the pasta is bubbling hot with bits of browned noodles on top. Pass the cheese of your choice at the table.

♦ Spaghetti Baked with a
Gutsy Roasted Tomato Sauce ♦

Serves 4 as a first course or 2 as a main course

Here is one pasta that doesn't play by the baked pasta rules. Rather than a sturdy macaroni, this recipe uses spaghetti. With her sister Camille in the 1970s, Portia Cimini owned a minuscule, remarkable restaurant, Casa Sorelle, which was one of the best places to eat in Providence. Customers waited for hours for one of the coveted seats. Portia made many delicious dishes—eggplant rolled with prosciutto and cheese baked under a film of tomato sauce was Johanne's favorite. George loved spaghetti simply tossed with tomato sauce and baked, brought to the table in a ceramic dish straight from the oven.

George devised this recipe with Portia in mind. It has a gutsy tomato sauce rich in olive oil and herbs with a hint of anchovy. There's no need for cheese here. Instead, give each serving a little sprinkle of toasted bread crumbs at the table.

1¾ cups canned tomato purée
4 coarsely chopped anchovy fillets
   (see Pasta Pantry)
¼ cup plus 1 tablespoon extra virgin olive
   oil
1 plump garlic clove, peeled and finely
   minced
1 tablespoon chopped fresh flat-leaf parsley
¼ teaspoon chopped wild fennel or bulb
   fennel fronds (or ¼ teaspoon ground
   fennel seeds)
¼ teaspoon best-quality dried oregano
¼ teaspoon sea salt
Pinch of crushed red pepper flakes
4 turns of the pepper mill
⅓ cup homemade unflavored bread crumbs
8 ounces dried spaghetti

1. Heat the oven to 350 degrees. Bring a large pot of water to a boil for the pasta.

2. Combine the tomato purée, anchovies, ¼ cup olive oil, garlic, parsley, fennel, oregano, salt, red pepper flakes, and black pepper in a large ceramic casserole. Bake for 30 minutes.

3. Toast the bread crumbs by heating the remaining tablespoon of olive oil in a small, heavy sauté

pan—cast iron is ideal. When the oil is very hot, toss in the bread crumbs and stir for 1 to 2 minutes, or until they are browned a bit but not too dark. Transfer immediately to a small bowl. Set aside.

4. When the tomatoes have been in the oven for 25 minutes, generously salt the boiling pasta water and drop in the spaghetti. Cook, stirring often, to parboil, about 5 minutes (or 1 minute more than half the recommended cooking time on the spaghetti package). Drain the spaghetti (it will be a little stiff), reserving ½ cup water.

5. Remove the tomatoes from the oven; toss the spaghetti on top of the tomatoes. Add ¼ cup reserved cooking water and toss together. There should be plenty of moisture in the dish. If not, add a tablespoon or more pasta water and toss again. Bake for 5 minutes until bubbly and hot. Serve right away with toasted bread crumbs passed at the table.

Fresh Pasta

◆ George's Fresh Pasta ◆

Makes about 1 pound

Homemade fresh pasta is glorious and well worth the effort. Nothing compares to the silky, light, slippery noodles you can produce in your own kitchen. This is a quick recipe. The dough is mixed in a food processor and a pasta machine kneads and rolls the dough.

There will be minor variations depending on the weather and the moisture content of the flour (you may have to knead in an extra tablespoon or two of flour), but by following these proportions you will have excellent pasta.

The organic eggs we buy at the farmers' market vary in size. The most reliable way to get an accurate measurement is with a portion scale (see page 12). The measuring-cup method will work, too (crack eggs into a small mixing bowl, whisk to combine, pour the required amount into a liquid measuring cup, and discard or save any excess for another use). In making pasta, skill is developed through practice and repetition. Each batch will be easier than the last and with a little experience exact measurements will become less important.

Don't fret if the final dimensions of the pasta are different from those specified in the recipe. The strips coming through the rollers of the pasta machine may be longer and/or not as wide. The ends may also be narrow rather than perfectly square. For instance, the edge going through the rollers first will be u-shaped (they can be cut later to square the noodle, if you like). Practice does make a difference in developing a feel for the process. Try to roll the dough as wide as possible—a little less than the width of the rollers, but don't be discouraged if that doesn't happen the first time. You may end up with narrower sheets of lasagne noodles, for instance; that's okay.

1 teaspoon fine sea salt
2 jumbo eggs, weighing 4½ ounces in their shells, lightly beaten (slightly over ½ cup but less than ⅔ cup lightly beaten eggs measured in a liquid measuring cup)
2 cups plus 2 tablespoons (10 ounces) flour (see Pasta Pantry)
1 tablespoon hot tap water

1. Lightly whip the salt into the beaten eggs. Set aside.

2. Put the flour in the bowl of a food processor fitted with the steel blade. With the motor running, pour the eggs through the feed tube. Stop the machine as soon as the mixture resembles coarse cornmeal. Run the motor again, pouring the hot water through the feed tube. Pulse on and off for 10 seconds; stop the motor. The dough should stick together when pressed between your fingertips. If not, add another ½ to 1 teaspoon hot water and pulse again. Turn out onto a cool, smooth surface—marble is ideal. Knead for a minute or two until the dough is smooth and pliable. If it is sticky, knead in 1 to 2 tablespoons flour. Shape into a ball, cover the dough completely with plastic wrap, and allow to rest at room temperature for a minimum of 20 minutes or up to 2 hours in the refrigerator. If the dough is refrigerated, remove it from the fridge about 20 minutes before proceeding with the recipe.

3. Set up the pasta machine with the rollers at their widest opening.

4. Divide the dough in half. If the dough is sticky, dust it with flour. Flatten the dough half with the heel of your hand, and feed it through the rollers of the pasta machine. Fold the dough in half lengthwise, and feed it through the rollers again. Repeat 20 to 30 times, occasionally folding the dough widthwise to fit between the guides. This kneads and smooths the dough further, creating silky and supple pasta.

5. Now you can roll the pasta into thin sheets by feeding it through each successive setting of the pasta machine until you have passed it through the second thinnest opening (dust with just enough flour as necessary to keep the dough from sticking). This process is done without folding. If the sheet of pasta becomes cumbersomely long, cut it crosswise into 2 pieces to make it more manageable. Repeat with the second half of the dough. Lay the dough out on a barely floured counter or clean, dry kitchen towels. Each half of dough will yield 2 strips of pasta, roughly measuring 3 feet by 4 inches.

Cutting the Shapes

For ravioli or any filled pasta, use the dough right away while it is soft, pliable, and slightly moist. Start immediately with one strip and cover the other strip with a length of plastic wrap and a clean, dry kitchen towel. Trim the first strip to eliminate any uneven ends. Cut across into 4 or 5 pieces. Leaving ½ inch of dough on each end, quickly place small mounds, roughly a rounded ½ teaspoon, of filling at 1-inch intervals on the bottom half of each piece of dough just below the center. Fold the top of the dough over the filling so the top and bottom edges of dough meet. Press down firmly on the pasta between the dollops of filling and all edges to seal the ravioli. With a pastry cutter, pizza wheel, or knife, cut between the mounds and check again to be sure the edges are sealed. Transfer the ravioli to a floured surface—large baking sheets work well. Keep them in a single layer without allowing them to touch; do not stack. Repeat with the remaining dough. Ravioli should be cooked as soon as possible after being made. If you are not using them right away, cover with plastic wrap and store in the fridge for no more than 2 hours.

Troubleshooting: Try to press out as much air as possible when folding the dough over the filling. If filled with air, the ravioli will stubbornly float on the surface of the boiling water when you cook them. If that happens, gently push them down into the water periodically so they will cook evenly.

If you have trouble getting the pasta layers to seal, you can brush the dough just before filling with beaten egg; or after placing the mounds on the dough, drag a pastry brush moistened with water over the outside edges of the dough and between the mounds. Either method will help keep the layers together.

For flat noodles, allow the pasta to dry, uncovered, for about 15 minutes, turning the sheets over once (the pasta should remain pliable without being brittle at all). Cut the pasta strips crosswise into 8- to 10-inch lengths (lasagne noodles can be longer; see below).

For narrow pasta, you can run the dough through the cutting attachment on the pasta machine—the wide cutter makes tagliatelle (¼ inch wide); the narrow one makes tagliolini or tonnarelli (square spaghetti). The wider shapes are easy to cut by hand with a fluted pastry cutter, pizza wheel, or sharp chef's knife. They can be a little irregular; they should not look machine made.

For fettuccine, cut each pasta strip lengthwise, into ⅜-inch-wide ribbons. Pappardelle are broader; cut them ¾ to 1 inch wide.

Pasta hankies can be 3- or 4-inch squares. Maltagliati are a good alternative to hankies: Cut the dough into wide strips, then cut the strips crosswise on a diagonal into parallelograms—these are nicest cut with a fluted wheel.

Cut lasagnette into 5-inch squares or rectangles measuring roughly 4 by 6 inches.

Try to make lasagne noodles as wide as your pasta machine allows (4 to 5 inches); cut the lengths that are the most appropriate size for the pan you plan to use—anywhere from 8 to 12 inches long, longer if you like, or shorter if smaller noodles are easier for you to handle. (Lasagne noodles can be cut and patched together in assembly.) Keep in mind the pasta will expand when it boils, increasing its dimensions.

After you have cut the noodles, you can cook them right away or lay them out in a single layer without touching on a lightly floured surface or on clean, dry kitchen towels until ready to cook (flour-dusted or towel-lined baking sheets work well if you don't have counter space). For thin ribbons, you can use a pasta drying rack made from wooden dowels placed in an area away from drafts (otherwise the pasta dries too quickly, becomes brittle, and breaks into small pieces.) If you are not using the pasta the same day, allow it to dry completely, then transfer to long, shallow containers with lids. You can keep it in a cool, dry place for 1 week.

◆ Ribbon Pasta with Fresh Lemon ◆

Serves 6 to 8 as a first course or 4 to 6 as a main course

Our friend Flaminia Mazziotti is brilliant, beautiful, and an excellent cook. She is a physician with a private practice, a professor at the University of Rome Medical School, the mother of two children, and she manages to participate in her family's wine estate, which produces the most delicious Est! Est!! Est!!!—a refreshingly crisp and snappy DOC white wine from Lazio made with Trebbiano and Malvasia grapes.

Flaminia and her husband, Alessandro Laurenzi, love good food, and some of our fondest memories are the meals we have shared with them. When we mentioned we were writing a book about pasta, Flaminia said we must include this lemon-scented one because everyone loves it.

Buy organic lemons for this recipe as you will be using the zest, or yellow outer skin. If you cannot find organic lemons, wash the lemons well before removing the zest.

8 tablespoons (1 stick) unsalted butter
1 rounded teaspoon grated lemon zest
Pinch of sea salt
1 batch George's Fresh Pasta (page 212), cut into pappardelle or tagliatelle
6 tablespoons freshly squeezed lemon juice
1 cup freshly grated Parmigiano-Reggiano

1. Bring a large pot of water to a boil.

2. Melt the butter with the lemon zest and salt in a large straight-sided sauté pan over low heat.

3. Generously salt the boiling water and drop in the pasta. Cook, stirring often, until al dente. Drain the pasta, reserving about 1 cup of the cooking water.

4. Swirl the lemon juice into the butter and lemon zest. Transfer the pasta to the sauté pan and toss to coat every noodle. If it seems dry, add a little pasta water, a tablespoon at a time, until you have a creamy consistency. Sprinkle on the Parmigiano-Reggiano and toss again. Serve right away in heated bowls.

◆ Pappardelle with Poached Eggs and Caviar ◆

Serves 6 as a first course

We don't often use luxury ingredients in our pasta dishes, but there are certain occasions that warrant a bit of indulgence—like New Year's Eve or a big birthday celebration. That's when we seek out caviar for this pappardelle and choose the best quality our pocketbook can afford. This kind of opulence is best when complemented by a nice sparkling wine—a crisp and frisky Italian Prosecco or even a vintage Champagne.

Although we normally do not use cheese with any fish-based pasta, the light sprinkling of Parmigiano-Reggiano works well with caviar.

¾ batch George's Fresh Pasta (page 212), cut into pappardelle
6 large eggs
4 tablespoons unsalted butter, softened
⅓ cup freshly grated Parmigiano-Reggiano
6 heaping tablespoons osetra, sevruga, pressed, or domestic black caviar

1. Bring a large pot of water to a boil for the pasta. Fill a large straight-sided sauté pan with water and bring to a gentle simmer for poaching the eggs.

2. Add a generous amount of salt to the large pot of boiling water and drop in the pappardelle. Cook, stirring often, to prevent the pasta from sticking together.

3. At the same time, crack the eggs, one by one, into a saucer, gently letting each one slide into the simmering water in the sauté pan before adding another. Poach the eggs until the whites have solidified but the yolks are still soft and runny. With a slotted spoon, remove the cooked eggs to a warmed plate.

4. When the pasta is al dente—soft, but with some resistance left—drain it in a colander, reserving about 1 cup of the cooking water. Return the pasta to the empty pot and toss with 2 tablespoons cooking water, the butter, and grated cheese. The butter and cooking water will create an emulsion the consistency of heavy cream. Toss to coat every ribbon of pasta. If it seems too dry, add a few more tablespoons of the cooking water and toss again. Divide the pappardelle among 6 warmed serving bowls, top each portion with a poached egg and a heaping tablespoon of caviar. Serve right away.

◆ Tagliatelle with Tomato and Gorgonzola ◆

Serves 6 to 8 as a first course or 4 to 6 as a main course

This sauce works well on both freshly made pasta or dried pasta. It is a snap to put together, so if you have spent time making your own tagliatelle or pappardelle, preparing the sauce is like walking to home plate.

3½ cups canned crushed tomatoes
½ cup plus 2 tablespoons crumbled Gorgonzola
Sea salt (optional)
1 batch George's Fresh Pasta (page 212), cut into tagliatelle, or 1 pound dried tagliatelle packed in nests
6 tablespoons unsalted butter

1. Bring a large pot of water to a boil for the pasta.

2. Combine the tomatoes and 1 cup water in a large straight-sided sauté pan. Bring to a boil, reduce the heat, and simmer for 8 minutes. Add the Gorgonzola and stir over low heat until the cheese is completely melted. Taste the sauce and add salt if necessary.

3. Meanwhile, add a generous amount of salt to the boiling water and drop in the pasta. Cook, stirring often, until al dente. Drain the pasta and transfer to the sauté pan. Add the butter and toss until the butter melts into the sauce and the pasta is nicely coated. Serve right away.

• Pasta Hankies with Broth and Mushrooms •

Serves 4 as a first course or 2 as a main course

In Tuscany, mushrooms are almost always sold with a tiny bouquet of nepitella—wild mint that grows through most of Italy and Provence—because they go together so well. A combination of cultivated fresh mint and marjoram (or oregano) will give you a fraternal taste twin.

3 tablespoons finely minced pancetta
4 tablespoons unsalted butter
1 tablespoon extra virgin olive oil
2½ to 3 cups sliced white, brown, cremini, or portobello mushrooms
¼ teaspoon sea salt
1 tablespoon chopped fresh marjoram or oregano
2 cups homemade chicken stock (see Pasta Pantry)
8 ounces (½ batch) George's Fresh Pasta (page 212), cut into hankies
5 to 6 large fresh mint leaves
Freshly grated Parmigiano-Reggiano

1. Bring a large pot of water to a boil. Use a pasta cooker with a built-in strainer if you have one.

2. Heat the pancetta with 2 tablespoons of the butter and the olive oil in a large straight-sided skillet. Cook over moderate heat until the pancetta begins to brown. Add the mushrooms and salt. Stir and toss with the pancetta until the mushrooms brown on the edges. (If the mushrooms absorb all the fat and seem dry, lower the heat until they begin to give off some of their liquid, then raise the heat to brown.) Add the marjoram and stock. Bring to a boil, lower the heat, and gently simmer on the lowest possible heat.

3. Meanwhile, generously salt the boiling water in the pasta pot. Drop in the noodles and cook until al dente. Drain the pasta and slide the noodles into the skillet. Cut the mint leaves into a chiffonade and add to the skillet with the remaining butter. Toss gently and serve right away with freshly grated Parmigiano-Reggiano.

on top of spaghetti...

Lasagnette with Broccoli Rabe in a Buttery Garlic Sauce

Serves 6 to 8 as a first course or 4 to 6 as a main course

Broccoli rabe, sometimes called rapini, has a bitter, peppery taste, giving it a reputation as an adult vegetable. It pairs well with anchovy, garlic, or sausage. Broccoli rabe can be eaten on its own as a side dish, tossed with pasta, or sautéed with lots of olive oil and garlic, and then packed into a loaf of Italian bread for a finger-licking sandwich.

For this pasta, broccoli rabe's peppery edge is amplified with a dose of crushed red pepper. Delicate palates may decrease the amount or eliminate it altogether. A sprinkling of Parmigiano-Reggiano is not a necessary component, but its nutty taste and creamy texture are welcome.

---

6 tablespoons extra virgin olive oil
1 tablespoon finely minced garlic
1 teaspoon crushed red pepper flakes
2¼ cups homemade, full-flavored chicken stock (see Pasta Pantry)
½ teaspoon sea salt
4 tablespoons unsalted butter, at room temperature
6 cups coarsely chopped fresh broccoli rabe
1 batch George's Fresh Pasta (page 212), cut into lasagnette or hankies
Freshly grated Parmigiano-Reggiano (optional)

---

1. Bring a large pot of water to a boil for the pasta.

2. Heat the olive oil in a large straight-sided sauté pan. Add the garlic and red pepper flakes, and sauté over moderate heat until the garlic is golden. Add the stock and salt. Bring to a boil, lower the heat, and simmer for 3 minutes. Add 2 tablespoons of the butter and the broccoli rabe and simmer for 5 minutes, or until the greens are tender.

3. Generously salt the boiling water and drop in the pasta. Cook, stirring often, until al dente.

Drain the noodles and add them to the broth in the sauté pan. Fold in the remaining butter and gently toss over low heat for 1 to 2 minutes, allowing the noodles to absorb some of the broth.

Transfer the noodles to individual heated bowls. Pour over the broth and broccoli rabe. Serve right away with Parmigiano-Reggiano passed at the table if you wish.

on top of spaghetti...

• Maltagliati with Cinnamon and Lemon Zest •

Serves 4 as a first course or 2 as a main course

Rome is one of our favorite cities. Not only are the art and architecture unparalleled, it is also a great food town. There is nothing quite as restorative after an exhausting morning of awe-inspiring visits to monuments, churches, and museums than a leisurely paced lunch at one of Rome's many neighborhood restaurants. And what could be more pleasant than sitting al fresco in Piazza Farnese trying to decide which pasta to order while gazing upon a masterpiece like Palazzo Farnese (architects: Antonio da Sangallo, Michelangelo, and Giacomo della Porta).

Our time in the Eternal City is divided between the cultures of art and food. And sometimes it's difficult to tell which one draws us more strongly. As restaurateurs, we are always on the prowl for interesting food and spend an inordinate amount of time reading menus! Often it is a fruitful pursuit, and a menu description of a dish will be enough to spark an idea for a new recipe to bring home to Al Forno. Such is the case with this cinnamon and lemon pasta and its saffron variation. Seen on separate menus and at different times, both notions sounded interesting enough to travel back to our kitchen.

½ cup heavy cream
2 cinnamon sticks
½ batch George's Fresh Pasta (page 212), cut into maltagliati or pappardelle
½ teaspoon freshly grated lemon zest, preferably from an organic lemon
2 tablespoons unsalted butter
Freshly grated Parmigiano-Reggiano

1. Combine the cream and cinnamon sticks in a small saucepan. Scald the cream, remove from the heat, and set aside to steep for 15 to 20 minutes.

2. Bring a large pot of water to a boil for the pasta. Generously salt the water and drop in the maltagliati. Stir often so the noodles do not stick together.

3. Meanwhile, transfer ¼ cup of the hot pasta water to a large straight-sided sauté pan, add the lemon zest, and bring to a boil over moderately high heat. At the same time, reheat the scalded cream to a simmer over low heat (do not let it boil or reduce at all).

4. When the pasta is al dente—it should only take a few minutes to cook—drain and transfer to the sauté pan. Toss in the lemon-flavored water for about 30 seconds over moderate heat to coat the noodles. Add the cinnamon-scented cream and butter and continue to toss and coat the pasta. The cream can get bubbly hot, but don't allow it to boil down or the pasta will become cloyingly rich. Remove the cinnamon sticks and serve right away with a little sprinkle of Parmigiano-Reggiano on each portion. Pass more cheese at the table.

Pasta with Saffron and Lemon Zest

Eliminate the cinnamon and substitute ½ teaspoon or more saffron threads in the cream in step 1. Proceed with the remainder of the recipe, leaving the saffron in the cream when you toss it with the pasta.

on top of spaghetti...

Sweet Potato and Pumpkin Lasagnette with Black Olive Purée

Serves 8 as a first course or 4 as a main course

Sweet potatoes, pumpkin, rosemary, and olives—sounds like a wacky combination, but they really do work in this pasta. Roasting the vegetables enhances their flavor and concentrates their sugar, making the combination a good substitute for the sweeter, denser Italian pumpkins.

Choose a baking dish nice enough to come from the oven to the table for easy serving.

6 medium sweet potatoes, washed
1 small (5- to 6-inch-diameter) sugar pumpkin, cut in half and seeded
1 small butternut squash, cut in half and seeded
Sea salt
¼ cup extra virgin olive oil, plus additional olive oil for the baking dish
½ cup pitted Kalamata olives
½ teaspoon finely minced fresh rosemary leaves
1 batch George's Fresh Pasta (page 212), cut into lasagnette or hankies
6 tablespoons unsalted butter, softened
Freshly grated Parmigiano-Reggiano

1. Heat the oven to 425 degrees.

2. Lay the sweet potatoes on a small, foil-lined baking sheet. Lay the pumpkin and squash on another foil-lined sheet, cut side down. Roast the vegetables until very tender, 30 to 45 minutes, then remove from the oven and set aside. (Leave the oven on to reheat the vegetables later.) As soon as the vegetables are cool enough to handle, peel and purée (or mash) the pumpkin, squash, and potatoes. Mix together and season with salt. Transfer the purée to a large, lightly oiled baking dish. Leave peaks and valleys rather than smoothing out the surface (when reheated, the peaks will brown a bit while the lower parts will remain soft, creating an interesting textural difference). Set aside.

3. Bring a large pot of water to a boil for the pasta and make the olive purée. Combine the olives, olive oil, and rosemary in a blender. Whir until you have a chunky purée, with bits of olive remaining. Transfer to a large mixing bowl and set aside.

4. Put the baking dish with puréed vegetables in the oven and heat for about 15 minutes, or until the highest points of the purée brown. Turn the oven off and set the door ajar while you cook the pasta.

5. Generously salt the boiling water and drop in the noodles. Cook, stirring often, until al dente. Drain and toss the pasta and butter with the olive purée in the bowl until they are evenly coated. Remove the vegetables from the oven and drape the noodles over them in the baking dish. Sprinkle with cheese and bring to the table. Serve right away on heated plates.

on top of spaghetti...

◆ Folded Hankies in Tomato-Flavored Broth ◆

Serves 6 to 8 as a first course

Think of this dish as the ultimate reverse chicken noodle soup. For those of us who, as children, slurped their soup as fast as possible so as to savor the yummy pile of noodles at the end, here the noodles are the main event with just enough satisfying broth to keep them moist.

We cook the pasta in an abundant amount of broth, which will leave you with leftovers. A smaller amount may result in the hankies sticking together and giving them a gummy rather than silky texture.

½ batch George's Fresh Pasta (page 212), rolled into 2 sheets roughly measuring 3 feet by 4 inches
1 large egg, lightly beaten
1 cup freshly grated Parmigiano-Reggiano, plus more for serving
Freshly grated nutmeg
Freshly ground black pepper
Sea salt
8 cups homemade chicken broth (see Pasta Pantry)
½ to 1 cup tomato juice, preferably organic

1. Lay the pasta sheets on a clean, smooth, dry surface covered in the barest dusting of flour. Lightly brush each pasta sheet with beaten egg. Top with a sprinkle of cheese, nutmeg, black pepper, and salt.

2. Carefully fold the dough lengthwise to enclose the filling, patting all over the surface with your fingers. Flatten gently with a rolling pin. Cut crosswise into squares about 1½ inches or rectangles measuring 1 by 2 inches (the ends may form squares where the dough is not as wide; the middle portion will form rectangles). You will have about 50 little folded hankies.

3. Bring the chicken broth to a boil in a large saucepan. Bring the tomato juice to a simmer in a small saucepan.

4. Drop the pasta into the boiling chicken broth. Cook, stirring often, until the hankies are soft and silky. With a slotted spoon, transfer the pasta to individual heated bowls. Ladle about ½ cup broth over each serving. Top with 1 to 2 tablespoons hot tomato juice and a generous dusting of Parmigiano-Reggiano. Serve right away.

Note: The leftover chicken broth will be flavored by the cheese, nutmeg, and pepper that have escaped from the pasta hankies. It makes a lovely scented soup to reheat as a little first course for another meal.

Ravioli

◆ Ricotta Ravioli ◆

Makes 4 to 5 dozen ravioli to serve 6 to 8 as a first course or 4 to 6 as a main course

Light and delicate, these versatile ravioli can be combined with a variety of sauces. In the summer, try them with Classic Ligurian Pesto (page 55) as they are served at the beach restaurants in San Remo. In cooler months, cook up a batch of Sunday Gravy (page 126) for the ravioli—and don't forget to make the meatballs to eat alongside. Other good choices are the Simple Tomato Sauce (page 72), Delicate Tomato Sauce (page 71), or Little Girl's Tomato Sauce (page 75), enriched with butter.

Drain the ricotta in a mesh strainer for at least 2 hours before beginning the recipe. If the cheese is too moist, the ravioli dough may absorb the excess liquid and end up gummy. Have extra Parmigiano-Reggiano on hand to pass at the table.

8 ounces fresh ricotta
4 ounces (about 2 cups loosely packed) freshly grated Parmigiano-Reggiano
½ teaspoon fine sea salt
Freshly grated nutmeg
1 egg, lightly beaten
1 batch George's Fresh Pasta (page 212)
1 batch Classic Ligurian Pesto (page 55), half batch Sunday Gravy (page 126), or any of the sauces suggested in the headnote
½ cup or more freshly grated Parmigiano-Reggiano

1. Put the ricotta in a fine-mesh sieve nested in a bowl. Cover loosely with plastic wrap and allow the ricotta to drain for 2 to 3 hours or more in the refrigerator.

2. Mix the drained ricotta with the Parmigiano-Reggiano and salt. Grate enough nutmeg into the mixture so that you can just perceive its presence. You want a hint of its flavor without imposing too much on the delicate nature of the filling. Add a bit more salt if necessary. Fold in the beaten egg gently but thoroughly.

3. Follow the instructions for rolling the pasta dough and filling ravioli on page 213.

4. Bring a large pot of water to a boil. Use a pot with a built-in strainer if you have one. Generously salt the water and drop in the ravioli. Cook, stirring often, until the ravioli are silky, tender, and a bit softer than al dente. Do not undercook or the ravioli will have a rubbery mouth-feel.

5. Drain the ravioli without shaking them bone-dry, transfer to a heated bowl, and layer with the sauce of your choice and ½ cup of Parmigiano-Reggiano. Pass more cheese at the table.

Ricotta and Watercress Filling

Cook ½ pound watercress in boiling salted water until tender, 3 to 5 minutes. Drain in a colander. When cool enough to handle, press down on the greens in the colander to remove as much moisture as possible. Finely chop and add to the drained ricotta mixture in step 2. Proceed with filling and cooking the ravioli. Serve with any of the sauces listed above. Or serve the ravioli with sage butter instead: Melt 6 tablespoons unsalted butter in a skillet. Add 8 to 10 large fresh sage leaves (do not substitute dried sage). Cook for a minute or two over moderately high heat until the sage is aromatic (it's okay if the butter begins to brown, but don't let it get too dark). Pour half the sage butter over half the ravioli in a large heated bowl. Dust with Parmigiano-Reggiano and top with the remaining ravioli and sage butter. Finish with another sprinkling of cheese and serve.

◆ Chicken and Herb Ravioli ◆

Makes 4 to 5 dozen ravioli to serve 6 to 8 as a first course or 4 to 6 as a main course

We often make this ravioli when we have leftover roasted chicken. It works well with boiled chicken, too. Try it with Little Girl's Tomato Sauce (page 75), or simply dress it with melted butter and Parmigiano-Reggiano. Pass additional grated cheese at the table.

½ cup coarsely chopped celery
1 cup coarsely chopped carrots
½ cup loosely packed fresh flat-leaf parsley leaves
2 small sprigs rosemary, spiky leaves only
10 young, tender sage leaves
¾ cup minced onions
½ teaspoon sea salt
3 to 4 tablespoons extra virgin olive oil
12 ounces skinned and boned boiled or roasted chicken
½ cup dry white wine
1 cup loosely packed freshly grated Parmigiano-Reggiano, plus more to pass at the table
1 egg, lightly beaten
1 batch George's Fresh Pasta (page 212)
1 batch Little Girl's Tomato Sauce (page 75)

1. Combine the celery, carrots, parsley, rosemary, and sage in the bowl of a food processor. Pulse on and off until finely chopped. Transfer to a large straight-sided skillet. Add the onions, salt, and 3 tablespoons olive oil. Sauté over moderately low heat until the vegetables are very soft. This could take 15 to 20 minutes. If the mixture seems dry, add the remaining tablespoon olive oil.

2. While the vegetables are cooking, cut the chicken into chunks and toss into the bowl of

the food processor. Pulse on and off until the chicken is very finely chopped, but not so long that it becomes a purée. Set aside.

3. When the vegetables are soft, add the chicken to the skillet. Sauté over moderate heat for a few minutes, stirring to combine. Add the wine; raise the heat and cook, stirring constantly, until the wine has cooked away and completely evaporated, 3 to 4 minutes. Set aside to cool.

4. Add the cheese to the cooled chicken and vegetable mixture. Taste and add more salt if necessary. Fold in the beaten egg gently but thoroughly.

5. Follow the instructions for rolling the pasta dough and filling ravioli on page 213.

6. Bring a large pot of water to a boil. Use a pot with a built-in strainer if you have one. Generously salt the water and drop in the ravioli. Cook, stirring often, until the ravioli are silky, tender, and a bit softer than al dente. Do not undercook or the ravioli will have a rubbery mouth-feel.

7. Drain the pasta, without shaking the ravioli bone-dry, transfer to a heated bowl, and layer with the sauce of your choice and a sprinkling of Parmigiano-Reggiano. Pass more cheese at the table.

◆ Pork and Watercress Ravioli ◆

Makes 4 to 5 dozen ravioli to serve 6 to 8 as a first course or 4 to 6 as a main course

Pork makes a tasty filling for ravioli, especially when combined with smooth and creamy mortadella. We add cooked watercress to the filling to cut through the richness of the meat and echo the taste of the greens in the sauce, where its sharp, peppery flavor perks up the butter and cheese.

12 ounces leftover roasted pork or cooked ground pork
6 ounces mortadella
1½ teaspoons sea salt
1 large bunch (½ pound) watercress
½ cup loosely packed fresh flat-leaf parsley leaves
5 to 6 sprigs fresh chervil
¾ cup finely minced onions
3 tablespoons extra virgin olive oil
2 tablespoons unsalted butter
2 cups freshly grated Parmigiano-Reggiano, plus more to pass at the table
1 egg, lightly beaten
1 batch George's Fresh Pasta (page 212)
6 to 8 tablespoons unsalted butter, softened

1. Cut the roasted pork and mortadella into chunks (if using cooked ground pork, it can go into the food processor as is). Put into the bowl of a food processor (this can be done in 2 or 3 batches) and pulse on and off until finely chopped, but not so long as to reduce the meat to a mushy purée. Set aside.

2. Bring a medium pot of water to a boil. Add 1 teaspoon salt. Set aside a small handful of watercress and add the rest to the boiling water. Lower the heat and simmer until the watercress is tender, 3 to 5 minutes. Drain in a colander. When the cress is cool enough to handle, squeeze out as much water as possible. Finely chop it and set aside.

3. Finely chop the parsley and chervil. Put into a large straight-sided skillet with the onions, olive oil, and butter. Sauté over moderately low heat until the onions are very soft, being careful not to let them brown. Add the meats with the cooked and chopped watercress and continue to sauté for about 5 minutes, stirring often. Set aside to cool.

4. Mix 1½ cups of the Parmigiano-Reggiano into the cooled pork mixture. Taste and add more salt if necessary. Fold in the beaten egg gently but thoroughly. Set aside.

5. Follow the instructions for rolling the pasta dough and filling ravioli on page 213.

6. Bring a large pot of water to a boil. Use a pot with a built-in strainer if you have one. Generously salt the water and drop in the ravioli. Cook, stirring often, until the ravioli are silky, tender, and a bit softer than al dente. Do not undercook or the ravioli will have a rubbery mouth-feel.

7. Drain the ravioli without shaking them bone-dry. Transfer half the pasta to a large heated bowl. Add half the butter and sprinkle with half the remaining Parmigiano-Reggiano. Toss. Add the remaining ravioli, butter, and cheese. Finely chop the reserved watercress and sprinkle over the ravioli. Toss gently and serve right away with more cheese passed at the table.

◆ Duck and Olive Ravioli ◆

Makes 4 to 5 dozen ravioli to serve 6 to 8 as a first course or 4 to 6 as a main course

An old, traditional dish from Perugia for spit-roasted wood pigeons served with a savory sage and olive sauce inspired this recipe. We adapted the idea to duck, which is readily available, and transformed it into a filling for ravioli rather than a main course. When we have leftovers from a roast duck, we use them in this dish or we cook duck legs or breast specifically for the ravioli.

You can use spinach for the greens as we have suggested, or Swiss chard, escarole, or watercress if you prefer. Have extra grated cheese to pass at the table when serving the pasta.

6 cups gently packed (about ½ pound) young, tender spinach leaves
½ pound skinned and boned cooked duck breast or legs
3 tablespoons finely minced pancetta
¾ cup finely minced onions
½ cup finely minced carrots
6 large fresh sage leaves
2 tablespoons extra virgin olive oil
6 tablespoons unsalted butter
½ teaspoon sea salt
¼ cup finely chopped pitted green olives
1½ cups gently packed freshly grated Parmigiano-Reggiano, plus more to pass at the table
Freshly grated nutmeg
1 egg, lightly beaten
1 batch George's Fresh Pasta (page 212)
1 cup rich duck or chicken stock
1 cup peeled, seeded, and chopped fresh tomatoes

1. Cook the spinach in boiling salted water until tender. Drain in a colander. When cool enough to handle, push down on the spinach with the back of a large spoon to extract as much moisture as possible. Finely mince the spinach by hand or in a food processor. Set aside.

2. Cut the duck meat into chunks and transfer to the bowl of a food processor. Pulse on and off until chopped into small pieces, being careful not to allow the meat to dissolve into a purée.

3. Combine the duck, pancetta, onions, carrots, sage, olive oil, 2 tablespoons of the butter, and salt in a large straight-sided skillet. Sauté over moderately low heat until the onions and carrots are soft and beginning to brown. Add the olives and stir to combine. Transfer to a mixing bowl and set aside to cool.

4. Add 1 cup Parmigiano-Reggiano to the cooled mixture and just enough freshly grated nutmeg to give a hint of its presence. Taste and add more salt if necessary. Fold the beaten egg gently but thoroughly into the mixture. Set aside.

5. Follow the instructions for rolling the pasta dough and filling ravioli on page 213.

6. Bring a large pot of water to a boil for the ravioli. Use a pot with a built-in strainer if you have one.

7. In a large straight-sided sauté pan, combine the stock and tomatoes. Bring to a boil and set aside over low heat while you cook the ravioli.

8. Generously salt the pasta water and drop in the ravioli. Cook, stirring often, until the ravioli are silky, tender, and a bit softer than al dente. Do not undercook or the ravioli will have a rubbery mouth-feel.

9. Drain the ravioli without shaking them bone-dry. Transfer half the pasta to the skillet with the hot stock and tomatoes. Add 2 tablespoons butter, ¼ cup Parmigiano-Reggiano, and toss gently. Top with the remaining ravioli, ¼ cup Parmigiano, and the remaining butter. Toss again and serve right away in heated bowls. Pass more cheese at the table.

◆ Braised Beef Ravioli ◆

Makes 4 to 5 dozen ravioli to serve 6 to 8 as a first course or 4 to 6 as a main course

The inventive cooks of Piemonte turn their highly seasoned, wine-enriched leftover braised beef—brasato—into a filling for agnolotti, the tiny, delicate ravioli of the region. The meat is ground with choice bits of vegetables and herbs into a smooth purée before adding cheese and egg to the mixture. We prefer a coarser texture and chop the beef and mortadella into small pieces instead. Serve these ravioli with butter and cheese; they are tasty enough simply adorned. Lucky Piemontese shave white truffles over the pasta just before serving.

3 cups tightly packed young, tender spinach leaves

14 to 16 ounces leftover beef from Brasato al Barolo (page 151) or any roast

3 ounces mortadella

½ teaspoon sea salt

½ teaspoon finely chopped fresh rosemary leaves

2 cups freshly grated Parmigiano-Reggiano, plus more to pass at the table

1 egg, lightly beaten

1 batch George's Fresh Pasta (page 212)

6 to 8 tablespoons unsalted butter, softened

1. Blanch the spinach in boiling salted water until tender. Drain in a colander. When cool enough to handle, squeeze out as much moisture as possible, transfer to a cutting board, and finely chop. Set aside.

2. Trim away and discard any fat from the beef and cut up into cubes. Cut the mortadella into chunks. Put the meats into the bowl of a food processor (this can be done in 2 or 3 batches) and pulse on and off until finely chopped, but not so long as to reduce the meat to a mushy purée. Transfer to a large mixing bowl. Add the chopped spinach, salt, rosemary, and 1½ cups of the Parmigiano-Reggiano. Taste the mixture and

on **top** of spaghetti...

add more salt if necessary. Add the beaten egg and mix thoroughly.

3. Follow the instructions for rolling the pasta dough and filling ravioli on page 213.

4. Bring a large pot of water to a boil. Use a pot with a built-in strainer if you have one. Generously salt the water and drop in the ravioli. Cook, stirring often, until the ravioli are silky, tender, and a bit softer than al dente. Do not undercook or the ravioli will have a rubbery mouth-feel.

5. Drain the ravioli without shaking them bone-dry. Transfer half the pasta to a large heated bowl. Add half the butter and sprinkle with half the remaining Parmigiano. Toss. Add the remaining ravioli, butter, and cheese. Toss gently and serve right away with more cheese passed at the table.

Lasagne

◆ Artichoke Lasagne ◆

Makes 8 to 10 generous servings

Artichokes are much loved in Italy and thrive in fields along the coasts. The markets offer all sizes from the largest (called *mammas*) to the smallest *nipoti* (nephews). Italians feast on the tiny, chokeless ones, thinly sliced and served raw in salad—simply dressed with extra virgin olive oil and lemon. Cleaned and quartered tender artichokes are also served in *pinzimonio,* the peasant-dish-turned-chic-antipasto, an unctuous dip of the best-quality olive oil, salt, and pepper. Larger artichokes can be boiled, stewed, braised, deep-fried, pickled, stuffed, roasted, or featured in pasta or risotto. There is even an artichoke liqueur, Cynar, which makes a super aperitivo mixed with freshly squeezed orange juice.

Here is one of our favorite recipes for artichokes, our version of a lasagne we enjoyed in Rome thirty years ago. This light, white-sauced vegetable lasagne is completely different from the Italian-American red-sauce-meat-and-cheese lasagne we grew up on (and love, too).

Johanne likes this lasagne lightly browned on top. George thinks the taste of the crisped noodles is too strong for delicate pasta and prefers all soft noodles with no browning. To cook it George's way, bake the lasagne covered with foil for 35 minutes and uncovered for the last 5 to 10 minutes in the oven.

Filling
1 lemon
8 to 10 large fresh artichokes
1½ cups finely chopped onions
4 tablespoons extra virgin olive oil
½ teaspoon fine sea salt

Béchamel with Mint
2 cups milk
6 large fresh mint leaves
1 cup chicken stock or vegetable broth
3 tablespoons unsalted butter
3 tablespoons flour
¼ teaspoon sea salt

Pasta and Assembly
1 batch George's Fresh Pasta (page 212), cut into lasagne noodles (4 to 5 inches wide by 12 to 13 inches long)
2 to 3 tablespoons unsalted butter
1 cup freshly grated Parmigiano-Reggiano

1. Cut the lemon in half. Squeeze the juice of one half into a bowl of cold water. Trim the artichokes down to their hearts, cut in half, remove the feathery choke, and rub all surfaces with the other half lemon. Drop the artichokes into the acidulated water to prevent them from browning.

2. To make the filling, cut the artichokes into thin, lengthwise slices and combine them with the onions, olive oil, and salt in a large straight-sided sauté pan. Cook over moderate heat, stirring from time to time, until the artichokes are tender and the onions are soft and completely cooked without any hint of browning. Be patient here as it can take 20 minutes or more. Set aside until ready to assemble the lasagne.

3. To make the béchamel, combine the milk and mint in a small saucepan. Scald and set aside, off the heat, for 20 minutes to infuse the milk with the mint flavor. Remove and discard the mint and reheat the milk.

4. Heat the stock in another small saucepan.

5. Melt the butter in a medium heavy-bottomed saucepan over moderate heat. Add the flour and stir continuously with a wooden spoon for about 2 minutes until the mixture is completely smooth and the flour is cooked. Slowly add the hot milk to the butter-flour mixture, whisking continuously to prevent lumps. When all the milk is incorporated and the mixture is smooth, bring to a boil over moderate heat, stirring all the while with a wooden spoon. Lower the heat and simmer for about 5 minutes, stirring, until the béchamel is the consistency of thick cream.

Add the stock and salt and boil an additional 2 to 3 minutes. Set aside until ready to assemble the lasagne. Stir the béchamel every few minutes to prevent a skin from forming on top.

6. Heat the oven to 375 degrees.

7. Bring a large pot of water to a boil for the lasagne. Put a bowl of ice water near the stove, and set out a few towels next to the bowl to drain the pasta.

8. Drop a few noodles at a time into the boiling water. Cook at a rolling boil for 1 minute. The noodles will be very firm; they will cook further in the oven. Transfer the pasta to the ice water with a long-handled flat skimmer or strainer. As soon as they are cool to the touch—less than a minute—lift them out, shaking off excess water, and lay the noodles out on towels to drain. Repeat the process until all the pasta is cooked.

9. Generously butter a 10 × 14-inch rectangular baking dish.

10. Line the bottom and sides of the dish with 3 of the noodles so that they overhang on all sides. Top with another layer of noodles cut to fit the bottom of the pan without an overhang. Cover with ½ cup of the béchamel and half of the artichoke filling. Sprinkle about ¼ cup of the Parmigiano-Reggiano. Cover with another layer of pasta cut to fit inside the pan without an overhang (odds and ends of the cut pieces can be used as part of the layers). Top with ½ cup of the béchamel and ¼ cup of the Parmigiano-Reggiano. Repeat with another layer of pasta,

the remaining artichoke filling, ½ cup of the béchamel, and ¼ cup of the cheese. Cover with a final layer of pasta (you may not have used every scrap of pasta—leftovers are delicious shredded and floated in soup). Top with the remaining béchamel and cheese. Bring the overhanging noodles up and over the top layer to enclose the filling. Dot with the remaining butter and cover loosely with foil.

11. Bake the lasagne for 25 minutes, uncover, and continue to bake until very lightly browned and bubbling hot, an additional 10 to 15 minutes. Let cool for 5 minutes before cutting and serving.

◆ Mushroom Lasagne ◆

Makes 8 to 10 generous servings

Use white, brown, cremini, portobello mushrooms, or a combination in this recipe. If you're a forager, wild mushrooms would be superb.

Filling
1½ cups chopped onions
2 tablespoons unsalted butter
1 tablespoon extra virgin olive oil
¼ teaspoon sea salt
5 to 6 cups sliced mushrooms (about 1 pound)

Marjoram Béchamel
2 cups milk
1 sprig fresh marjoram or ¼ teaspoon best-quality dried oregano
1 cup chicken stock or vegetable broth
3 tablespoons unsalted butter
3 tablespoons flour
¼ teaspoon sea salt

Pasta and Assembly
1 batch George's Fresh Pasta (page 212), cut into lasagne noodles (4 to 5 inches wide by 12 to 13 inches long)
2 to 3 tablespoons unsalted butter
1 cup freshly grated Parmigiano-Reggiano

1. Prepare the filling by combining the onions, butter, olive oil, and salt in a large straight-sided sauté pan. Cook over moderate heat, stirring from time to time, until the onions are soft and completely cooked without any hint of browning. Be patient here as it can take 20 minutes or more. Raise the heat. When the oil and butter are sizzling, toss in the mushrooms. Cook over moderately high heat, stirring often until the mushrooms are soft and cooked through. Initially, they may give off their juices, but over time they will reabsorb them. You want the mushrooms to be tender and moist but not swimming in liquid. The juices can be reduced over high heat if the mixture is too soupy. Set aside until ready to assemble the lasagne.

2. To make the béchamel, combine the milk and marjoram in a small saucepan and scald. Remove from the heat, let steep for 20 minutes, then remove and discard the marjoram, and reheat the milk.

3. Heat the chicken stock in another small saucepan.

4. Melt the butter in a medium heavy-bottomed saucepan over moderate heat. Add the flour and stir continuously with a wooden spoon for about 2 minutes until the mixture is completely smooth and the flour is cooked. Slowly add the hot milk

to the butter-flour mixture, whisking continuously to prevent lumps. When all the milk is incorporated, bring to a boil over moderate heat, stirring all the while with a wooden spoon. Lower the heat and simmer for about 5 minutes until the béchamel is the consistency of thick cream. Add the stock and salt and boil an additional 2 to 3 minutes. Set aside until ready to assemble the lasagne. Stir the béchamel every few minutes to prevent a skin from forming on top.

5. Heat the oven to 375 degrees.

6. Bring a large pot of water to a boil for the lasagne. Put a bowl of ice water near the stove, and set out a few towels next to the bowl to drain the pasta.

7. Drop a few noodles at a time into the boiling water. Cook at a rolling boil for 1 minute. The noodles will be very firm; they will cook further in the oven. Transfer the pasta to the ice water with a long-handled flat skimmer or strainer. As soon as they are cool to the touch—less than a minute—lift them out, shaking off excess water, and lay the noodles out on towels to drain. Repeat the process until all the pasta is cooked.

8. Generously butter a 10 × 14-inch rectangular baking dish.

9. Line the bottom and sides of the dish with 3 of the noodles so that they overhang on all sides. Top with another layer of noodles cut to fit the bottom of the pan without an overhang. Cover with ½ cup of the béchamel and half of the mushroom filling. Sprinkle about ¼ cup of the Parmigiano-Reggiano. Cover with another layer of pasta cut to fit inside the pan without an overhang (odds and ends of the cut pieces can be used as part of the layers). Top with ½ cup of the béchamel and ¼ cup of the Parmigiano-Reggiano. Repeat with another layer of pasta, the remaining mushroom filling, ½ cup of the béchamel, and ¼ cup of the cheese. Cover with a final layer of pasta (you may not have used every scrap of pasta). Top with the remaining béchamel and cheese. Bring the overhanging pasta up and over the last layer of pasta to enclose the filling. Dot with the remaining butter and cover loosely with foil.

10. Bake the lasagne for 25 minutes, uncover, and continue to bake until very lightly browned and bubbling hot, an additional 10 to 15 minutes. Let cool for 5 minutes before cutting and serving.

Note: George prefers this lasagne baked without any browned noodles on top. To cook it his way, bake the lasagne covered with foil for 35 minutes and uncovered for the last 5 to 10 minutes in the oven.

◆ Zucchini Lasagne ◆

Makes 8 to 10 generous servings

Roasted zucchini is nestled into this light and fresh lasagne with creamy mozzarella and Parmigiano-Reggiano. Perfect for summer—or anytime you find exceptional zucchini at the market.

Filling
1 teaspoon unsalted butter
4 tablespoons extra virgin olive oil
3 cups halved and thinly sliced onions
½ teaspoon sea salt
8 young, tender zucchini (2 pounds), trimmed and cut lengthwise into ¼-inch-thick slices

Béchamel
3 cups milk
3 tablespoons unsalted butter
3 tablespoons unbleached flour
¼ teaspoon sea salt

Pasta and Assembly
1 batch George's Fresh Pasta (page 212), cut into lasagne noodles (4 to 5 inches wide by 12 to 13 inches long)
2 to 3 tablespoons unsalted butter
1 cup freshly grated Parmigiano-Reggiano
1 cup cubed mozzarella

1. Heat the oven to 450 degrees.

2. To make the filling, heat the butter and 1 tablespoon olive oil in a large skillet. Add the onions and ¼ teaspoon salt, and sauté over low heat until the onions are very soft without browning, about 20 minutes. Set aside.

3. With a pastry brush, lightly coat one or two baking sheets with 2 tablespoons olive oil. Lay out the zucchini slices in a single layer, brush the tops with the remaining tablespoon olive oil, sprinkle with ¼ teaspoon salt, and roast for 10 to 15 minutes, or until tender and cooked through. The zucchini slices should be translucent—don't worry if the edges brown a bit; it will add a nice flavor to the lasagne. Set aside.

4. Lower the oven temperature to 375 degrees.

5. To make the béchamel, scald the milk in a small saucepan.

6. Melt the butter in a medium heavy-bottomed saucepan over moderate heat. Add the flour and stir with a wooden spoon until the mixture is smooth. Continue to stir until the mixture has bubbled for 2 minutes and the flour is cooked. Take care not to allow the flour to darken. Very slowly pour the hot milk into the flour-butter mixture, whisking continuously to prevent lumps.

When all the milk is incorporated, bring to a boil, stirring with a wooden spoon. Lower the heat and simmer for about 5 minutes until the béchamel has thickened to the consistency of heavy cream. Stir in the salt, remove from the heat, and set aside. Stir every few minutes to prevent a skin from forming on top.

7. Bring a large pot of water to a boil. Put a bowl of ice water near the stove, and set out a few towels next to the bowl to drain the pasta.

8. Drop a few noodles at a time into the boiling water. Cook at a rolling boil for 1 minute. The noodles will be very firm; they will cook further in the oven. Transfer the pasta to the ice water with a long-handled flat skimmer or strainer. As soon as they are cool to the touch—less than a minute—lift them out, shaking off excess water, and lay the noodles out on towels to drain. Repeat the process until all the pasta is cooked.

9. Generously butter a 10 × 14-inch rectangular baking dish.

10. Line the bottom and sides of the dish with 3 of the noodles so that they overhang on all sides. Top with another layer of noodles, cut to fit the bottom of the pan without an overhang. Cover with ½ cup of the béchamel, half the zucchini slices, and half the onions. Sprinkle with ¼ cup of the Parmigiano-Reggiano. Cover with another layer of pasta, cut to fit inside the pan without an overhang (odds and ends of the cut pieces can be used as part of the layers). Top with ½ cup of the béchamel, ¼ cup of the Parmigiano-Reggiano, and half the mozzarella. Repeat with another layer of pasta, the remaining zucchini and onions, ½ cup of the béchamel, ¼ cup of the Parmigiano-Reggiano, and the rest of the mozzarella. Cover with a final layer of pasta (you may not have used every scrap of pasta). Top with the remaining béchamel and cheese. Bring the overhanging pasta up and over the top of the lasagne to enclose the filling. Dot with 2 tablespoons butter and cover loosely with foil.

11. Bake the lasagne for 25 minutes, uncover, and continue to bake until very lightly browned and bubbling hot, an additional 10 to 15 minutes. If you prefer the lasagne without a browned top, bake the lasagne covered with foil for 35 minutes and uncovered for the last 5 to 10 minutes in the oven. Let cool for 5 minutes before cutting and serving.

◆ Zucchini Flower Lasagne ◆

Makes 8 to 10 generous servings

We buy zucchini flowers from Raymond, a kind and generous farmer. When we ask for a dozen, he tosses fifteen into the sack. We either dip the flowers in batter and fry them in olive oil, or use them to make this stunning lasagne.

Béchamel
10 large fresh basil leaves
3 cups milk
4 tablespoons unsalted butter
4 tablespoons flour
Pinch of sea salt
Tiny pinch of cinnamon
Pinch of freshly grated nutmeg
Freshly ground white pepper

Filling
2 cups finely chopped onions
2 tablespoons unsalted butter
2 tablespoons extra virgin olive oil
½ teaspoon sea salt
48 fresh zucchini flowers with stems
  attached

Pasta and Assembly
1 batch George's Fresh Pasta (page 212), cut
  into lasagne noodles (4 to 5 inches wide
  by 12 to 13 inches long)
4 tablespoons unsalted butter
1½ cups loosely packed freshly grated
  Parmigiano-Reggiano

1. Steep the basil in the milk, covered and refrigerated, for 4 to 5 hours.

2. Bring the milk to the verge of a boil. Pour through a fine-mesh strainer into a heatproof measuring cup or bowl. Discard the basil.

3. Melt the butter in a heavy-bottomed saucepan over moderately low heat. Add the flour and cook, stirring constantly with a wooden spoon. Let the mixture bubble for about 2 minutes until the flour is cooked. Adjust the heat low enough so that the flour remains uncolored. Slowly add the hot milk, whisking constantly to avoid lumps. After all the milk has been added, continue to whisk to keep the béchamel smooth and creamy. Stir in the salt, cinnamon, and nutmeg. Add white pepper to taste. Cook over low heat, stirring with a wooden spoon, until the béchamel has thickened to the consistency of heavy cream. Set aside, stirring every few minutes to

prevent a skin forming, until ready to assemble the lasagne.

4. To make the filling, sauté the onions in the butter and the olive oil in a large straight-sided sauté pan over moderate heat for 8 minutes. Season with salt, cover the pan, and continue to cook for another 10 minutes, or until the onions are very soft without a hint of browning.

5. Coarsely chop the flower stems and add to the onions. Sauté for 3 minutes. Add the flowers, cover, and sauté over low heat until they are wilted and softened, 3 to 5 minutes. Taste for salt and add more if necessary. Set aside.

6. Heat the oven to 375 degrees.

7. Bring a large pot of water to a boil. Put a bowl of ice water near the stove, and set out a few towels next to the bowl to drain the pasta.

8. Drop a few noodles at a time into the boiling water. Cook at a rolling boil for 1 minute. The noodles will be very firm; they will cook further in the oven. Transfer the pasta to the ice water with a long-handled flat skimmer or strainer. As soon as they are cool to the touch—less then a minute—lift them out, shaking off excess water, and lay the noodles out on towels to drain. Repeat the process until all the pasta is cooked.

9. Generously butter a 10 × 14-inch rectangular baking dish.

10. Line the bottom and sides of the dish with 3 of the noodles so that they overhang on all sides. Top with another layer of noodles cut to fit the bottom of the pan without an overhang. Cover with ½ cup béchamel and half of the zucchini flower mixture. Sprinkle with ¼ cup Parmigiano-Reggiano. Cover with a layer of lasagne cut to fit over the filling without an overhang (odds and ends of the cut pieces can be used as part of the layers). Top with ½ cup béchamel and ¼ cup Parmigiano-Reggiano. Repeat with another layer of pasta, the remaining zucchini flower mixture, ½ cup béchamel, and ¼ cup Parmigiano. Add another layer of pasta, ½ cup béchamel, and ¼ cup Parmigiano. Cover with a final layer of pasta sheets (you may not have used all the pasta). Top with the remaining béchamel and cheese. Bring the overhanging pasta up and over the top of the lasagne to enclose the filling. Dot with the remaining butter and cover loosely with foil.

11. Bake the lasagne for 25 minutes, uncover, and continue to bake until very lightly browned on top and bubbling hot, an additional 10 to 15 minutes. If you prefer the lasagne without a browned top, bake the lasagne covered with foil for 35 minutes and uncovered for the last 5 to 10 minutes in the oven. Let cool for 5 minutes before cutting and serving.

◆ Fennel and Endive Lasagne ◆

Makes 8 to 10 generous servings

~~~~~~

The delicate flavor of fennel bulb becomes more assertive with slow cooking. The bitter, aggressive taste of endive mellows in the same process. Together the sautéed vegetables compose the filling for this unusual lasagne.

If you are lucky enough to find fennel with its fronds attached, chop up the feathery, tender parts and add a few tablespoons to the filling with the ground fennel seeds.

~~~~~~

Filling
6 tablespoons unsalted butter
3 cups halved and thinly sliced onions
4 cups trimmed and thinly sliced fennel bulbs (3 to 4 medium bulbs)
6 medium endive, trimmed and sliced crosswise into ¼-inch rounds
¼ teaspoon or more sea salt
1 teaspoon ground fennel seeds

Béchamel
3 cups milk
3 tablespoons unsalted butter
3 tablespoons flour
Pinch of sea salt
Freshly ground white pepper

Pasta and Assembly
1 batch George's Fresh Pasta (page 212), cut into lasagne noodles (4 to 5 inches wide by 12 to 13 inches long)
3 tablespoons unsalted butter
½ cup heavy cream
1 cup freshly grated Parmigiano-Reggiano

1. To make the filling, melt the butter in a large skillet. Add the onions, fennel, endive, and salt. Sauté over low heat, stirring from time to time, until the vegetables are very soft, about 25 minutes or more. Add the ground fennel seeds and stir to combine. Taste and add more salt if necessary. Set aside until ready to assemble the lasagne.

2. To make the béchamel, heat the milk in a small saucepan to scald.

3. Melt the butter in a medium heavy-bottomed saucepan. Add the flour and stir with a wooden spoon until the mixture is smooth. Continue to stir until the mixture has bubbled for 2 minutes and the flour is cooked. Adjust the heat so the flour does not color at all.

4. Slowly add the hot milk to the flour-butter mixture, whisking constantly. When all the milk has been added and the mixture is smooth, continue to stir continuously with a wooden spoon,

over low heat, until the béchamel has thickened to the consistency of heavy cream. Season with salt and white pepper, remove from the heat, and set aside. Stir every few minutes to prevent a skin from forming on top.

5. Heat the oven to 375 degrees.

6. Bring a large pot of water to a boil. Put a bowl of ice water near the stove, and set out a few towels next to the bowl to drain the pasta.

7. Drop a few noodles at a time into the boiling water. Cook at a rolling boil for 1 minute. The noodles will be very firm; they will cook further in the oven. Transfer the pasta to the ice water with a long-handled flat skimmer or strainer. As soon as they are cool to the touch—less than a minute—lift them out, shaking off excess water, and lay the noodles out on towels to drain. Repeat the process until all the pasta is cooked.

8. Generously butter a 10 × 14-inch rectangular baking dish.

9. Line the bottom and sides of the dish with 3 of the noodles so that they overhang on all sides.

Top with another layer of noodles, cut to fit the bottom of the pan without an overhang. Cover with ½ cup béchamel and half of the fennel and endive mixture. Drizzle with half the cream. Sprinkle with ¼ cup Parmigiano-Reggiano. Cover with a layer of lasagne cut to fit over the filling without an overhang (odds and ends of the cut pieces can be used as part of the layers). Top with ½ cup béchamel and ¼ cup Parmigiano-Reggiano. Repeat with another layer of pasta, the remaining fennel and endive mixture, the remaining cream, ½ cup béchamel, and ¼ cup Parmigiano. Add another layer of pasta, ½ cup béchamel, and ¼ cup Parmigiano. Cover with a final layer of pasta sheets (you may not have used all the pasta). Top with the remaining béchamel. Bring the overhanging pasta up and over the lasagne to enclose the filling. Dot with the remaining butter and cover loosely with foil.

10. Bake the lasagne for 25 minutes, uncover, and continue to bake until very lightly browned on top and bubbling hot, an additional 10 to 15 minutes. To cook the lasagne without browning the top layer, keep it covered for 35 minutes and uncovered for the last 5 to 10 minutes in the oven. Let cool for 5 minutes before serving.

on top of spaghetti...

◆ Roasted Asparagus Lasagne ◆

Makes 8 to 10 generous servings

Roasting asparagus is one of the most satisfying ways to enjoy them. The flavor becomes concentrated with none of the loss of taste that boiling causes, and there is no excess moisture from steaming, which gives this lasagne plenty of character.

If you are unable to find organic lemons, be sure to wash the lemon well before removing the peel.

Lemon Béchamel
3 cups milk
3 tablespoons unsalted butter
3 tablespoons flour
One 3-inch strip fresh lemon peel, preferably from an organic lemon
½ teaspoon sea salt
Freshly grated nutmeg

Filling
2 tablespoons unsalted butter
2 tablespoons plus 1 teaspoon extra virgin olive oil
2 large onions (1 pound), halved vertically and thinly sliced
1 teaspoon sea salt
2 pounds fresh asparagus, trimmed

Pasta and Assembly
1 batch George's Fresh Pasta (page 212), cut into lasagne noodles (4 to 5 inches wide by 12 to 13 inches long)
3 to 4 tablespoons unsalted butter
½ cup heavy cream
1¼ cups freshly grated Parmigiano-Reggiano

1. Heat the oven to 500 degrees.

2. To make the béchamel, combine the milk and lemon peel in a small saucepan. Scald, remove from the heat, and set aside for 20 minutes to infuse the milk with lemon flavor. Remove and discard the lemon peel and reheat the milk.

3. Melt the butter in a medium heavy-bottomed saucepan over moderate heat. Add the flour and stir continuously with a wooden spoon for about 2 minutes until the mixture is completely smooth and the flour is cooked. Slowly add the hot milk to the butter-flour mixture, whisking continuously to prevent lumps. When all the milk is incorporated and the mixture is smooth, bring to a boil over moderate heat, stirring all the while with a wooden spoon. Lower the heat and simmer for about 5 minutes, stirring, until the béchamel is the consistency of thick cream. Season with salt and just enough nutmeg to perceive its

presence in the béchamel. Set aside until ready to use. Stir the béchamel every few minutes to prevent a skin from forming on top.

4. To make the filling, melt the butter and 1 tablespoon olive oil in a large skillet. Add the onions and ½ teaspoon salt, and sauté over moderately low heat until the onions are very soft, about 20 minutes or more. Do not allow the onions to brown. Set aside.

5. With a pastry brush, lightly coat a baking sheet with 1 teaspoon olive oil. Lay out the asparagus in a single layer, brush with the remaining tablespoon olive oil, and roast for 7 to 10 minutes, or until the asparagus are tender (the tips may brown, but that's okay). When cool enough to handle, thinly slice them on a diagonal and toss with the onions. Taste and add more salt if you like.

6. Lower the oven temperature to 375 degrees.

7. Bring a large pot of water to a boil for the lasagne. Put a bowl of ice water near the stove, and set out a few towels next to the bowl to drain the pasta.

8. Drop a few noodles at a time into the boiling water. Cook at a rolling boil for 1 minute. The noodles will be very firm; they will cook further in the oven. Transfer the pasta to the ice water with a long-handled flat skimmer or strainer. As soon as they are cool to the touch—less than a minute—lift them out, shaking off excess water, and lay the noodles out on towels to drain. Repeat the process until all the pasta is cooked.

9. Generously butter a 10 × 14-inch rectangular baking dish.

10. Line the bottom and sides of the dish with 3 of the noodles so that they overhang on all sides. Top with another layer of noodles cut to fit the bottom of the pan without an overhang. Cover with ½ cup béchamel and half of the asparagus filling. Drizzle with half the cream and sprinkle with ¼ cup the Parmigiano-Reggiano. Cover with another layer of pasta, cut to fit inside the pan without an overhang (odds and ends of the cut pieces can be used as part of the layers). Top with ½ cup béchamel and ¼ cup Parmigiano-Reggiano. Repeat with another layer of pasta, the remaining asparagus filling and cream, ½ cup béchamel, and ¼ cup cheese. Cover with a final layer of pasta (you may not have used every scrap of pasta). Top with the remaining béchamel and cheese. Bring the overhanging pasta up and over the top of the lasagne to enclose the filling. Dot with the remaining butter and cover loosely with foil.

11. Bake the lasagne for 25 minutes, uncover, and continue to bake until very lightly browned and bubbling hot, an additional 10 to 15 minutes. If you prefer the top layer without any browned areas, bake the lasagne covered with foil for 35 minutes and uncovered for the last 5 to 10 minutes in the oven. Let cool for 5 minutes before cutting and serving.

on top of spaghetti...

◆ Mary's Lasagne ◆

Makes 8 to 10 generous servings

"If you want to make lasagne, first you gotta make meatballs!" We repeat this quote to each other and chuckle whenever we get ready to prepare this recipe. We remember it coming from the famous actor Tony Danza, in a magazine article with some of his favorite Italian-American recipes. George's mom, Mary, must have agreed with Tony because her lasagne always included her delicious meatballs.

Be sure to remove all the bones from the pork chops in the Sunday Gravy (page 126) before making the lasagne.

4 tablespoons unsalted butter
1 cup (8 ounces) fresh ricotta
1 egg
2 tablespoons finely chopped fresh flat-leaf parsley
4 or 5 large fresh basil leaves
¼ to ½ teaspoon sea salt or more to taste
½ batch Sunday Gravy with Sausages and Meatballs (page 126)
1 recipe George's Fresh Pasta (page 212), cut into lasagne noodles (4 to 5 inches wide by 12 to 13 inches long)
1½ cups freshly grated Pecorino Romano
1 ball of fresh mozzarella (see Pasta Pantry), drained and sliced

1. Heat the oven to 375 degrees.

2. Bring a large pot of water to a boil for the noodles. Put a bowl of ice water near the stove, and set out a few towels next to the bowl to drain the pasta.

3. Generously butter a 10 × 14-inch baking pan. Set aside.

4. In a small bowl, mix the ricotta, egg, and parsley together. Rip up the basil leaves and fold them into the ricotta mixture. Season with salt and set aside.

lasagne   253

5. With a slotted spoon, transfer the pieces of pork, sausage, and meatballs from the Sunday Gravy to a separate bowl. They will be coated with some of the tomato gravy. That's okay. Set the remaining gravy and bowl of meats aside.

6. Generously salt the boiling water and cook the lasagne sheets, a few at a time, at a rolling boil for 1 minute. The noodles will be very firm; they will cook further in the oven. Transfer the pasta to the ice water with a long-handled flat skimmer or strainer. As soon as they are cool to the touch—less than a minute—lift them out, shaking off excess water, and lay the noodles out on towels to drain. Repeat the process until all the pasta is cooked.

7. Cover the bottom of the baking pan with a layer of lasagne sheets, allowing the pasta to hang over all sides of the pan. Top with another layer of lasagne sheets cut to fit the bottom of the pan without an overhang.

8. Cover the pasta with half of the reserved meats. Spoon over enough gravy to moisten well, about 1 cup. Sprinkle with a rounded ¼ cup Pecorino Romano. Cover with another layer of pasta cut to fit without an overhang. Top with 1 cup gravy. Dollop half of the ricotta mixture over the gravy and top with half of the mozzarella and a rounded ¼ cup Pecorino Romano. Repeat the pasta and meat layer and the pasta and ricotta mixture layer.

9. Cover with a final layer of pasta (you may not have used all the lasagne sheets) cut to fit the inside of the pan without an overhang. Top with the remaining gravy and Pecorino Romano. Bring up the overhang of pasta and fold over the top of the lasagne to enclose the filling. Dot with the remaining butter and loosely cover with foil.

10. Bake the lasagne for 25 minutes, uncover, and continue to bake until very lightly browned and bubbling hot, an additional 10 to 15 minutes. To keep the top noodles soft without browning, bake the lasagne covered with foil for 35 minutes and uncovered for the last 5 to 10 minutes in the oven. Let cool for 5 minutes before serving.

♦ George's Toss-and-Tumble "Cheater's" Lasagne ♦

Serves 8 to 10 as a first course or 6 as a main course

George always looks for the most direct route to achieve results. His toss-and-tumble method for lasagne will make you say, "Why didn't I think of that?!"

After the noodles are prepared and boiled, this is a very easy dish to put together. Don't try to smooth out the surface when you plop the noodles into the pan. Hills and valleys will reward you with crunchy bites from the peaks of pasta sticking up and mouthfuls of velvety soft noodles underneath. The play of flavors and textures in the filling will delight you, too—bits of meaty sausage, nutty Parmigiano-Reggiano, and resilient, creamy mozzarella. For an over-the-top occasion, fold in the optional ricotta.

2 tablespoons unsalted butter
1 batch (about 5 cups) Spicy Sausage Red Sauce (page 135)
1 batch George's Fresh Pasta (page 212), rolled and cut into 8-inch-long lasagne sheets
1 large (4 ounces) ball of fresh mozzarella (see Pasta Pantry), drained and cut into ½-inch dice
1½ cups freshly grated Parmigiano-Reggiano
1 cup (8 ounces) ricotta (optional)

1. Bring a large pot of water to a boil and heat the oven to 425 degrees.

2. Smear some of the butter on the bottom and sides of a 10 × 14-inch baking pan. Cover the bottom of the pan with 1 cup sauce. Set aside. Put 2 cups sauce into a large mixing bowl. Set aside.

3. Generously salt the pasta water and cook half the lasagne noodles in batches. Drain and transfer the pasta to the mixing bowl with the sauce. Toss gently but thoroughly to ensure the sauce covers all surfaces of the noodles to prevent them from sticking together. Add half the mozzarella and half the Parmigiano-Reggiano. Toss together without making a homogeneous mix. Gently

fold in the ricotta if you like—also being careful to leave the mixture patchy. Tumble the whole thing into the baking pan without smoothing out the surface.

4. Repeat the process with the remaining sauce, the other half of the pasta, mozzarella, Parmigiano-Reggiano, and optional ricotta. Toss and tumble into the baking pan, purposely leaving high and low spots. Dot with the remaining butter and bake for 25 minutes, or until bubbling hot with portions of the top nicely browned. Cool for about 5 minutes and serve.

on top of spaghetti...

◆ Jo's Fast "Cheater's" Lasagne ◆

Serves 8 as a main course

Don't be put off by the length of this recipe. Once you have all your ingredients together it takes less time to assemble the lasagne than to read all the blah blah directions.

If you have a not-too-seasoned tomato sauce on hand—like Pomodoro—Al Forno's Tomato Sauce (page 70) or a Simple Tomato Sauce (page 72)—use it. Otherwise choose a good-quality canned tomato purée and doctor it up with a little salt.

For the béchamel, you can make 1 to 1½ cups of your favorite recipe or ½ batch of the béchamel for fresh Zucchini Lasagne.

1 batch George's Fresh Pasta (page 212), cut into lasagne noodles (4 to 5 inches wide by 9 inches long)
4 tablespoons extra virgin olive oil
2½ to 3 cups Veal Ragù (page 139)
2 cups canned tomato purée
Fine sea salt
½ batch Béchamel (page 245)
1 cup freshly grated Parmigiano-Reggiano
8 tablespoons (1 stick) unsalted butter, cut into 16 pieces

1. After you have made and kneaded the pasta dough, and stretched it to the next to thinnest setting on the rollers, run the pasta sheets through the same setting again—this will lengthen and thin the sheets just a little more (but not as much as the thinnest setting). Cut the pasta into 16 pieces, measuring roughly 5 to 6 inches wide by 8 to 9 inches long. Set aside to dry for 20 minutes, in a single layer without touching, on a barely floured surface.

2. Preheat the oven to 475 degrees. Brush the bottoms and sides of 2 large well-seasoned or nonstick baking sheets (we use commercial half-sheet pans measuring roughly 13 by 17½ inches) or jelly-roll pans with the olive oil. They should be nicely coated so the bottom layer of pasta doesn't stick. (This could happen if you are using an aluminum pan that is not well seasoned.) Set aside.

3. Bring a large pot of water to a boil to cook the pasta. Put a bowl of ice water near the stove, and set out a few towels next to the bowl to drain the pasta.

4. Generously salt the water and cook the lasagne sheets, a few at a time, at a rolling boil for 1 minute. The noodles will be very firm; they will cook further in the oven. Transfer the pasta to the ice water with a long-handled flat skimmer or strainer. As soon as they are cool to the

touch—less than a minute—lift them out, shaking off excess water, and lay the noodles out on towels to drain. Repeat the process until all the pasta is cooked.

5. Lay out the baking pans lengthwise in front of you. The short ends of the pans will be nearest you and the longer sides will be perpendicular to you and stretching out before you. Leave about 10 inches of empty space between the pans. Also, leave empty space on the outside edges of the pans—to your far left and far right, as the noodles will hang over the rim of each side and drape onto the counter during the assembly process.

6. With the thumb and index fingers of each hand, gently lift two corners of one of the noodles so that the longest dimension is stretched between your hands. Lay the noodle out on the top left quadrant of the baking pan so that the right-hand side of the noodle, hanging from your right hand, is placed in the center of the pan, with the rest of the noodle covering the left side of the pan and hanging over the left rim of the pan to drape onto the counter. Repeat with another noodle, this time laying the noodle on the upper right side of the pan so that the left side of the noodle butts up to the first noodle in the center and the right-hand side hangs over the right side of the baking pan and onto the counter. Repeat with 2 more noodles laid out in the same manner on the lower quadrants of the pan. The rectangular noodles will be laid out perpendicular to the baking pan and hanging over on the left and right sides. There should be enough room on the pan so that the noodles butt up to each other but do not overlap. Whew! Have a sip of wine and repeat with the second baking pan and 4 more noodles.

7. Spread the inside half of each noodle—the portion sitting in the pan—with 2 to 3 tablespoons each of ragù. It needn't be a smooth layer or be spread from edge to edge.

8. Fold the outside portion of each pasta sheet—the part hanging over the pan and onto the counter—over the ragù so the outside edge of each noodle meets the inside edge in the center of the pan—like a folded sheet of paper. Top each with 2 tablespoons tomato purée and a sprinkle of salt.

9. Create another layer with the remaining noodles by repeating steps 6 and 7. Drizzle 1 tablespoon béchamel onto each portion over the ragù and fold the outside portion of each pasta sheet over as you have done in step 8.

10. Cover the top of each portion with 2 tablespoons tomato purée and drizzle each with another tablespoon béchamel. Sprinkle the Parmigiano-Reggiano equally over the tops, dot with butter, and bake for 10 to 12 minutes, or until the lasagne is bubbly hot and some bits of noodle and cheese have browned on top. Transfer each individual lasagne to heated plates and serve right away.

Index